# CENTRAL BANKING IN DEVELOPING COUNTRIES

*Also by Anand Chandavarkar*

KEYNES AND INDIA

# Central Banking in Developing Countries

Anand Chandavarkar

First published in Great Britain 1996 by
**MACMILLAN PRESS LTD**
Houndmills, Basingstoke, Hampshire RG21 6XS
and London
Companies and representatives
throughout the world

A catalogue record for this book is available
from the British Library.

ISBN 0–333–62915–9

---

First published in the United States of America 1996 by
**ST. MARTIN'S PRESS, INC.,**
Scholarly and Reference Division,
175 Fifth Avenue,
New York, N.Y. 10010

ISBN 0–312–16352–5

Library of Congress Cataloging-in-Publication Data
Chandavarkar, Anand G.
Central banking in developing countries / Anand Chandavarkar.
p. cm.
Includes bibliographical references and index.
ISBN 0–312–16352–5 (cloth)
1. Banks and banking, Central—Developing countries. I. Title.
HG3550.C47 1996
332.1'091724—dc20 96–18826
CIP

---



10 9 8 7 6 5 4 3 2 1
05 04 03 02 01 00 99 98 97 96

Printed and bound in Great Britain by
Antony Rowe Ltd, Chippenham, Wiltshire

For Neil and Mark

# Contents

# List of Tables and Figures

**Tables**

**Figures**

# Preface

'We do not need central banks but we shall certainly continue to have them.' — *Milton Friedman*

'Economists find bankers fascinating. After all, you are the white mice we study.' — *Paul A. Samuelson*

The monetarist messiah's acceptance of the inevitability of central banks happily controverts Keynes's celebrated epigram – 'The inevitable never happens. It is always the unexpected' – and deftly swivels the debate away from the rationale of central banks towards the burning contemporary issues of their status, objectives and functions amidst globalized financial liberalization and the evangelical litany of independence for central banks. The small, albeit distinguished, minority of free bankers remains, as always, a stubbornly permanent loyal opposition. At no other time in monetary annals have central banks been so much in the public forum – academic, institutional and political – as in recent years, beginning with the widely acclaimed reform and statutory independence of the Reserve Bank of New Zealand in 1989. For the first time there is a fully fledged periodical on central banking. Even in the Augustan age of monetary controversy in nineteenth-century England which engaged some of the most seminal contemporary economists, the battle lines in the classic debates between the Currency and Banking Schools were drawn around the monetary standard rather than the intrinsic role of the central bank. Central banking today is in a state of genuine transition which, even more than institutional reform, is witnessing the abandonment of what Robert Roosa once trenchantly called the systematic ad hocery of central banking policies.

But the burgeoning literature on central banking has focused mostly on the industrial democracies. Even de Kock's standard text on *Central Banking* although updated in successive editions till 1974 (the last) has only peripheral references to developing countries. The problems of central banking in developing countries have attracted a long line of writers since the pioneering contributions of Warren Hastings (1773) and James Steuart (1776) in the Indian context, which has had worthy successors, individual and institutional, notably the meticulous inquiries of Royal Commissions on

Indian monetary problems. The subsequent treatment of central banking problems in developing countries falls into three distinct groups, namely the country-specific monographs like those of Gupta (1934) and Raj (1948); regional studies as in Wagle (1937) and Plumptre (1947) which dealt with the British Dominions, followed by Tamagna (1965), Olakanpo (1965) and Basu (1967) on Latin American, the Commonwealth and African countries, respectively. The third group of a comparative study of 'Central Banking in Undeveloped Money Markets' was pioneered by Sen in 1952 and his last revised edition (1967) has had no successors. The extant literature on central banking in developing countries has been overtaken by the sheer speed of far-reaching institutional developments. The present monograph therefore attempts to fill a long-standing gap in the literature by providing a comprehensive descriptive, analytic, and normative framework drawing on the state of the art and the author's experience as a member of an epistemic community and a participant-observer in central banks and the international civil service.

The approach of this study is necessarily a blend of the historical and institutional. As even the high priest of economic theory remarked:

> Monetary theory is in 'history'... Monetary economics try as economists will to reduce it to a pure theory is in fact the study of a particular social institution ... which has inevitably developed in different ways in different milieux. (Hicks, 1982, pp. 132–3)

Central banks are in fact an archetype of 'a particular social institution' that is now faced with a variety of pressing challenges, which are addressed in this study. Among the principal issues are: the primacy of price, exchange and financial stability as objectives; the relative scope of monetary, regulatory, advisory, and developmental roles of central banks; the transition to indirect monetary policy instruments; the conflict between monetary policy and other roles; the fiscalization of central banks; the case for divestiture of their quasi-fiscal activities, which are a potent source of central bank losses; the macroeconomic implications of central bank losses; scope and limitations of central bank independence and of ceilings on credit to government; organizational reform of central banks including the partial privatization option. It aims at a *tour d'horizon* of the developing countries (including the Islamic and transitional economies) and views central banking as a policy-making process, central banks as organisations and central bankers as human capital. The empirical evidence draws on a sufficiently representative sample of central banking experience, regional and functional, with due regard to the perils of what social anthropologists call the Pago Pago principle – there is always an exception to every generalization in a sufficiently remote part of the globe. The analysis and prescriptions are not offered in any dogmatic stance. They aim, in the spirit of Francis Bacon, 'to excite the judgment briefly, rather than to inform it tediously', by exploring the grammar of argument. This book points to an agenda of country-specific issue-orientated research and reform, invoking the insights of analytic and institutional economics, particularly public choice and bureau theory as well as historical experience. Its key message: central banks as autonomous rather than independent knowledge-based but market-orientated public interest bureaux have to divest their fiscalization and aim at effective central banking. The white mice are fated to be perennial learners and doers.

ANAND CHANDAVARKAR

**Note**: As used in this book, the term 'country' does not in all cases refer to a territorial entity that is a state as understood by international law and practice. As used here, the term also covers some territorial entities that are not states but for which statistical data are maintained on a separate and independent basis.

# Acknowledgements

The author wishes to express his grateful thanks to:

J.A.H. de Beaufort Wijnholds, Executive Director, International Monetary Fund, for useful information on the central banks of Netherlands, Bulgaria, Cyprus and Israel.

J.D. Dorrington, former Alternate Executive Director, UK, for facilitating access to the Bank of England archives.

Philip Davies for prompt and helpful supply of material from the Bank of England archives.

The staff of the Joint Bank-Fund Library, Washington DC for unfailingly courteous and highly professional assistance, particularly: Beverly Tait and Deirdre Shanley, for excellent bibliographic services; Owi Jayanan for expeditious supply of inter-library material; Southamini Borlo and Jean Lachance Ntonme for cheerful and efficient circulation services. This marvellous bibliotheca provided the perfect milieu of monastic calm and friendly staff to assuage the Loneliness of the Long Distance Writer at Desk 1.

Melissa Little for timely and professional reformatting of the typescript.

Permission to use copyright material from the following sources is gratefully acknowledged:

Ian S. McDonald, Chief Editor, for tables from publications of the International Monetary Fund, Washington, DC.

Carol C. Rosen, Chief, Editorial and Production Services Unit, World Bank, Washington, DC, for tables from World Bank publications.

J.R.T. Footman, Secretary, Bank of England, for tables from the Bank of England Central Banking Symposium, June 1995, and the Bank of England *Quarterly Bulletin*.

R. Pringle, Editor, Central Banking Publications, London for tables from Morgan Stanley Central Banking Directory, 1996.

Blackwell Publishers, Oxford and Cambridge, Mass., for a table from 'Informal Financial Markets in Developing Countries', 1994.

Arnaldo Mauri, Editor, for a table from *Savings and Development*, 1988.

# 1 Nature, Objectives and Functions

'. . . both the ends and the means of central banking are multiple and there can therefore not be any golden rule for its conduct.' —*R. S. Sayers*

'Anyone who has studied carefully the evolution of Central Banking will have noted the steady broadening of its functions and goals.' — *Paul Samuelson*

## 1.1 THE NATURE OF CENTRAL BANKS

It has been rightly said 'defining central banking is problematic' but 'we recognize it when we see it' (Capie *et al.*, 1994, p. 5), rather like the phenomenon of fundamental disequilibrium in the balance of payments, which although not defined in the IMF Articles of Agreement is recognized by the Fund in providing adjustment finance. Therefore the more practical approach is to discuss the objectives and functions of typical central banks, which are best regarded as organizations rather than institutions following the illuminating dichotomy of Douglas North, who differentiates them as follows: Institutions are 'the humanly devised constraints that structure human interaction' and are made up of formal constraints like rules, laws, constitutions, informal constraints like norms and conventions, self-imposed codes of conduct, and their enforcement characteristics, which together define the incentive structure of economies and societies' (1994, p. 361). Organizations, on the other hand, comprise 'groups of individuals bound together by some common purpose to achieve certain objectives' and include political bodies (such as political parties, the Senate, a city council, regulatory bodies), economic bodies (such as, firms, trade unions, family farms, cooperatives), social bodies (for example, churches, clubs, athletic associations), and educational bodies (such as, schools, universities, vocational training centres) (ibid., p. 361). North defines institutions as the rules of the game in which organizations are the players and argues that 'organizations that come into existence will reflect the opportunities provided by the institutional matrix' (p. 361). This dichotomy can be further refined in so far as 'organizations have constitutions, are collective actors and are also subject to social rules' (Rutherford, 1994, p. 182), features which are readily applicable to central banks but, surprisingly, they do not figure in either the old nor the new institutionalism (see Rutherford's survey of the literature, 1994). An even more illuminating approach is to regard a central bank as an autonomous public interest bureau with a constitution, operating rules and a managerial bureaucracy. But to date the applications of bureau theory have been largely confined to an analysis of the US Federal Reserve System and other industrial country central banks (for example, Chant and Acheson, 1972; Goodfriend, 1988; Boyes *et al.*, 1988). In so far as a central bank acts as a fiscal agent for the government its behaviour is also amenable to agency theory which is concerned broadly with the interaction between principals and agents. On the other hand, a central bank has also to function as a cost-effective financial institution which also approximates it to a firm which aims not at profit, *per se*, but at an operating surplus and adequate reserves while meeting economic policy objectives. In sum, a central bank is very much an amalgam of an autonomous knowledge-based public interest bureau and a cost-effective financial entity.

## 1.2 OBJECTIVES

The contemporary debate happily no longer concerns the rationale of central banking except perhaps for the small core of unreconstructed 'free bankers' who would rely on the Invisible Hand even in monetary affairs, and even those argue that 'economic theory does not yield decisive arguments for and against laissez faire in bank-issued money' (Selgin and White, 1994, p. 1744). Rather the contemporary focus is on the range and scope of the objectives and functions of central banks. The literature has focused on issues such as: should central banks have a hierarchy of objectives with stability of the domestic currency (price stability) as the overriding aim? Should central banks concentrate on the so-called core functions of monetary policy and lender of last resort or should they also assume other responsibilities such as prudential regulation and supervision, exchange rate policy and developmental activities?

Central bank objectives may be usefully classified into:

(1) the tactical or conjunctural (macroeconomic) objectives of short-term and medium-term price stabilization (monetary management); sustainable balance of payments (exchange rate management);
(2) the long-term strategic objectives of development (payments systems, financial infrastructure);
(3) sectoral objectives (microeconomic) for example, prudential supervision, deposit insurance.

The conjunctural objectives are spelt out in all central bank statutes whereas promotional and developmental objectives are stated explicitly in the case of developing countries and exceptionally in the case of developed countries, as under the US Federal Reserve Act in conjunction with the Full Employment and Balanced Growth Act of 1948.

The stipulation of objectives is not necessarily a statutory requirement of central banks and barring a few exceptions such as the US Federal Reserve System, the statutes of the older central banks, – both in developed and developing countries – were confined to a listing of the 'general business' which they were permitted or expected to conduct (as for instance, in the earliest enactments of Bulgaria, Chile, Colombia, Estonia, Latvia, Lithuania (Kisch and Elkin, 1932). In contrast, the newer central banks founded in the late 1930s and the post-Second World War era invariably specify the objectives or purposes without always establishing a hierarchy of purposes. The objectives of central banking policy could be best described as statutory variations of four or five main objectives: price stability, viable exchange rates, sustainable balance of payments position, economic growth and development, full employment, and even general welfare. For instance, the central bank acts in the Caribbean region define their purposes in different ways, which may be generalized as follows: preservation of the internal and external value of the currency; promotion of a healthy financial system and economic development; development of capital markets (Blackman, 1993, pp. 91–2). Among the Caribbean central banks, the Barbados Central Bank Act seems to give equal weight to them; Jamaica and Guyana assign priority to economic development, while the Bahamas and the East Caribbean Central Bank Acts suggest the priority of price stability over economic development. Generally speaking, central banks which have less formal policy independence tend to have objectives which are more broadly defined in their statutes, covering a range of macroeconomic objectives or making general references to promote welfare. In contrast, banks with greater formal independence tend to have more narrowly focused specific statutory macroeconomic objectives emphasizing stability in the domestic and also the external value of the currency. On closer examination this apparent paradox dissolves because 'when monetary policy aims at several objectives simultaneously, with the need for choice and balance between them, policy will be subject to greater political oversight and the central bank will be subservient' whereas 'greater autonomy is more likely when central banks are asked to achieve a single macro outcome, such as the maintenance of the gold standards up till 1914, or price stability now' (Goodhart, 1994, p. 1427). But the primacy of price stability was in fact advocated as early as 1923 by Keynes, who argued that the Bank of England 'should adopt the stability of sterling prices as their primary objective – though this would not prevent their aiming at exchange stability also as a secondary objective' (1971, vol IV, p. 147). Keynes also acknowledged that Irving Fisher was the pioneer advocate of price stability as against exchange stability' in the shape of his 'compensated dollar', which was to be automatically adjusted by reference to an index number of prices without any play of judgment or discretion' (ibid., p. 147).

Typically, the drafters of central bank statutes of developing countries list several desirable objectives without seeking to establish any rank or order among them, thus leaving it to the policymakers to determine the relative importance of the policy objectives. This neutral posture is understandable given the lack of any guidance from the theory of hierarchial choice in economics which to date has been limited to analysing the implications of hierarchial preferences for demand theory, Engel curves, the theory of the firm and social choice and its possible applications to the economics of taxation and bargaining theory (Drakopoulos, 1994). The hierarchial choice paradigm has yet to be applied to analysing the objectives of central banks. In the absence of any ordering of objectives, one can only infer their relative importance by observation of revealed preference. Thus, a recent Bank of England survey of forty-four selected central banks in developing countries (BOE group) showed that although in virtually all cases the statutory objective included preservation of the (external and internal) value of the currency, only three countries, Chile, Cyprus, and Mexico, gave it the same priority as did the European System of Central

Banks (ESCB), who are required by the protocol of the Maastricht Treaty to make price stability the primary objective 'with support for other government objectives only possible when price stability has been attained (a lexicographic ordering)' (Bank of England, 1995, pp. 8–9). Despite the high priority given to price stability in the BOE group, their median level of inflation has been high (11.3 per cent over 1989–93) compared with the OECD countries over the same period (6.4 per cent). The failure of the central banks in the group to meet the statutory requirement of price stability is ascribed to the fact that they were not well placed to resist government pressures to finance their budgetary deficits and to provide financial subsidies to specific sectors by undertaking quasi-fiscal activities (ibid., p. 12). However, the contention that 'since inflation is a monetary phenomenon, central banks must bear a considerable responsibility for the state of affairs' (ibid., p. 12) is highly debatable. For one thing, there are other equally strong causes of inflationary pressures, notably fiscal imbalances and supply-side cost-push factors, and monetary policy alone cannot be expected to bear the entire onus of adjustment. It is also arguable whether mere statutory objectives are a cast-iron safeguard against central bank transgressions of its own laws, which are known to occur even in the most developed countries – for example, in the USA where the Federal Reserve's legal obligation, under the Humphrey–Hawkins Act 1978, to take steps to reduce unemployment whenever it is above 4 per cent has not always been fulfilled.[1] It is also the case that central bank statutes *per se* do not seem to constrain discretionary choice of additional objectives and activities not specifically covered in the law, and there is a subtle yet effective doctrine of implied powers. Central bank governors tend not to be strict constructionists in discharging their duties.[2] It is arguable whether sanctions and penalties can be imposed under the law of torts on any central bank for acts of omission and commission as a body corporate in relation to its defined objectives as distinct from actionable wrongs committed by its employees. The so-called purposes of central banks which are ritually set out in their statutes have therefore to be treated as more in the nature of hortatory guidelines, rather like the directive principles of political constitutions, than legal obligations.

The growing consensus in support of price stability as the prime objective of a central bank, however, carries the risk of obscuring that 'successful management comprises the simultaneous attainment of at least the four major objectives of high, if not full employment, growth, satisfactory balance of payments, reasonable stability of wages and prices (Kaldor, 1971, p. 2). Even in the context of a developing country like India it has been argued that: 'the primary function of the Central Bank is to ensure that the expansion of bank credit proceeds fast enough to exploit an economy's true potential for growth; so that the true economic potential of the economy can be reasonably fully exploited but this is neither ensured nor prevented by attempts to control the vagaries of the money supply' (Kaldor, 1984, p. 16). The analytics of the Kaldor approach and the best practice of central banks in developing countries would seem to argue against any lexicographic ordering of objectives. Given the desirability of the various social and macroeconomic objectives, and the fact that macroeconomic policies in simultaneous pursuit of different objectives inevitably create conflicts and trade-offs, there has to be a rational division of labour between the central bank and other public agencies, such as the treasury, concomitantly with the provision of a flexible and expeditious machinery for resolution of conflicts. This implies a proper orchestration of instruments and targets, although exceptionally the same instrument can secure the attainment of more than one target simultaneously. But a central bank, equally with the treasury, is obligated to follow the four commandments:

1. Keep your eye at all times on the probable effects of different policies on real income (corrected where necessary for distributional effects).
2. Do not multiply proximate targets without need, but, equally, do not drop legitimate objectives simply because you do not have sufficiently numerous or sufficiently effective policy instruments to attain them all.
3. . . . do not be hypnotized by the alleged importance of attaining a few fixed targets, often of a macroeconomic character, into forgetting the real income effects of misallocations of resources and distortions of demand.
4. Realize the inevitability of second-best or compromise solutions to policy problems. (Fleming, 1968, pp. 401–2)

Central bankers, like other technocrats, are only too prone to overlook the fourth commandment which also carries the corollary 'that policies be centrally coordinated, but 'in each country there is a limit to the number of policies that can be successfully coordinated by the political and administrative machine' (Ibid., p. 402). The targets most amenable to central bank instruments are price levels and exchange rates, which creates a strong presumption in favour of according priority to price stability as a 'single, quantifiable, easily recognized, measured and understood outcome' that facilitates greater autonomy as well as monitoring and accountability (Goodhart, 1994, p. 1427). A single goal like price stability has the advantage that it avoids any public expectations that a Central Bank can maximize employment without risking inflation. In the case of developing countries the trade-off and policy concern in the context of price stability is not so much with regard to cyclical employment, because of their typical occupational structure of predominantly self-employed farmers and artisans, as it is with structural and disguised unemployment which can only be addressed through rising growth and development. But even the strongest commitment to price stability is no assurance of growth and development, as shown by the experience of the United States and Great Britain under the gold standard which did not result in rapid growth. Since central bank statutes are amended only at long infrequent intervals, only a few (for example, Chile, Cyprus and Mexico) have set price stability as the priority target. But the absence of specific statutory embodiment in no way constrains the central bank from according it primacy in practice. The operative question then is whether the target should be expressed in terms of a desired level or range of prices or a desired rate of change of prices. Whatever the theoretical advantages of a target expressed in terms of levels, all the quantified targets so far adopted have been set, for practical reasons, in terms of the rate of increase of the retail or consumer price index expressed as a band-width (for example, 2 per cent in New Zealand). The measured inflation target should, however, be allowed to move outside the stipulated range (as in the Policy Targets Agreement of New Zealand) in certain exceptional circumstances such as major changes in terms of trade, a major natural disaster, material changes to indirect taxes, or a major divergence between the measured index and a version of the index that excludes interest rates. This could well be the cost of living index in the case of the developing countries, a figure which is more easily perceived in the popular consciousness. Its accepted deficiencies (such as the omission of asset prices (land, housing, and equities, and quality changes) are of less consequence in developing countries and could to a considerable extent be supplemented by using the exchange rate as an intermediate target.

While the acceptability of the cost of living index may not pose problems, a more difficult technical issue is whether it overstates or understates inflation, an aspect which has triggered a spirited controversy in the USA, where Alan Greenspan, the Chairman of the Federal Reserve and Senator D.P. Moynihan (Senate Finance Committee), among others, have argued that the consumer price index overprotects both tax-payers and social security beneficiaries because it overstates inflation within a plausible range of 0.7 per cent to 2 per cent as estimated in the interim report of the US Advisory Commission to study the Consumer Price Index (Michael J. Boskin, Chairman, 1995). There is also the problem that 'measured (RPI) inflation is conceptually mismatched with core inflation: the difference is more than just measurement error', when 'core inflation is defined as that component of measured inflation that has no (medium-to) long-run impact on real output – a notion that is consistent with the vertical long-run Philips curve interpretation of the commencement in inflation and output' (Quah and Vahey, 1995, p. 1130). It could also be argued that for all middle-income developing countries and emerging market economies one can put a 'development premium' on the consumer price index in as much as 'in growing economies the prices of services rise more rapidly than the average price of goods' and 'even with price stability in tradable goods, developing countries experience a positive increase in the CPI . . . . which is in fact positively associated with . . . economic growth' (Cooper, 1990, p. 147). For instance, Korea, a high-performance economy, had until the mid-1980s an increase in the consumer price index of between 10 and 20 per cent a year.

More important than the issue of a technically adequate price index is the overriding question: how does a central bank ensure the achievement of assigned targets of price stability since it involves not only monetary policy but also the entire panoply of macroeconomic management (exchange rates, fiscal policy, income policies, supply-side measures)? What are the sanctions in the event of failure? Among the possible sanctions are non-renewal of the Governor's term of office and relating the 'remuneration of senior central bank officials to their success' as was recommended (but rejected by the Bank) by Goodhart as an external adviser to the Reserve Bank of New Zealand before the 1989 Act (1994, p. 1432).

Whatever the theoretical merits of this proposal it does seem invidious to single out only the Governor (or staff) of the central bank for such a Draconian job contract which is not applied to any other public functionary. Would a similar dispensation apply to a finance minister who fails to balance the budget or introduces a tax which is unpopular and distortionary in its economic effects (such as, poll tax)?

## 1.3 FUNCTIONS

Central banks perform a variety of functions, which vary with the degree of institutional and market development of an economy. These are not all limited to the achievement and maintenance of price stability but may also include the more wide-ranging prudential, developmental, advisory and representational functions. It is possible to classify the list of more or less conventionally agreed central banking functions as follows.

### 1.3.1 Core Functions

1. Issue and regulation of legal tender currency (coinage is a government responsibility)
2. Banker and fiscal agent for the government (this may still leave the government the option to use commercial banks as depositories)
3. Banker for commercial banks
4. Lender of last resort
5. Management of foreign exchange reserves
6. Macroeconomic management of the cost (interest rates) availability and supply of money and credit

### 1.3.2 Optional or Peripheral Functions

1. Regulation and supervision of banks and/or the rest of the financial system; deposit insurance and credit guarantee schemes
2. Development of clearing, payments, and settlements systems and financial infrastructure
3. Full or partial responsibility for the regulation of foreign exchange markets, involving the determination of the exchange

rate at least within bounds; this latter role may depend on the choice of the exchange rate regime

4. External financial relations agent – for example, as fiscal agent and/or depository for the International Monetary Fund or in regional clearing and payments arrangements
5. Quasi-fiscal activities – for example, micro allocation of credit, credit subsidies to preferred sectors and so on (The divestiture of these activities may be an important precondition of effective central bank autonomy.)
6. Macroeconomic research, collection of monetary, financial data and balance of payments data (and acting as an statistical correspondent for international agencies such as the International Monetary Fund)
7. Surveillance of the banking and financial system including credit card companies, semi-formal and informal finance, and guarding the interests of users of banking and financial services
8. Fostering inter-central bank co-operation, including the international supervisory or prudential entities (such as the Basle Accords of the Bank for International Settlements)

As in the case of targets, the core functions of central banks can conflict with the peripheral, for instance, monetary policy considerations may conflict with developmental as well as prudential objectives.

# 2 Central Banks: Origins and Variants

'Another argument often used . . . complains that the "Currency Board" system common to many colonial territories is unduly rigid and that it makes the provision of additional currency unreasonably burdensome for the colonial territory.' — *R.S. Sayers*

## 2.1 ORIGINS

The genesis of the theory, organization, and practice of central banking is traditionally associated with the industrial countries which witnessed the foundation of the very first central bank, the Sveriges Riksbank in Sweden (1668), followed by the Bank of England (1694) and the European central banks in the nineteenth century, like the Bank of France (1980), the Bank of Finland (1811), the Netherlands Bank (1814), Austria and Norway (1816), and Denmark (1818) (see Appendix A.1). The origins of central banking doctrine date back to Bishop Berkeley's pioneering plan of a National Bank for Ireland (1735) in the first edition of his classic *The Querist* which was followed by the writings of a number of British economists, notably Ricardo (1828), Palmer, Henry Thornton, and Walter Bagehot. But it is hardly known even among the *cognoscenti* that by far the most extended discussion of central banking in different guises was undertaken in the context of the Indian subcontinent and, most remarkably, almost parallel to the celebrated monetary controversies in England. The unquestioned pioneer was the noted Scottish political economist, Sir James Steuart (1713–80), who, as an adviser to the East India Company, wrote the *Principles of Money Applied to the State of the Coin in Bengal* (India) in 1772. He even anticipated many modern developments including the rationale for detailed state intervention into virtually every aspect of economic life, particularly money and banking, which led an Indian economist to describe him as 'in a way the first Economic Adviser to the Government of India' (S.R. Sen, 1957, p. v). The earliest scheme to set up a bank in India with some characteristics of a central bank was the Plan for a General

Bank in Bengal and Bahar' (1773), the main British territories in India at that time, prepared by Warren Hastings, the Governor-General. It was envisioned as a government's bank to facilitate revenue collection and remittances, propagate the standard coin (Sicca) and remedy the contraction of currency at the time of revenue collection. Strangely, the bank, which achieved its objectives and even made a considerable profit during its short life – of which the Government took half – was abolished in February 1775 for reasons unconnected with economics (Reserve Bank of India, 1970, p. 9). Thereafter there was a succession of still-born schemes for a central bank in India beginning with Robert Rickards 'scheme for a General Bank' (1807–8), and the proposal for a 'Great Banking Establishment for British India' submitted by a body of merchants in England to the East India Company, followed by proposals for a National Banking Establishment presented by James Wilson, India's first Financial Member (1860). The proposed Bank, which was to be modelled on the Banking Department of the Bank of England, remained only on paper (ibid., p. 13). In 1870, Mr Ellis, a member of the Viceroy's Executive Council, suggested the setting up of a State Bank of India on the model of the Bank of France, which was followed by yet another still-born scheme (1884) to set up a central bank of issue on the model of the Netherlands Bank. One witness before the Indian Currency Committee (Fowler), de Rothschild, also outlined a scheme for creation of a bank in India similar to the Bank of England.

The first and most detailed blueprint for a State Bank in India was submitted by Keynes (1913) (in collaboration with Sir Ernest Cable) to the Royal Commission on Indian Finance and Currency (Chamberlain) in tandem with a similar scheme prepared by Lionel Abrahams, Assistant Under-Secretary of State for India. Both these schemes were shelved – much to the chagrin of Keynes, who noted, with some acerbity but with great perception, that successive proposals for a state bank in India were so often 'smothered in the magnificent and empty maxims of political wisdom' which clearly implied that there were no valid economic arguments against the creation of a central bank in India (Chandavarkar, 1985a, p. 284). Thereafter, the International Financial Conference (Brussels, 1920) passed a resolution to the effect that 'in countries where there is no central bank of issue, one should be established' which was followed by a similar recommendation by the second conference in Genoa (1922). In the wake of these resolutions, several countries established central banks, for instance, South Africa (1921), Colombia (1923), Hungary and Poland (1924). But once again the fates seemed to conspire against a central bank for India. When the Royal Commission in Indian Currency and Finance (Hilton Young) was appointed (1926) the setting up of a central bank was not one of its terms of reference. Nevertheless, the Commission strongly recommended the establishment of a central bank to be called the 'Reserve Bank of India'. It was ably supported by two eminent expert witnesses, (later Sir) Cecil Kisch, a noted authority on central banking, and (later Lord) Montague Norman, Governor of the Bank of England. But it was not until 1935, over a century and a half after Warren Hastings' pioneering scheme, that the Reserve Bank of India was set up as a full-fledged central bank. In fact, there is no parallel in monetary history anywhere to the phenomenally long period of gestation of the Reserve Bank of India, despite some of the most persuasive economic advocacy by eminent academics and bankers. The tangled history of 'The Delay in the Formation of the Reserve Bank of India' (Mathur, 1988) offers a piquant contrast to the creation of the two oldest central banks in the developing countries as early as 1828, without any political or intellectual fanfare in the two Dutch colonies – the Bank of the Netherlands Antilles and the Bank of Java (later nationalized as the central bank under the name Bank Indonesia).

As if to redress this historical imbalance, the Princely State of Hyderabad in India witnessed a most innovative experiment in central banking with the expeditious creation of the State Bank of Hyderabad (1941) which combined the functions of a bank of issue, banker to government, and a commercial bank, operating an exchange standard linked to the British Indian rupee at the standard ratio of Hyderabad rupees 116–10–8 = British Indian rupees 100, based on a paper currency reserve, two-thirds of which was held in metallic coin, while the maximum cover by securities was fixed at one-third of the total issue. This was a 'bank born and brought up under completely Indian auspices' (Iyengar, 1943, pp. 279–80), being largely the work of a notable member of the Hyderabad Civil Service, Nawab Mir Nawaz Jung, the Finance Secretary, who brought to his task a unique blend of practical experience and academic expertise, derived, ironically, as a pupil of two eminent free bankers, Hayek (London School of Economics) and von Mises (Geneva).

## 2.2 CURRENCY BOARDS

Now that every independent developing country has a fully-fledged central bank it might sound somewhat academic and even irrelevant to ask the question: are there any alternatives or variants of national central banks which developing countries, particularly the so-called mini states, need to consider? This argument has also acquired prominence in contemporary discussion, with the advocacy of currency boards or independent currency authorities (ICAs) as a technique to achieve monetary and price stability, convertibility, and the general promotion of foreign trade, saving and investment (Williamson, 1995; Hanke and Schuler, 1991, 1994). They have also been advocated as being particularly suitable for the emerging market economies in Eastern Europe and the former Soviet Union (Hanke and Schuler, 1991). The attempt to revive currency boards, although based on very sophisticated analysis, is nevertheless richly ironical if one recalls that there was a time when even noted academic economists and advisers to newly independent former colonies reviled the currency board as a part of 'The Mechanism of Neo-Imperialism' (Balogh, 1974) which amounted to a perverse export of capital from the colonies to the metropolis and inhibited conscious policies of stabilization and development in the dependencies.[1] Another issue which merits examination is the scope and limitations of central banking in unified currency areas such as the CFA Franc Zone (Central and West Africa) and the Eastern Caribbean Currency Area. It is possible to view a monetary union with a common central bank as a feasible alternative to multiple national central banks, particularly for the so-called mini states.

The conventional currency boards which were once widespread in the colonial territories of Africa, Asia, and the Caribbean, are now operative only in a few, mostly dependent, countries (Table 2.1). But they have been grafted on to existing central banks in Estonia and Lithuania and Argentina. The central issue is whether the potential advantages of a currency board are substantial enough to warrant its adoption on a universal scale by developing countries and the transition economies.[2] These advantages depend on the key elements and operating principles of a typical currency board, the distinguishing feature of which is the issue and redemption of legal tender currency on demand against a foreign reserve currency at a preannounced rate of exchange through a 100 per cent foreign reserve cover against the entire stock, or alternatively a 100 per cent marginal backing. Such an arrangement can also operate as part of a fully-fledged central bank, as in Malaysia, where the issue department of the Bank Negara maintains a 100 per cent foreign exchange cover. Singapore still retains the Board of Commissioners of Currency as an autonomous body operating a 100 per cent reserve currency.

*Table* 2.1 Existing currency boards (1995)

| *Country/territory* | *Date of establishment* | *Currency peg* |
|---|---|---|
| Argentina | 1991 | US dollar |
| Bermuda[a] | 1915 | US dollar |
| Brunei | 1967 | Singapore dollar |
| Cayman Islands[a] | 1972 | US dollar |
| Estonia | 1992 | Deutsche mark |
| Falkland Islands[a] | 1899 | Pound sterling |
| Faroe Islands[a] | 1940 | Danish krone |
| Gibraltar[a] | 1927 | Pound sterling |
| Hong Kong[a] | 1983 | US dollar |
| Lithuania | 1994 | US dollar |

[a] Dependent territories.
*Sources*: International Monetary Fund publications.

A currency board issues base money (notes and coin, which may also include some or all of the other reserves held by commercial banks) in exchange for foreign assets (reserve currency) at a fixed rate of exchange. The board operates on the rule 'that changes in the monetary base will be equal to the country's overall balance of payments surplus or deficit' which 'gives the country a highly credible mechanism for defending a fixed exchange rate, but at the cost of abandoning its monetary sovereignty because it has no discretion as regards its monetary policy' (Williamson, 1995, p. 1). The rationale for a currency board is best seen in a historical perspective because many of the arguments for its initial introduction are not really valid today. An example in point is the emphatic recommendation of the IMF mission to Libya (1950–1) that 'reserves of 100 percent in foreign exchange be maintained for the new Libyan currency in order to ensure a sound currency' and 'inspire the confidence in it which is so desirable in the case of a new country desirous of economic development' (Blowers and McLeod, 1952, pp. 456–7). The mission also justified their recommendation on the additional ground that 'the paucity of political experience and the lack of any past history of monetary and banking practice under domestic management, make us feel certain that inclusion of a discretionary element in the currency system is not desirable' (ibid., p. 460). The mission was, of course, mindful of the standard criticisms of the currency board system, which it was able to refute convincingly. For instance, the foreign exchange reserves 'that could be reasonably released by abandoning the 100 per cent reserve provision would be approximately equal to the necessary budgetary grant-in-aid during one bad year' and given the total currency circulation in Libya of about £3 million, the amount possibly available from this source was 'relatively unimportant' and the psychological disadvantages of reducing the reserve below 100 per cent would far outweigh any practical advantages' (Ibid., pp. 459–60). The mission also argued that any adverse developments resulting from drought or low export prices do not offer any scope for increasing real income through monetary and fiscal policies because these are not caused by a deficiency of internal effective demand. Any deflationary effects could be partially offset by the injection of new purchasing power from abroad through the operations of the Stabilization Fund (based on external grants-in-aid and budgetary subsidies). This situation was not dissimilar to that of the currency boards in British dependencies, which were able to maintain reserves at 100 per cent only because the governments had ready and preferred access to the London capital markets (under the British Trustee Investments Act) for long-term capital, and to the resources of large British banks like Barclays for meeting seasonal demands for credit through their branches in the dependencies. This mechanism, coupled with the fact that the local bank branches could create additional credit because of the fractional reserves system, ensured that the apparently rigid relation between the dependency's balance of payments and its currency circulation was considerably modified in practice. Likewise, the Bank of England's technical assistance and advice to the newly independent colonies and dependencies to retain currency boards or similar arrangements was intended as a half-way house to fully-fledged discretionary banking.[3]

It is also interesting to note that the currency board system in Libya was retained by the newly set up central bank, the National Bank of Libya (1956), by transferring its assets to the Issue Department. But the retention of the 100 per cent foreign exchange cover by the National Bank of Libya did not prevent the emergence of inflationary pressures in the economy subsequently because of the heavy expenditure of the oil companies and inappropriate fiscal policies, coupled with an inability to allow the exchange rate to appreciate, which was also a material factor, given the high import content of wage-goods (Chandavarkar, 1960).[4] The rigidity of the exchange rate pegged as it was to the pound sterling proved a real constraint on the flexibility of macroeconomic policies. It is, therefore, important to view the advantages of a currency board system in proper perspective. The four major advantages commonly invoked in support of currency boards as opposed to central banks are that they:

- assure convertibility;
- instil macroeconomic discipline;
- provide a guaranteed balance of payments adjustment mechanism; and because of these features
- they create confidence in the monetary system and thereby promote trade, investment and growth (Williamson, 1995, p. 13).

The currency board's ease and simplicity of operation makes it particularly suitable for the former centrally planned economies in their transition to full central banking in a market-orientated economy. It also ensures fiscal responsibility inasmuch as if the budget is not balanced, the government can no longer have recourse to print money through the central bank. Barring the ultimate option of overriding the statute of the currency board, governments may compel commercial banks to lend to the government at below market rates of interest by requiring them to hold part of their reserves in low-yielding government bonds. The difference between the actual yields and the free-market yields would then accrue as non-cash seigniorage to the government. Since the currency board is not obligated to convert demand deposits directly into legal tender currency, commercial banks would need to maintain extra reserves of domestic currency or of foreign assets that are easily convertible into domestic currency. The two possible options suggested to meet this requirement, namely 'to encourage international branch banking and to establish a separate monetary agency with substantial holdings of foreign reserves and credit lines abroad to back up the commercial banks' (Osband and Villanueva, 1993, p. 21) in fact only serve to expose the inherent limitations of the currency board system as a monetary mechanism for an autonomous country. It is argued that international banks could then supply reserve liquidity to domestic banks through an interbank market. This only suggests that no country can dispense with a domestic lender of last resort, that is, a full-fledged central bank, to meet liquidity requirements of its banks and financial institutions. The same objection applies to the creation of a separate monetary agency to provide discount facilities subject to strict limits which may include 'punitive interest rates, time limits on outstanding discounts, and requirements that repayments of reserve borrowings by the commercial banks take precedence over new credits to customers' (ibid., p. 213). In fact, there is something Gilbertian in the suggestion, first, to set up a currency board on grounds of simplicity of operation and then to seek to circumvent its limitations by creating a parallel agency and to depend on foreign banks to provide liquidity to domestic banks. Also, the corset of a currency board precludes variation of the exchange rate without undermining the board itself as is borne out by the overvaluation of the Argentine peso from levels of inflation which are above the levels in the USA, to whose dollar the peso is pegged, resulting in an appreciation of the peso in real terms. To correct the overvaluation of the peso would mean the adoption of the politically more difficult option of restraining wages and prices – that is, an incomes policy, the thorniest of all nettles to grasp, even in the most sophisticated industrial countries. Such a scenario is more probable and more risky in large economies, whereas inflation in non-traded goods and services, the usual source of currency overvaluation, is much less probable in smaller open economies, which are price-takers because the bulk of their prices are set by international price-makers. This explains why the most successful experiences of using a currency board are those of the small and highly open economies – Brunei, Hong Kong, Estonia and Singapore – whereas Argentina, the largest of the group, is very much of an outlier. This assessment probably also explains the rejection of the currency board option by Brazil and the fact that to date the currency board has had very limited appeal to the majority of developing countries. In fact,

> the steady sequence of reforms being introduced by the authorities in Hong Kong is testimony to the constraining nature of such an arrangement. While these constraints are a virtue when central banking experience is scarce, or in times of crisis, currency boards are likely to evolve

over time into more conventional arrangements, as experience is gained and crises fade (Bennett, 1994, p. 210).

Meanwhile, the somewhat overzealous advocacy of the merits of currency boards has only served to divert attention from key policy objectives like fiscal consolidation and balancing the budget. 'In sum, a currency board would seem a good device to reinforce a commitment to fiscal discipline, but it is not clear that it could create such a commitment where it does not already exist' (Williamson, 1995, p. 29). In this context, it is instructive to contrast the lopsided contemporary advocacy of currency boards to the exclusion of equally important fiscal reforms with the broad-based recommendations of the successive Kemmerer financial missions to American countries in 1917 and 1930 which, in addition to the establishment of central banks in Peru (1922), Colombia (1923), Chile (1925), Ecuador (1927) and Bolivia (1020), gave equal importance to budgetary reform.[5] According to Kemmerer only a balanced budget was consistent with the maintenance of a fixed gold standard peg and typically he recommended adoption of 'modern and scientific procedures for the imposition, collection, and disbursement of taxes, the abolition of special subsidies, and the accumulation of a reserve of surplus funds, with centralized budgetary control in a single ministry of public finance.' Kemmerer also recommended limiting the right of note issue to central banks and going on to the gold standard, precluding monetization of budget deficits to ensure effective control of note circulation and maintenance of monetary stability.

In the final analysis, policy-makers have to balance 'seven actual or potential disadvantages of currency boards,' namely, 'the seigniorage problem, the start-up problem, the transition problem, the adjustment problem, the management problem, the crisis problem, and the political problem' against their putative advantages (Williamson, 1995, pp. 19–29). These may be elaborated as follows:

(1) The seigniorage cost of using a foreign currency to back the domestic money supply would depend on the difference between the yield on its foreign assets and the return on any alternative marginal domestic investment. This is the familiar problem of the opportunity costs of foreign exchange cover for domestic money supply, which is a matter for empirical deter-

mination rather than a priori analysis. However, the argument that 'if a currency board increases confidence that the domestic currency will maintain its value and so encourage substitution of domestic for foreign currency, seigniorage will actually be higher under a currency board' (ibid., p. 20) is not really decisive. The strength of a currency depends on the productivity of the economy and its balance of payments position, rather than on the composition and magnitude of its foreign exchange backing. Hot money flights, for instance, are unconnected with the foreign cover of a currency. Otherwise, there would not be hot money movements between highly prosperous currency area or countries.

(2) The start-up problem of mobilizing sufficient gold or convertible currency to back the entire monetary base can pose severe difficulties, although it is feasible to launch a currency board with less than cent-per-cent cover, as in Argentina (of net reserves) and Estonia. Admittedly, the cover in both those cases rose very quickly to more than 100 per cent, but this was a result of fortuitous exogenous factors, namely the Brady Plan Settlement (Argentina) and the restitution of Second World War gold by the Bank of England and the Swedish Riksbank in the case of Estonia. It is arguable that for medium-sized and large countries the sheer magnitude of the required start-up cover would be a daunting hurdle.

(3) The transition problem refers to the risk of overvaluation of the fixed exchange rate 'if a currency board is introduced in a country with a high inflation rate' and the related questions of 'how large the overvaluation will be and how long the transitional period will be' since 'the evidence does not suggest that fixing the exchange rate has typically brought inflation screeching to a halt' (Williamson, 1995, p. 21).

(4) The adjustment problem arises because currency boards are precluded from using the exchange rate to secure balance of payments adjustment, and this can arise at any time, and not necessarily during an initial transitional period due to inflationary hysteresis 'The economic adjustment costs as a result of an inability to . . . change the real exchange rate through a change in the nominal rate could call into question the credibility of the commitment to a fixed rate' (ibid., p. 23). Therefore, as suggested by the optimal currency area literature,

small, open economies 'are well advised to fix or at least peg their exchange rates to the country of their major trading partner, while less open economies have more to gain by allowing some form of exchange rate flexibility' (ibid.).

(5) The management problem arises because currency boards cannot operate a proactive discretionary monetary policy. Monetary policy therefore tends to be necessarily procyclical and if capital movements are volatile, 'the government may even find it necessary to tighten fiscal policy' as in Argentina (1995) in the wake of the Mexican crisis (ibid., p. 24).

(6) This, in turn, poses the political problem 'whether fiscal policy will in fact be disciplined by the establishment of a currency board' (ibid., p. 28).

(7) Perhaps an even more decisive consideration is the crisis problem inasmuch as a currency board cannot act as a lender of last resort and 'it is not fail-safe' once there is a flight of domestic capital.

Finally, it is only realistic to recognize the political dimensions of the issue which suggests that the 'price is sufficiently high as to make monetary sovereignty as dysfunctional as possible as most other aspects of this curious social institution called national sovereignty' but 'monetary sovereignty is likely to provide a net economic benefit to large countries, except when there is no alternative way of reestablishing a measure of credibility for economic policy' (Williamson, 1995, p. 42). The message is clear: currency boards are not a panacea; they are best suited for small open economies and as interim contrivances for transitional economies.

Currency boards have historically been the precursors of transitional central banking institutions, the so-called 'monetary authorities' set up in Fiji (1973), the Solomon Islands (1976), the Seychelles (1976), Belize (1979), the Maldives (1981), and Bhutan (1982). The title 'monetary authority' was selected deliberately to suggest that the new institutions were not expected immediately either to carry out all the functions or to have the operational independence of a full central bank (Collyns, 1983, pp. 10 and 22). Paradoxically, the Monetary Authority of Singapore is a solitary case of a pioneer which has retained the title despite graduation to being a full central bank (except for the currency issue) whereas virtually all the others have shed the title on assumption of full central banking functions.

## 2.3 NATIONAL OR MULTINATIONAL CENTRAL BANKS

The historic role of currency boards as halfway houses towards discretionary central banking poses the related question: should emergent countries, particularly the so-called mini-states, opt for national currencies and national central banks, or for membership of a unified currency area with a common central bank, like the West African Monetary Union (WAMU), the Central African Monetary Union (CAMA) and the East Caribbean Currency Area

*Table* 2.2 Currency areas

| *Currency areas* | *Members* | *Currency peg* |
|---|---|---|
| 1. West African Monetary Union (WAMU) (7 members) | Benin, Côte d'Ivoire, Mali, Niger, Burkina Faso, Senegal, Togo | French franc |
| 2. Central African Monetary Union (CAMA) (6 members), | Cameroon,Congo, Central African Republic,Equatorial Guinea,Chad | French franc |
| 3. Eastern Caribbean Currency Area (ECCA) (7 members) | Antigua, Dominica,Grenada, Montserrat, St. Kitts-Nevis,St. Lucia, St. Vincent | US dollar |
| 4. Rand Area[a] | South Africa, Lesotho, Swaziland | South African rand |

[a] The currencies of Lesotho and Swaziland are both pegged to the South African rand, which is also legal tender in Lesotho. But the three currencies are otherwise distinct, and the parity of both of the smaller countries can be changed without agreement of the other.

*Source*: Author's compilation from IMF sources.

(ECCA) (Table 2.2) Does mere smallness of area and population warrant membership of a currency union, or in any way modify the nature of central banking. This question has been decisively answered by a former Governor of the Central Bank of the Solomon Islands:

> Some of the most interesting and difficult functions are not explicit in the structure, staffing, accounts of the bank. This observation is just as true of large central banks. If you set aside the staff list and the balance sheet, and look at the statutes setting up these banks, and the functions they are expected to perform, there is no significant difference between the smallest and the largest. Clearly smallness does not mean narrower legal definition or formal boundaries, or less comprehensive objectives of financial stability, systemic soundness, balanced growth and so forth.
>
> Current moves to narrow the focus of central banking onto price stability above all else, would also logically apply regardless of size . . . But while institutional smallness is real enough, and certainly affects the way we operate – mainly in positive ways, I think – I don't believe it is the smallness of the central bank itself that makes central banking 'at the small end' different, as much as the smallness of the political economy in which it operates. We are performing conventional central banking functions in economies that are often tiny by world standards, only partially monetized, very open to external influences, often making heavy use of foreign aid, lacking in financial and industrial complexity or depth, and where politics is highly personalized. (Hughes, 1992, pp. 23–4)

Thus, it is not the smallness of the central bank but the smallness of the environmental political economy that explains the differences between the Central Bank of the Solomon Islands and the Monetary Authority of Singapore. The monetary evolution of the mini states in the Pacific and in the Eastern Caribbean has followed divergent paths, with the former region opting for national currencies and central banks and the latter for membership of common currency areas with a supraregional central bank (Table 2.3). The membership of the two currency areas and the two supranational banks in the CFA Franc Zone has been determined more by historical, political and geographic factors than by strict economic criteria, since there is a high degree of economic diversity among the countries in the zone, with each region being dominated by a relatively large country accounting for about a quarter of the region's output; Côte d'Ivoire (West Africa) and Cameroon (Central Africa). Of the thirteen countries, nine are classified as low income and three oil exporters (Cameroon, the Congo and Gabon) have much higher levels of per capita GDP, with Côte d'Ivoire as an intermediate case. Benin, Côte d'Ivoire, Senegal, and the Congo

*Table* 2.3 Institutional Arrangements of the CAMA and ECCA 1990

| | | *CAMA/BEAC* | *ECCA/ECCB* |
|---|---|---|---|
| 1. | *Reference dates* | | |
| | Creation | 1960 | 1965 |
| | Last major reforms | 1972; 1990 | 1983 |
| 2. | *Basic provision* | | |
| | Currency unit(s) | Common currency (CFAfranc) issued by common central bank (BEAC) | Common currency (EC dollar) issued by common central bank (ECCB) |
| | Monetary policy | Co-ordinated policy | Common policy |
| | External exchange rate | Common external rate | Common external rate |
| | parity | Collective fixed peg to the French franc (CFAF 50 = FF1) | Collective fixed peg to the US$ (EC$2.7 = US$1) |
| | regime of convertibility | Fully guaranteed under co-operation agreement with France | No external guarantee |
| | Capital restrictions | None (harmonized) within (outside) the Franc zone | Prevail within and outside the ECCA |
| | Interest rate policy | Common policy | Common policy |
| 3. | *Organizational structure* | | |
| | Highest body | Monetary Committee composed of finance ministers | Monetary Council composed of finance ministers |
| | Policy-making body | National Monetary Council | Board of Directors |
| | Executive body | | |
| 4. | *Voting powers* | Weighted vote among members | Equal vote among members |
| 5. | *Statutory limits on central bank-operations* | | |
| | Foreign currency cover[a] | 20 per cent of sight liabilities of the BEAC (minimum) | 60 per cent of currency and other demand liabilities of ECCB (minimum) |
| | Claims on government (gross) | 20 per cent of previous year's budgetary revenues (ceiling) | 10 per cent on T-bill holdings; plus 5 per cent on other securities holdings; plus 5 per cent for advances |

*Notes*: CAMA: Central African Monetary Area
ECCA: Eastern Caribbean Currency Area
BEAC: Banque des Etats de l'Afrique Centrale
ECCB: Eastern Caribbean Central Bank (replaced East Caribbean Currency Authority on 1 October 1983).
[a] Gross official reserves of the common central banks, in per cent of liability base defined in the respective coloumns.

*Source*: Adapted from Nascimento, 1994, p. 31.

have had substantial recourse to market borrowing while the remaining countries are classified as primarily official borrowers. The most significant feature of the CFA Franc Zone 'is that by itself it does not constitute an optimal currency area by any of the accepted criteria such as: that members should be affected similarly by disturbances; should have a high degree of intercountry factor mobility and intra regional trade; reasonable flexibility of prices and wages; and similarity in regard to policies towards inflation' (Boughton, 1991, pp. 6–7). This is only a classificatory scheme and 'there are no formal or parametric standards for evaluating the appropriateness or effectiveness of any particular currency union' (ibid., p. 6).

The CFA Franc Zone is a virtually unique combination of a currency union and monetary standard of sovereign countries with a fixed peg to the currency of a co-operating foreign country (France). The exchange rate stability of the CFA franc against the French franc since 1948 (CFAF50 = FF1) is a remarkable performance for so diverse a group of developing countries and is regarded as a major determinant of the region's economic performance and stability. This means that the countries in the zone have abjured the exchange rate as a policy instrument and operate monetary discipline through:

- interest charges on overdrafts;
- credit rationing by raising the cost of rediscounting and reducing its availability when balances fall below target levels;
- ceilings on credit to each government to a maximum of 20 per cent of the previous year's revenue.

The heavy reliance on rediscounting reflects the narrowness of the domestic financial markets and the absence of reserve requirements. Each regional central bank maintains an operations account of at least 65 per cent of reserves other than working balances with the French Treasury.

It is also instructive to compare and contrast the performance of monetary policy under the two different institutional arrangements of the central banks for Central Africa (BEAC) and the East Caribbean (ECCB), which have as their main objective, '[to] safeguard the common pool of resources in order to preserve the parity of the fixed collective peg' (Nascimento, 1994, p. 10, Table 2.3). Although the ECCB is called upon to assist economic development of member countries, the BEAC is not assigned such objectives, which come within the purview of national monetary authorities. There is a major difference in the mandate of the respective central banks: to harmonize members' monetary policies in the case of the BEAC, whereas the ECCB aims at a common monetary policy for the group. This accounts for the decentralization in the formulation of monetary policy in the CAMA and the centralization in the case of the ECCA, and also explains the differences in their respective programming techniques. Thus the BEAC formulates its targets at the national level and the national authorities submit the monetary targets (such as, rediscount ceilings, foreign reserves, and so on) to the Board for approval. The Monetary Council of the ECCB determines monetary aggregate (or areawide) targets (for example, foreign reserves, rediscount ceilings, aggregate credit ceilings). Among other things it aims at maintaining a foreign currency cover of about 75 per cent of its own sight liabilities in order to protect the common pool of reserves. Although both BEAC and ECCB use statutory rules and discretionary tools to implement monetary policy, the rules and design of instruments differ markedly, with discretionary controls being more limited in the case of the ECCB (Table 2.4). The main finding on the conduct of their monetary policies during 1976–88, is that 'due to disparities in their institutional and structural setup, the ECCB and BEAC achieved opposite results with regard to controlling the area's domestic credit and thus preserving the area wide external position' (Nascimento, 1994, p. 28). This study comments on the inability of the BEAC to protect the net foreign reserves (1976–90), allowing for exogenous shocks like drought and fall in export prices, as being due to inadequate design and use of rediscounting – the main monetary control instrument – capital flight due to rigid interest rates, erosion of public confidence in the banking system, and lack of co-ordination of fiscal and monetary policy. But the study does not explain why the BEAC has not used reserve requirements as a policy instrument though it is empowered to do so. In contrast, the ECCB was able to strengthen the net foreign reserve position by pursuing a flexible interest rate policy to prevent capital flight. The empirical analysis of the results for the ECCA 'support the hypothesis of a speedy external adjustment process when the central bank relies on interest rate management' (ibid., p. 29).

*Table* 2.4 BEAC and ECCB: monetary policy instruments, 1976–90

| I. | BEAC | *ECCB* |
|---|---|---|
| 1. Foreign currency cover[a] | 20 per cent | 60 |
| 2. Limit(s) on central bank financing of governments | Single limit on BEAC credit, equal to 20 per cent of previous year's budgetary revenues, applied uniformly to all governments. Any modification requires revision of statutes (none so far). | Three limits set on: (a) holdings of national treasury bills, equal to 10 per cent of estimated recurrent budgetary revenues over the current year; (b) holdings of other government securities, equal to 15 per cent of ECCB's sight liabilities; (c) temporary advances, equal to 5 per cent of governments' annual average recurrent revenues over the three preceding years. |
| II. *Discretionary tools* | | |
| 1. Rediscount ceilings | Set on short-term, medium-term, and long-term rediscounts for each member which, in turn, allocates them among banks[b] | Not used. ECCB has relied on moral suasion which has been sufficient because of limited dependence on rediscounts by banks which rely on the money market |
| 2. Reserve requirements | Not used | 6 per cent of bank's total deposit liabilities |
| 3. Interest rate | Set: (a) rediscounts and penalty rates and (b) a 'reference' deposit rate ('*taux crediteur de base*') | Set (a) the charge on its overdrafts; (b) the rate of bankers' deposits with ECCB; (c) the 'money market' rate. Banks are free to determine their lending and nearly all deposit rates but there is a minimum of 4 per cent for savings deposits set by the ECCB |

[a] Official reserves of the common central bank in per cent of its sight liabilities
[b] Selective credits are rediscountable outside these ceilings.
*Source*: Adapted from Nascimento, 1994, p. 12.

What can one conclude about the efficacy of the CFA Franc Zone as a currency union? Although far from being an optimum currency area because of limited intra-regional trade, some rigidity of prices and wages, diversity of incidence of variations in terms of trade, and the non-availability of the exchange rate as a policy tool – which places an extra burden on fiscal policies – the CFA Franc Zone authorities have been able to stabilize economic activity (Boughton, 1993, p. 105). There are, however, no studies of the efficacy of other central banking functions such as prudential supervision in the currency unions, which makes it difficult to evaluate central banking as a whole as distinct from analyses of monetary policy. Even these studies do not explain why certain available instruments of monetary policy such as reserve requirements have not been used. Nor is one enlightened on matters like the failure to develop interbank money markets in the Franc Zone on the lines of the ECCA. But such arrangements which are an offshoot of special factors such as political and geographic consanguinity are unlikely to be replicated, and, not surprisingly, some long-projected currency unions like the UMA (L'Union du Maghreb Arabe) comprising Algeria, Libya, Morocco, Mauritania and Tunisia, have not gone beyond the drawing board.

# 3 Monetary Policy: Instruments and Issues

> 'Milton, Milton, we set up the Fed to adjust the quantity of money to the needs of the economy.' — *Paul Samuelson*
>
> 'There is no single objective by which all monetary policy can be conditioned.' — *Radcliffe Committee*

The prime policy objective of a central bank in a market economy which is being increasingly accepted as the internal and external stability of the national currency in the medium term, was pioneered by Keynes in his classic exposition of domestic price stability as the sole aim of monetary policy (1924). In attempting to regulate the cost, availability and supply of money and credit a central bank can operate in two ways: directly through its regulatory power, or indirectly through its influence on money market conditions and the monetary variables as the sole source of central bank money (that is, legal tender currency and balances with the central bank). This distinction is based on their respective channels of transmission (Table 3.1).

Direct instruments are targeted to either prices (interest rates) or quantities of credit through regulation and are mainly aimed at the balance sheets of commercial banks. The term 'direct' connotes the one-to-one correspondence between the instrument (for example, credit ceiling) and the policy objective (for example, domestic credit). Indirect instruments, on the other hand, are targeted at the balance sheet of the central bank and operate through the money market by influencing the underlying demand and supply conditions. Hence they are also described as market-based instruments as they generally influence the supply of bank reserves through banks and non-bank financial institutions at market-related prices on a voluntary basis. But even indirect market-based instruments have a modicum of regulation to govern the terms and conditions of their use – for instance, specifying the forms of auctions, the eligibility of counterparties, and the modes of payment at settlement. Nevertheless, within the framework it is the market forces that, through the operation of indirect instruments, influence variations in central

*Table* 3.1 Monetary policy: instruments and process

| *Instruments* | |
|---|---|
| *Direct* | *Indirect* |
| 1. Interest rate controls | 1. Reserve requirements[a] |
| 2. Credit ceilings (bank-by-bank) | 2. Rediscount window |
| 3. Rediscount quotas (bank-by-bank) | 3. Lombard (overdraft) window |
| 4. Statutory liquidity ratios | 4. Public sector deposits |
| 5. Selective credit controls | 5. Credit auctions |
| 6. Moral suasion | 6. Open market operations<br>(a) Primary market sales of<br>(i) central bank securities<br>(ii) government securities<br>(b) Secondary market operations (outright purchases and sales or repurchase (and reverse repurchase) operations |
| | 7. Foreign exchange swaps |

*Process*

Intermediate target (monetary/credit aggregate, exchange rate)

| Instruments (prices or quantities reserve ratios) | Operating target | Ultimate target | Price stability |
|---|---|---|---|

Indicators (or information variables)

[a] Reserve requirements have features of both direct and indirect instruments but are conventionally classified by central banks as indirect because reserve money creation is most directly monitored and controlled through the central bank's balance sheet.

bank money. Equally, it is misleading to impose a rigid dichotomy between direct and indirect instruments since they may be used concurrently during the usually prolonged periods of transition to full reliance on market-based instruments, both in developing countries and the transition economies. Thus, statutory liquidity ratios are still used in many market-orientated countries but mainly for prudential reasons. Likewise, moral suasion, although essentially a supplementary instrument, can be used under both monetary policy regimes, direct and indirect.

Perhaps a more significant distinction than that between direct or indirect is whether an instrument is statutory or market-based, meaning whether it is voluntarily held at a certain price. But given market imperfections the resultant interest rates may not be representative: as, for instance, interbank rates when all banks are subject to credit ceilings and have excess liquidity, or where banks are obliged to hold statutory reserves in government securities at controlled rates. Given the armoury of instruments, the challenge for central banks is to find an appropriate balance between rules and discretion in order to handle possible conflicts between the dual aims (internal and external) of monetary policy, taking due account of the ratchet-like character of several prices such as public utility rates and wages.

## 3.1 DIRECT INSTRUMENTS

The recourse to direct instruments reflects a combination of technical, administrative, and political factors, coupled with the fact that 'they seem to have performed well at least in some industrial countries, until the mid 1980s without any immediately apparent negative side-effects', as noted in an IMF study (Alexander *et al.*, 1995, p. 9). It is, however, debatable whether any developing country was even remotely influenced by the experiences of any industrial country. For instance, prudential considerations do not seem to have been influential in developing countries in instigating ceilings on interest rates as much as the need to keep interest rates low to facilitate government borrowing and overall investment. More to the point is the fact that given their undeveloped financial systems direct instruments were the only feasible instrument until the markets and framework for indirect instruments had been developed. They are also more amenable to a monetary programming format of instruments targets and have greater transparency, relatively low fiscal costs, and attractiveness as a vehicle of directed credit to priority sectors. They are easier to 'implement and explain to politicians and the public' (ibid., p. 9). Moreover, in the absence of alternative domestic sources of credit, bank-by-bank credit ceilings have the great merit of being workable regardless of the exchange rate regime. Generally, like direct controls in the real sector, direct monetary instruments are a useful, 'second best or supplemental instrument in situations of severe specific or general market failures,' and therefore, 'should be part of any central bank's arsenal even if not normally used' (Lindgren, 1991, p. 323). But this line of thought overlooks that such a conjuncture may equally reflect the passivity of central banks and their failure to take positive initiatives to develop money markets on the lines of the Bank of Canada in the 1950s and 1960s.

But the core elements of direct monetary instruments, bank specific credit ceilings and highly differentiated interest rate limits, are both potent sources of distortion, inefficiency and inequity, which have to be set off against their perceived advantages. Among the typical major distortions and problems associated with direct instruments are the following. First, interest rate ceilings often result in low or negative real rates, discouraging savings and thus the availability of total credit. They also cause domestic disintermediation and lead to flight of capital abroad, or into real assets like land, real estate, gold, or consumer durables. Attempts to manage monetary conditions at the micro level often create an excessively complex tiered structure of interest rates differentiated by categories and maturities, as in Korea, Kenya, Indonesia, Mexico and Tunisia. For instance, Korea, before the reforms of September 1965, had no fewer than eleven classes of deposits with rates ranging from 0 to 1.8 per cent on money accounts and from 3.5 per cent to 16.8 per cent on savings accounts. 'So fine a distinction between accounts implies a knowledge by banking officials about the public's elasticities of demand for deposits of different maturity, with slight differences also in some other characteristics, that must be fictitious' (Gurley *et al.*, 1965, p. 53). Similarly, in Indonesia in the year prior to reform and liberalization, there were over twenty different categories of refinance credits each with its own interest rate. India presents a curious anomaly where only the lending rates of commercial banks for small advances (Rs. 25 000–Rs. 200 000) are still fixed administratively (12–13.5 per cent) since 18 October 1994, although banks are free to determine the rate for all advances above Rs. 200 000. This arrangement is obviously a disguised subsidy to the so-called small borrower. Such excessive fine-tuning of interest rates by fiat cannot be based on any rational economic criteria. Second, direct controls tend to proliferate in an attempt to cope with evasions of initial controls, as in Argentina, Hungary, and Egypt, where interest rate controls had to be buttressed by credit ceilings, a textbook illustration of the policy consequences of Goodhart's Law – controls of monetary aggregates breed substitutes and lead to more controls. In turn, credit ceilings pose their own problems in so far as they are related to amounts extended by specific institutions or are earmarked to finance specific key or priority sectors as of a certain base period (as in Egypt, Ghana and Jamaica). 'Such ceilings perpetuate market shares, independent of a bank's competitiveness, and reduce the incentive for banks whose ceilings are binding to finance profitable projects' (Alexander *et al.*, 1995, p. 9). More importantly, direct controls are ineffective in determining the intended end-use of credit because of the fungibility of credit and finance and, in any event, tend to lose their effectiveness over time, particularly as controls on international capital movements are eased or circumvented.[1] Also, the recourse to direct controls can be positively misleading because 'policy objectives are often defeated in practice, even if monetary targets are met' (ibid., p. 14). Finally, direct controls hamper price competition among banks, and the development of money markets, and by involving the central bank in micro management issues lead to conflicts with its macroeconomic and prudential role. In so far as they are effective, they lead to financial repression, disintermediation, and an overhang of liquidity because of limits on bank credit, while the growth of deposits is funnelled by an expansion of reserve money caused, among others, by monetization of fiscal deficits.

## 3.2 INDIRECT (MARKET-RELATED) INSTRUMENTS

Indirect monetary instruments offer many decisive advantages over direct instruments, notably greater flexibility and effectiveness in the implementation and conduct of monetary policy – more effectiveness because they work through markets and permit small, frequent and timely changes in instrument settings, enabling the authorities to respond rapidly to shocks and to correct policy errors, thereby obviating the need for more massive shifts in policy. Such timely and appropriate responses are infeasible in respect of direct instruments like credit ceilings which are usually set on a quarterly or annual basis. Market instruments also help to depoliticize the formulation of monetary and exchange rate policy and the allocation of credit and foster the development of competitive financial markets, which in turn increase financial savings and improve the efficiency of investment. Additionally, they ensure consistency between monetary, fiscal and exchange rate policies. On the other hand, the simple one-to-one correspondence between instruments and policy targets, as in the case of direct instruments, does not obtain in regard to indirect instruments because of the longer lags which therefore necessitate intermediate targets or indicators that can be gauged more frequently, such as monetary and credit aggregates and short-term interest rates. There are also difficult transitional problems associated with the limitation of credit controls and interest rate liberalization.

## 3.3 INTEREST RATE MANAGEMENT

The key to a market-instrument-based monetary policy is a genuinely market-determined interest rate regime, but interest rate liberalization is not to be equated with a *laissez-faire* policy stance, since no monetary authority would be willing to accept as reasonable any structure or level of interest rates that is market-determined. It therefore requires the replacement of administratively determined interest rates by indirect monetary policy techniques operating through the market, while using a set of indicators, which together can help the central bank to judge whether prevailing interest rates are grossly out of equilibrium. There are, however, no unambiguous criteria for determining the appropriateness of nominal rates of interest. The most favoured guideline is that of positive expected real rate of interest, taking account of the taxation of interest incomes. Ideally, the most appropriate deflator of nominal rates is a representative price index that reflects the prices of current consumption goods as well as the prices of capital goods. But then due allowance has also to be made for the understatement of inflationary pressures due to subsidies and price controls and the lack of reliable consistent time series of prices and inflation rates. A comprehensive real interest rate series would also need to take account of relevant foreign rates of interest, exchange rate expectations, and the rate of return to domestic capital. A more basic limitation is that positive real rates help determine only the floor under nominal rates and there are no definitive criteria to determine the level of interest rates above the floor. The social rate of discount is unavoidably indeterminate, which makes interest rate policy necessarily judgemental, a rule of thumb at best.

The same caveats would apply to evaluating the appropriateness of the structure of interest rates, which should differ according to their intrinsic properties such as riskiness, maturity, liquidity and convenience but are subject to distortions arising out of market segmentation, selective credit controls, preferential rates for government borrowing and priority sectors, and excessively large spreads between the average cost of loanable funds and lending rates due to oligopoly, government intervention (high reserve and liquid asset requirements), high operating costs, and non-performing loans. For instance, the imposition of high statutory liquid assets ratios creates a captive market for government borrowing at preferential rates of interest, which is clearly inconsistent with the spirit of a market-orientated interest rate regime. Apart from the abolition of credit subsidies and all preferential rates, the other measures to promote a consistent interest rate structure would include reduction and unification of liquidity requirements of banks and other financial institutions, the intervention of a base lending (prime) rate coupled with means to improve the operating efficacy of financial institutions.

An integral part of interest rate and monetary management is the operation of rediscount and overdraft (Lombard) windows by central banks, particularly in conditions where open market operations are hampered by lack of paper. Rediscount windows have also the advantage that their initial impact is wider than with open market operations, which are necessarily limited to the counterparties of the central banks, and they can also help to develop demand for rediscountable paper. The designing of rediscount windows involves definition of eligible paper and the terms and criteria of access. If it is intended to discourage access to rediscount the rate has to be penal – that is, above-market – whereas if it is below market rates, the central bank has necessarily to use quantitative non-price rationing. The criteria for rediscountable paper and for access to windows are often used for selective credit policy and moral suasion: effectiveness is thus largely governed by the conditions of access. Although used in many countries as a standard monetary instrument, the rediscount window is not suited for precise targeting of base money since recourse to the window is normally at the initiative of banks, which also complicates its usefulness for quantity transactions.

The Lombard (overdraft) window is a facility (usually collateralized) for very short-term loans, usually priced above any alternative source of funds, where the collateral and other conditions regarding maturity and access are defined by the central bank but actually access is at the discretion of commercial banks. The Lombard rate can be a key rate in announcing the central bank's changes in policy stance and the Lombard window is also an integral part of the payments system. Given the feature of a pre-announced rate facility where access is at the discretion of banks, it shares the disadvantage of a rediscount window.

## 3.4 RESERVE REQUIREMENTS

Variations in reserve requirements function as a monetary instrument by injecting or withdrawing liquidity, since an increase in the level or ratios of reserves obliges banks to purchase temporary liquidity from the central bank, raises their costs and reduces their credit activity leading to a reduction in the deposits held by the public. Conversely, a lowering of reserve requirements increases the margin for credit creation from any given monetary base. No doubt such variations have some advantages, primarily to 'accommodate structural changes in demand for resources' or as a useful instrument for 'one-off sterilization of excess liquidity' and 'to enhance the predictability of reserve demand' (Alexander *et al.*, 1995, p. 4). Marginal reserve requirements may also be appropriate when the central bank lacks flexible instruments and timely information and even more 'when the central bank wishes to change the level of reserve requirements substantially, but for some reason does not wish to adjust the stock of base money very rapidly' (Hardy, 1993, p. 15). On the other hand, varying reserve requirements to regulate aggregate money supply is not a particularly efficient means of conducting monetary policy, since 'even small changes could entail large adjustments in banks' portfolios, and so some forewarning is needed' and nor can they be 'readily used to offset short-term monetary fluctuations, if only because of lags in defining the reserve base and the length of the holding period (ibid., p. 8). Moreover, frequent changes and without adequate notice only serve to give an added incentive to banks to hold excess reserves or to innovate substitutes for deposits that are not liable to such requirements. Consequently, the money multiplier is rendered less sensitive to changes in reserve requirements, thereby weakening the link to ultimate targets. Analysts also point to a critical intrinsic asymmetry in the use of reserve variations in as much as while it is easy to raise them to absorb liquidity 'few occasions will be found to reduce them so reserve requirements will tend to drift upwards' and 'a point may be reached where any further increase is prohibitively costly and even this instrument becomes unusable' (ibid., p.9). This almost suggests that reserve requirements are subject to a ratchet effect: this is controverted by the experience of countries like Jamaica, where at one point they even reached their statutory limit of 25 per cent of deposits and where, concurrently, there was also a liquid asset requirement (LAR). Prior to 1985, the Bank of Jamaica relied on variations in the liquid asset ratio to 'adjust the distribution of credit between the private and public sectors' which, however, 'distorted the pattern of credit allocation' as noted by a former Governor (Arthur Brown, 1994, p. 327). Similarly, reserve requirements have been altered frequently in Sri Lanka, although they have remained well above the 5 per cent statutory minimum.

Reserve requirements, if they are carefully crafted, also serve as a prudential measure to maintain the liquidity of the banking system in the face of systemic risk. They have too a fiscal impact in so far as a high requirement imposes a tax on bank intermediation, which can, however, be neutralized by reserve remuneration at market rates. But under-remuneration can result in a widening of the spread between lending and deposit rates which, in turn, can induce disintermediation.

The current nature and level of reserve requirements in developing countries are hard to describe because of frequent changes. However, the available data broadly suggest that Latin American countries tend to impose highly complex reserve requirements, while the British Commonwealth countries often have a simpler system but in many cases are supplemented by liquid asset requirements (LAR). In several countries the measurement of the reserve base and the monitoring and enforcement of compliance are hampered by problems of staffing and information. The fact that non-bank financial institutions (NBFIs) in many countries such as Kenya enjoy zero or low reserve requirements on liabilities that are close substitutes for bank deposits creates an unequal playing field conducive to disintermediation. Some countries have made notable progress towards steady lowering of reserve requirements: for example, Indonesia (1988, 2 per cent), Bahamas (1991, 5 per cent), Bangladesh (1993, 5 per cent), Oman (1992, 5 per cent), and Tunisia (1992, 2 per cent). The main area of concern is LARs which create a captive market for government securities and impede the development of competitive money markets. For instance, in India, the statutory liquid assets ratio (SLR), despite reductions in the base, is still as high as 29.3 per cent of domestic demand and time liabilities (March 1995). There is no economic rationale for SLRs in the context of financial liberalization.

Reserve requirements are thus a multipurpose instrument which can be used for monetary policy, serve as a fiscal device, and also function as a prudential measure which guarantees the liquidity of banks and financial institutions. These purposes are not mutually exclusive provided the ratios are set according to the requirements of monetary policy over and above the floor level determined by prudential considerations and provided their remuneration generally approximates, or is equal, to a relevant market rate of interest like a pure riskless government borrowing rate. In proportion as the allocative and indicator role of market-driven interest rates increases, the desirable norm would be to set them at fairly low levels, approximating to the prudential minimum, and to phase out any tax element in them since reserve requirements are 'a poor way to impose a tax, albeit a politically convenient one' (Hardy, 1993, p. 24). But their overall macroeconomic effects in developing countries are still an unresearched aspect that merits attention in light of the interesting results of a study of US data which found 'that changes in changes in reserve requirements have statistically significant and quantitatively important impacts on real activity' (Loungani and Rush, 1995, p. 524).

## 3.5 PUBLIC SECTOR DEPOSITS

The shifting of public sector deposits between the central bank and commercial banks can serve as an effective instrument of monetary policy in developing countries where open market operations are infeasible or inefficient, with the added advantage that it is not likely to lead to the undesirable repercussions inherent in the variation of reserve requirements of commercial banks (Chandavarkar, 1972). If government deposits are treated as part of the money supply, then their transfer to the central bank acts like an increase in the reserve requirement on these deposits to 100 per cent. If these deposits are not counted as part of the money supply, the shift is more like a liquidity absorbing open market operation, except that the central bank does not have to pay a market-related rate of interest on its deposits as it would on regular sterilization bonds. A rise in commercial bank shares of government deposits increases the liquidity of banks just like expansionary open market operations. Conversely, a shift of government deposits back to the central bank has the opposite contractionary effect. The movement of government deposits as sterilization operations neither requires nor promotes the development of money markets, which, although a practical advantage, is also a consideration for not relying on them consistently or indefinitely. This type of operation has several advantages because it does not act like a tax on financial intermediation and nor does it tend to increase short-term interest rates to the same extent as bond sales. Moreover, there are no quasi-fiscal costs associated with such operations if the deposits are not remunerated; if they are paid at below market rates of interest there is no doubt a quasi-fiscal cost which, however, is still below the cost of sterilization through open market operations.

The provenance and usage of this instrument hark back to Europe, particularly in Germany, where it is described as the policy of '*Einlagen-Politik*'. The Deutsche Bundesbank is the sole depository of all government funds but Article 17(2) of the central bank law provides for the transfer of these funds to and from commercial banks. In Canada too this instrument has been widely used, a feature facilitated by the fact that there are only a few large banks. But it has not been much used in developing countries as a regular instrument, barring a few exceptions such as Indonesia and Malaysia. Twice in the deregulation era (in mid-1987 and again in early 1991) the Bank Indonesia shifted government-related deposits from commercial banks to its own books to sterilize the monetary impact of foreign exchange intervention aimed at controlling exchange rate pressures. The Bank Negara Malaysia makes even more active use of government deposits, including the deposits of the Employees' Provident Fund, as a monetary policy instrument. Such deposits account for more than 10 per cent, on average, and are allocated among commercial banks through an auction system, which gives the Bank Negara additional control over the reserves of commercial banks. In recent years, several developing countries and regions (for example, Indonesia, Malaysia, Taiwan Province of China and Thailand) have activated this instrument to sterilize the effects of abnormal capital inflows. In Mexico (1991) the government placed the proceeds of privatizations in the central bank to assist sterilization efforts.

The interesting question then is why has this instrument, which seems so well-tailored to the requirements of underdeveloped money markets, not been more widely used in developing countries? One obvious policy constraint is the persistent structural budget deficits in most developing countries, whereas this instrument presupposes budgetary surpluses. There are also other institutional limitations. In about 80 per cent of the countries surveyed in a study conducted by the International Monetary Fund, the government is allowed under law to maintain its deposits outside the central bank with commercial banks (Cottarelli, 1993, p. 9), which therefore, suggests that the initiative for shifting deposits between the central bank and commercial banks rests with the government rather than with the central bank. However, this feature in itself need not be a bar to the appropriate deployment of government balances between the central bank and the commercial banks for monetary policy purposes, provided there is full understanding and co-operation between the government and the central bank. On the other hand, government balances are not always a homogeneous *mass de manouevre* freely disposable for monetary policy purposes. Governments are typically required to maintain minimum working balances with central banks. Moreover, to the extent budgetary funds are earmarked for specific developmental and related purposes (as in Latin America and the cess funds for tea, cotton, jute, and small-scale industries in the Indian budget) they are not freely available for monetary policy purposes. For reasons of efficient financial administration such balances are distributed between the branches of the central bank and the government treasuries, and, similarly, between the central government and the state governments, particularly in federations, where states may not readily accede to the central bank's use of their balances as a monetary policy instrument. Given the pronounced seasonality of government finances in developing countries, priority has to be given to safeguarding the ways and means position of the government rather than to influencing the monetary situation. There is also the difficult problem of efficient and equitable distribution of government deposits between individual commercial banks. This makes the instrument more usable in oligopolistic financial systems with a few large banks, which is the case with most developing countries. It would be virtually unusable in countries with a large number of unit banks (for example, the Philippines) and as a monetary policy instrument it suffers from the same drawback of selectivity as foreign exchange swaps. Periodic shifts in government deposits also result in large and unforeseen changes in the cash base of commercial banks and thereby introduce an element of considerable uncertainty in their operations and even adverse effects, as for instance, 'when Indonesia forced state enterprises to move their deposits out of the state banks, these banks not only lost liquidity, but they also had to reduce their amount of loans outstanding' (IMF, 1995, p. 84). Once banks realize that they cannot depend upon the size and frequency of changes in government deposits held with them, they may soon begin to discount them altogether as a determinant of their lending policies. If trustee and provident fund deposits are shifted, as in Malaysia and Singapore, the related costs are borne by the contributors to the fund in so far as benefits from the funds are linked to the return on the funds, which therefore clearly suggests that there are hidden equity costs involved in such operations for monetary policy purposes. In fact being trustee funds such balances are best left out of such operations. Since changes in government deposits can also occur for reasons other than monetary policy it is correspondingly more difficult to determine the use of this instrument for monetary policy. On the other hand, it is important not to exaggerate the practical difficulties of manipulating government deposits, as borne out by the successful experience of Canada and Malaysia. In Canada, 'at no time has the division [of government deposits] frustrated or hampered seriously cash management by the central bank' (Neufeld, 1958, p. 61). Notwithstanding the associated practical problems the management of government deposits merits attention as a powerful auxiliary instrument of monetary policy in so much as their size and distribution will influence overall liquidity, regardless of whether they are consciously being used as an instrument of monetary policy.

## 3.6 CREDIT AUCTIONS

Central banks in developing countries rely on auctions of treasury bills and central bank securities to absorb liquidity but they also need a complementary instrument to inject liquidity at their initiative; this is somewhat infeasible given the shallowness of money markets and the lack of reference rates. To circumvent this constraint, several central banks (for example, the former Czechoslovakia, Indonesia, Romania, and Tunisia) have had recourse to auctions of refinance credit. Given the existence of a suitable security such as commercial bills of exchange or some form of government securities, auctions of repo contracts are also a possibility. Lending to the financial sector can be for specific monetary policy objectives like providing liquidity to commercial banks to meet specified monetary targets. It can also be a vehicle for targeted credit to finance investment and economic development in key sectors by provision of central bank credit to commercial and development banks for on-lending to targeted priority sectors. An innovative development is the auctioning of development credit to financial institutions that meet certain minimum eligibility requirements: this has been used in Bolivia, Chile, Honduras and Mexico and is also being considered in Argentina, Colombia, Ecuador, Jamaica and Peru (Guasch and Glaessner, 1993, pp. 170–1). Credit auctions are also well suited for establishing monetary control in financial systems with insolvent institutions (Mathieson and Haas, 1995) and in transition economies like those in Eastern Europe and the former Soviet Union countries.

Credit auctions have substantial advantages over conventional techniques of disbursing credit because of much greater transparency and equity, lower time and transaction costs, and their potential for inducing more competition and efficiency because the bidder has better information than the lender about the opportunity costs of capital. They help allocate central bank credit at market rates and provide a reasonable proxy or benchmark reference rate Consequently, auctions virtually eliminate rent-seeking opportunities, provided there are adequate safeguards against collusion among bidders, an ever present possibility given the oligopolistic character of financial systems in many developing countries. They also share some problems with conventional lending, particularly the inability of the lender to control the use of the funds by the borrower, and could also exacerbate the risks of adverse selection, which results in attracting the least desirable participants with the highest risks, who may bid up interest rates to appropriate a larger share of credit. This exposes the central bank to credit risks that are difficult to assess because adequate quality collateral may not be available and counterparties may fail.

Nevertheless, properly designed credit auctions can be regarded as a desirable and feasible option when:

- there are no efficient credit markets and no reasonable proxy reference interest rate;
- competition can be induced;
- state-owned banks do not dominate the banking sector; and
- supervisory agencies have demonstrated their competence and capacity to assess and monitor the credit risks of potential bidders (Guasch and Glaessner, 1993, p. 174).

For instance, the Bank of Ghana restricts the bidding to banks which are certified by the supervisory agencies. On balance, as concluded by an IMF study, 'central bank auctions can be considered a transitory tool until other instruments are established,' which therefore 'require special care to avoid their use for multiple purposes that undermine their value as monetary management instruments' like financing 'nonperforming assets in bank portfolios' or 'to use short-term central bank credit to finance banks' long-term loans' (Alexander *et al.*, 1995, pp. 8 and 32). Oddly, while the literature is rich in demonstrating the merits of credit auctions, it does not explain why they have not been used more widely, which suggests one more potential area for research and promotional initiatives by central banks.

## 3.7 FOREIGN EXCHANGE SWAPS

Foreign exchange swaps by central banks in which only the principal amounts are exchanged on the initial and maturity dates at predetermined exchange rates – that is, buying foreign exchange spot with a contract to resell it later – have been used to fine-tune domestic liquidity, manage foreign exchange reserves, and stimulate and develop domestic financial markets. The forward premium, or discount, also called a swap premium or swap rate, is the price of the instrument which 'reflects the corresponding differential between interest rates on the international markets, as risk-free arbitrage should ensure that no unexploited profit opportunities exist' (Hooyman, 1994).

Foreign exchange swaps are eminently suited as a money market instrument to conduct a market-orientated monetary policy and to target a monetary aggregate in countries, which, while lacking a well-developed market for short-term securities (because they have no securitized government debt) have both deep spot and forward foreign exchange markets. The critical condition is the availability of a deep and active forward exchange, which accounts for its widespread use in countries like Kuwait, Saudi Arabia and Malaysia. But the swap facility of the Saudi Arabian Monetary Agency, which provides liquidity through foreign exchange swaps using spot sales of US dollars to the agency, with a repurchase agreement based on the market-determined forward exchange rate, is not significant in terms of size and it has therefore been used to provide emergency liquidity to the market. In Oman the lack of a developed forward market in Omani rials means that the Central Bank of Oman is not in a position to reverse swaps to drain liquidity for fear of generating destabilizing expectations of exchange rate movements. The use of foreign exchange swaps to acquire reserves or to subsidize quasi- fiscal activities through provision of forward cover and exchange rate guarantees oblige the central bank to take open positions, thereby assuming an exchange rate risk that often culminates in substantial losses, which represent an injection of liquidity (see Chapter 11 for details). In proportion as short-term securities markets develop, swaps become less attractive as a money market instrument. This, coupled with the discouraging experience of countries that have resorted to swaps, has rendered 'most swap facilities restricted or dormant in recent years' (Hooyman, 1994, p. 161).

## 3.8 OPEN MARKET OPERATIONS

The term 'open market operations' refers broadly to the purchase and sale by central banks of specified assets, usually government securities, which are undertaken to influence the prices and yields of these assets and the cash base of the banking system. Open market operations can subserve one or more of the following objectives:

(1) to assist debt management and government borrowing;
(2) to provide seasonal or other finance for commercial banks;
(3) to create and maintain a desired pattern of yield and maturity; and

(4) to control the reserve base of the banking system.

The first objective is related to the fiscal aspects of open market operations; the other three have predominantly monetary significance. Although conceptually distinct, in practice these objectives tend to be closely intermixed because the purchase or sale of government securities by a central bank can simultaneously affect the debt position of government, the cash base of the banking system and the yields of government securities. When a central bank buys securities from banks, its purchase expands the cash base of the banking system and thereby enables it to expand credit. Similarly, by selling securities to banks for cash, it contracts the cash base of the banks, who are thereby obliged to restrict credit to their customers.

Open market operations can take the form of purchases and sales of a variety of assets such as foreign exchange, gold, commercial and treasury bills, government securities, securities issued by a central bank (as in Chile, Costa Rica, Ghana, Indonesia, Korea, Mauritius, Nepal, Poland, Philippines, and Sri Lanka) and even company shares, as in Jamaica where the Bank of Jamaica may, with the approval of the finance minister, buy and sell shares of companies specially authorized by the government to develop a local money or securities market or to improve the financial machinery for financing of economic development. But in practice, they are usually confined to government or central bank securities, because, in these cases, the degree of initiative by the central bank is greater than in respect of foreign exchange or gold where the volume of transactions depends largely on exogenous factors like the balance of payments position or the demand for gold, neither of which can be influenced directly by the central bank. Second, they are more prominent in the portfolios of banks and financial institutions (the largest normal transactors with the central banks) than any other single asset category and are, likewise, more sensitive to changes in interest rates and capital values than other assets. Finally, they have a more active market, even in the developing countries, than other assets. The second and third factors also explain why an asset like gold is not a convenient medium of normal open market operations. Although largely held by households, it hardly figures in the portfolios of banks and financial institutions, and therefore transactions in it cannot influence the credit base of the economy. The market for gold is largely a one-way market in developing economies where the demand for gold is so strong that while the market can absorb large amounts of gold, it does not easily disgorge it. Moreover, the use of gold in normal open market operations may have the unintended effect of undermining confidence in the legal tender currency itself. Central banks have resorted to gold sales to absorb excessive liquidity in exceptional circumstances, as, for instance, the wartime sales of gold and silver bars (of about 7.5 million ounces during 1943–6) by the Reserve Bank of India (Reserve Bank of India, 1970, p. 338) or the post-Second World War sales of gold sovereigns by the Bank of Greece. Similarly, central banks could undertake purchases of gold against legal tender currency or issue of special bonds, as in India, with a view to converting domestic gold into foreign exchange, though such an operation would be unconnected with either monetary or fiscal policy *per se*. Thus, by elimination, central banks are confined to government securities as the normal medium of open market operations, since they (a) are held by individuals as well as by the financial system, and (b) have an active reversible market.

The capacity of a central bank to conduct open market operations depends on the quantity and type of assets it can hold and the size and depth of the market: that is, the number of buyers and sellers as well as the ease with which transactions can be put through without undue fluctuations in security prices. But the problem is not really one of a shortage of ammunition in the arsenal of the central bank so much as one of the ability and willingness of the market to absorb different types of securities. Hence, the nature and size of the market is the principal limiting factor in open market operations. If, as in many developing countries, the market happens to be predominantly a broker's market rather than a dealer's market, it is naturally narrower. Dealers or jobbers who can operate on their own account and take positions in respect of purchases and sales of securities bear the risk of fluctuations in capital value of the securities and provide a continuous market. In their absence, transactions have to be directly between parties or through brokers acting as pure intermediaries who merely match orders and do not bear risks.

Another classification of open market operations is whether they represent primary sales of central bank and/or government paper or outright purchases and sales or repo operations in the secondary market. In addition to outright purchases and sales, central banks can resort to swap (or switch) operations which involve swaps of securities of different maturities as a means of changing the maturity pattern of government debt without altering its size. Such swaps figure prominently in the Reserve Bank of India open market operations, although no published data are available since 1964 (Chandavarkar, 1964).

Country experiences of open market operations divide into four categories (Quintyn, 1994, pp. 699–707) using representative examples. The first group consists of those that in practice have only resorted to central bank securities (Costa Rica, since the late 1970s; Indonesia since 1983; Korea since 1961). The second group includes central banks which have consistently used government securities – that is, treasury bills (Pakistan, 1991; Kenya, 1990; The Gambia, 1990; Israel, early 1970s; and Mexico, 1984). The third group consists of those that have used both central bank and government securities, but where the latter are currently the preferred instrument (Philippines, 1983; Sri Lanka, 1984, 1987; Poland, 1990; and Nepal, 1988, 1991–2). In the fourth group are countries that have used both types but which at present mainly rely on central bank securities (Mauritius, 1988, 1991; Ghana, 1988; and Chile, 1975). Among those the experience of Bank Indonesia is unique: first, because the 'Balanced Budget' rule prohibits the government from issuing any domestic debt instruments; second, Indonesia is probably the only developing country where private paper is used in open market operations in addition to the central bank's own debt instruments, SBIs (Sertificat Bank Indonesia) which are used mainly for draining liquidity, whereas the SBPUs (Surat Berhaga Pasar Uang – money market securities) are used to inject liquidity. The SBPUs include promissory notes issued by customers in borrowing from banks or non-bank financial institutions (NBFIs); or by banks and NBFIs for interbank borrowing; and trade bills. These SBPUs can be rediscounted directly with Bank Indonesia but rediscounting normally takes place through a market-maker working under the central bank's guidelines. On the other hand, the real success story is the Bank of Mexico which is the only central bank among the developing countries that relies entirely on genuine open market operations through secondary markets for government securities, as in the industrial countries.

The type of security, whether central bank or government securities, does not matter for the efficacy of open market operations, since what is significant are the characteristics rather than the origin of the instruments (Quintyn, 1994, p. 715). The critical condition is that these instruments should be properly designed to foster a wide and active market and meet the following necessary conditions:

(1) interest rates should be market determined, which requires that ownership be as broad-based as possible and easily transferable to stimulate competition and facilitate transmission of the monetary policy stance;
(2) simple, transparent and uniform taxation of all financial instruments, including private paper;
(3) appropriate maturities to stimulate trading; and
(4) clear and well-defined rules for rediscounting.

Since these features can be attached to both types of securities the choice has to be based on a careful balancing of other advantages and disadvantages. The central bank's use of its own securities enables separation of monetary policy objectives from public debt management and thereby strengthens the operational autonomy of the central bank, particularly if the treasury is unwilling to accept sufficient flexibility of interest rates. It offers a very flexible instrument for management of short-term liquidity at the discretion of the central bank, which can tailor the issuance, auction system, counterparties, maturities, and settlement rules. As against this, there are some disadvantages. Thus, if central bank securities are issued along with government securities it may pose problems of co-ordination, unless there is some complementarity between the two in terms of maturity. But the complications arise primarily in regard to treasury bills for which central bank securities are a close competing asset. Central bank securities do not generate any externalities and spill-over to foster development of financial markets because the volume of issue is necessarily much smaller relative to government securities and they are designed almost exclusively to absorb liquidity. They depend too much on ancillary features like eligibility for reserve requirements and rediscounting. Consequently the markets for central bank securities remain thin and secondary markets do not develop as in Indonesia and Korea. On the other hand, perhaps the potential for diversifying central bank securities into medium-term and long-term maturities has not been fully exploited, as, for instance, on the lines of Ghana and Chile where the central banks have tried to develop the markets by issuing a more varied range of securities. But 'these shortcomings should not be considered as inherent flaws in the use of central bank bills' since 'what they reveal is that when no government securities markets exist, the proper design of central bank paper is a crucial element for the reform process to be successful' (Quintyn, 1994, p. 722). But central banks have not been particularly innovative in the design of securities, as for instance, by issuing at least some undated and double-dated paper to serve as a bell-wether for the market, like the British consols or the Government of India 1986 or later rupee paper.

The dual issue of central bank and government securities can also lead to segmentation and compression in the market, as in the Philippines in the early 1980s and Poland in 1990, Costa Rica, and Nepal (where the Rastra Bank tends to pay higher interest rates on its bills than the treasury in parallel auctions, whereas the Central Bank of The Gambia's securities – otherwise identical to treasury bills – trade at a higher premium than the treasury bills). In Ghana and Mauritius the central bank paper and treasury securities have identical characteristics and the issues are co-ordinated, with the treasury and the central bank alternating the issue dates depending on the government's needs for fresh funds. The Bank of Israel has a unique arrangement whereby it uses a specific government security that is not used by the government for debt-financing purposes, with the interest cost being borne directly by the government, as in Kenya and The Gambia (and Mauritius before 1992). The Bank of Israel arrangement, while using government securities, has the added merit of largely separating monetary policy from public debt management. The Central Bank of the Philippines shares the larger part of the cost with the government. 'However, on a consolidated basis, all solutions approximately yield the same results, provided all central bank profits are transferred to the government, and the central bank does not artificially depress profits to dampen the transfer' (Quintyn, 1994, p. 733).

A major drawback of relying exclusively on central bank paper to absorb excess liquidity of domestic origin is the risk of central bank losses (as in Chile, Ghana and Philippines) or else a significant negative impact on the profit and loss account (Korea and Indonesia). Central bank losses not only erode the central bank's autonomy and credibility but also pose a major danger that the monetization of the losses and the large interest payments due on the outstanding debt undermine the effectiveness of monetary policy, thus, 'neutralizing the very effects sought by the issuance of central bank securities' (Quintyn, 1994, p. 716).

On the other hand, the use of government securities in open market operations has the comparative advantage of acting as a catalyst for the deepening and widening of financial markets and improving the transparency of operations, while obviating the risk of central bank losses. But even more critical to the efficacy of open market operations than the nature of the financial instrument is the establishment of effective co-ordinating and supporting arrangements between the central bank and the fiscal authority to manage and support the use of the appropriate instrument, which would also protect the operational autonomy of the central bank.

## 3.9 MORAL SUASION

The steady and successful transition to the use of indirect market-orientated monetary policy instruments in the developing countries poses a little discussed question: is there any scope for exercise of old-fashioned moral suasion by central banks through informal non-market channels of influence without invoking statutory or administrative controls? Moral suasion, an umbrella concept which fits snugly into the trilogy of policy instruments, has been picturesquely compared by Sir Dennis Robertson, to the three ways of 'getting a donkey to progress along a road by holding a carrot in front of his nose, by applying a stick to his behind and stroking his ears – in other words establishing a code by means of which the animal becomes aware of what is expected of him and behaves accordingly' (1992, p. 156). He calls earstroking a 'noble art, which has been developed in England to a pitch which may well be, and is indeed the envy of some other countries.' It has also been so successfully emulated in some other developed countries, notably by the Bank of Canada and in an even more distinctive way by the Bank of Japan through its administrative or window-guidance of commercial banking operations. It is no accident that in all these three countries the banking and financial systems are oligopolistic – which offers the most congenial environment for moral suasion, since it is possible for the central banks to communicate with and effectively direct a few large banks, a procedure which is simply infeasible in unit banking systems with large numbers of banks of varying sizes as in the United States or the Philippines. Moral suasion being an invisible essentially qualitative technique, is not amenable to standard econometric testing and nor has it been systematically researched in the descriptive and historical literature.

The exercise of moral suasion by the Bank of Canada for monetary policy and financial development is particularly instructive for developing countries, as it exemplifies not only 'the process whereby commercial banks cooperate with the central bank either for altruistic reasons or out of fear of administrative or legislative sanctions,' but also 'an exchange between the central bank and commercial banks in which the central bank provides information and other services which facilitate collusion among the commercial banks in exchange for their compliance with the goals of the central bank' (Breton and Wintrobe, 1978, p. 216). The Bank of Canada has made extensive use of moral suasion, in large part because of its 'reservations about the efficiency of price system', to introduce innovations like the 15 per cent ratio, the ban on term loans above specified limits by the chartered banks, allocations for housing finance, restrictions on chartered bank lending to finance companies and the lending policies of finance companies (Neufeld, 1958, p. 178).

There is also considerable scope for moral suasion as a central banking policy instrument not only for credit policies but also for prudential, and developmental purposes, particularly in small island economies and in developing countries which typically have oligopolistic financial systems with high ratios of financial concentration (see Table 6.8), and also fairly homogeneous face-to-face consensual societies, like Korea and South-East Asia, or such as Indonesia and Malaysia with their strong indigenous traditions of *mushawarah* (consultation leading to consensus). For instance, the Bank Negara Malaysia (central bank) during the prolonged terms of office of its distinguished Governor Tun Ismail, used to hold regular fortnightly meetings with commercial banks to discuss not only issues of credit policy and prudential problems but even sensitive managerial and personnel problems like the risks and consequences of poaching senior staff from the central bank. Given this background, it is all the more surprising that the useful innovation of using 'deliberation councils' adopted by Malaysia, on the lines of similar entities in Japan and Korea (World Bank, 1993, p. 14) for industrial policy has not been adopted by the Bank Negara. There is in fact considerable merit in institutionalizing central bank moral suasion through periodic but emphatically informal meetings with commercial bankers and financiers to address matters of concern which do not call for formal action. This would serve to improve the transparency of the policy-making process in the developing countries and deter lobbying and cabalistic procedures. But the efficacy of moral suasion depends, in the final analysis, on the leadership, professionalism, and credibility of the central bank. The success of the Bank Negara Malaysia was in no small measure due to the strong and highly professional leadership and personality of Governor Tun Ismail, matched only by the record of the Bank of Thailand under Governor Poey Ungphakorn.

There are, of course, limits to the use of moral suasion as in the case of any other instrument. 'Persuasiveness and persuadability are valuable things; but, like most valuable things, limited in supply. It is the duty of society to create a framework of monetary law and administration, and to operate a regime of incentives and disincentives, which will prevent these precious qualities of persuasiveness and persuadability from being wastefully squandered through being set tasks which it is outside their compass to perform' (Robertson, 1992, p. 168). Moral suasion is none the less a useful supplement to formal central banking techniques but one whose potential has not been fully tapped by developing countries.

## 3.10 INSTRUMENT AND POLICY MIX

The general, as distinguished from country-specific, criteria for determining the mix of instruments are, broadly (Alexander *et al.*, 1995, pp. 15–16):

(1) the flexibility, effectiveness, and predictability of the instrument in controlling the variable that the central bank wishes to influence, such as the levels of money, credit and interest rates;
(2) whether the use of the instrument interferes with financial markets and distorts the allocation of real resources even if aggregate credit is effectively controlled;
(3) the extent to which the instrument contributes to the overall development and stability of the financial system; and
(4) whether the instrument can be used to deal with bank-specific shocks and stresses (for example, a discount window).

The multiplicity of instruments and criteria requires an effective co-ordinating tool in the form of reserve money programming to analyse systematically the sources and uses of aggregate liquidity and determine how much each instrument will be used and how its use will affect overall liquidity. There is, however, considerable diversity in the choice and channels of instruments and policies because of country-specific historical, structural and macroeconomic factors like: the size and depth of interbank, money and securities markets; the efficiency and reliability of the payments systems; the aggregate and bank-by-bank level of excess reserves; and the sources, duration and expected duration of changes in bank reserves.

The IMF survey of the experiences of a representative sample of nineteen non-industrial countries in their transition to indirect monetary policy instruments (defined as from the commencement of central bank auctions of treasury or central bank bills to the point of elimination of interest rate controls and reduction of directed central bank credit to no more than 25 per cent of total credit) yields some interesting facts and inferences (Tables 3.2, 3.3 and 3.4).

*Table* 3.2 Initial conditions in selected countries in transition to indirect instruments

| *Condition* | *% of total 19 countries*[a] |
|---|---|
| *Initial institutional conditions* | |
| IMF-supported programme | 89 |
| Public ownership of banking sector greater than 50 % | 63 |
| Effective supervision | 32 |
| Independent central bank | 11 |
| Attainment of monetary policy targets | 63 |
| Existence of capital controls | 95 |
| *Initial macroeconomic conditions* | |
| Annual rate of inflation greater than 20 % | 47 |
| Negative real interest rates | 53 |
| Ratio of fiscal deficit to GDP greater than 5 % | 58 |
| Excess liquidity | 79 |

[a] Argentina, Burundi, Chile, Egypt, The Gambia, Ghana, Hungary, Indonesia, Israel, Jamaica, Kenya, Malaysia, Mexico, the Philippines, Poland, Sri Lanka, Thailand, Tunisia, and Venezuela.

*Source*: Table 4, IMF, Occasional Paper 126, p. 20.

*Table* 3.3 Features of transition to indirect instruments in selected countries

| *Feature* | *% of total 19 countries*[a] |
|---|---|
| Gradual | 58 |
| Reversal of monetary reforms | 47 |
| Fiscal consolidation | 68 |
| Fixed exchange rate regime | 53 |
| Abolition of capital controls[b] | 58 |

*Notes*: [a] Sample as in Table 3.2.
[b] Includes partial liberalization efforts.

*Source*: Table 5, IMF, Occasional Paper 126, p. 20.

*Table* 3.4 Monetary instruments in selected countries at the end of the transition

| *Instrument* | *% of total 19 countries*[a] |
|---|---|
| *Open market operations* | |
| Market | |
| Primary markets | 50 |
| Predominantly primary markets[b] | 30 |
| Predominantly secondary markets | 20 |
| Instrument | |
| Treasury bills only | 53 |
| Central bank bills only | 16 |
| Both | 31 |
| Maturity[c] | |
| 1–3 months | 63 |
| 3–6 months | 58 |
| More than 6 months | 21 |
| Weekly auctions | 95 |
| Type of auction | |
| Uniform price | 74 |
| Multiple price | 26 |
| Retains discretion to modify auction outcome | 63 |
| *Reserve requirements* | |
| Less than 15 per cent | 58 |
| Remunerated | 32 |
| *Rediscount facilities* | 90 |
| Access limited | 79 |

*Notes*: [a] Sample as in Table 3.2.

*Table* 3.4 Continued

[b] The central bank basically intervenes through the issue market but may sporadically also do repos or reverse repos with the banks or primary dealers.
[c] As some countries issue different maturities simultaneously the percentages do not add up to 100.

*Source*: IMF, Occasional Paper 126, p. 22.

The most noteworthy feature is the use of treasury securities as the underlying instrument of open market operations, although about one-third of the countries used both instruments simultaneously, mostly with weekly uniform price auctions (after experimenting with longer intervals). In about two-thirds of the cases, the central banks retained some discretion to modify the auction outcome in order to reject outlying bids or discourage collusion. Significantly, the money market interventions were conducted mainly through the primary (issue) markets in about three-quarters of the sample, because of the weakness of the secondary markets despite development of the supportive legal and technical procedures for clearing and settlement and a wide range of instruments. Only a fifth of the sample central banks relied entirely on open market operations in the secondary markets. Most central banks kept a rediscount facility in place with a rediscount rate above the market rate, while others limited the access to this facility.

All central banks, except Mexico, maintained reserve requirements, at different levels, but only in about a third of the sample were they remunerated. Consequently, the unremunerated reserve requirements imposed a substantial tax on financial intermediation while providing the authorities with a captive source of cheap finance. One of the more salient features of the experience is that more than formal independence of central banks (only 11 per cent of the sample) effective supervision and fiscal consolidation were among the key factors. The relative irrelevance of central bank independence is also borne out by the estimated monetary policy reaction function estimate by the Bank of England study for a sample of forty-one countries which found 'that greater government involvement in, and control over, central banks is associated with lower rates of domestic credit expansion, in part due to the neutralization of government borrowing on aggregate domestic expansion through reductions in private sector credit' (Bank of England, 1995, p. 27).

## 3.11 TECHNICAL CAPACITY

The technical capacity of central banks to implement an effective monetary policy depends upon several essential preconditions, of which the most important are whether the central bank has the appropriate legal framework and legal capacity to utilize all the instruments at its command. For instance, the scope and effectiveness of reserve variations would be determined by the permitted range of variations and differentiation of deposits, by types and regime, and the basis of calculation of reserves. Equally important for the central bank to enhance and refine its operational capacity is its ability to recruit and retain highly skilled economists, financial analysts and accountants in competition with the usually more attractive remuneration and incentive structure of the private financial sector. But even the most competent staff cannot deliver without adequate data.

A review of experience under IMF arrangements (IMF, 1995, p. 10), drew pointed attention to the poor quality of the data for many of the countries, instancing, among others, frequent and large revisions, national accounts based on poor survey techniques, wide variations in the coverage of fiscal accounts and incomplete data on quasi-fiscal activities, which together impair the efficacy of monetary programming. The growing sophistication of monetary programming based on projections of the demand and supply of reserves, their probable effects on broader monetary, credit and financial aggregates, the size and stability of the money and credit multiplier and the strategic behavioural relationships presuppose timely and accurate compilation and reporting of basic money supply and interest rate data. But central banks show insufficient awareness of the real quality of primary monetary data supplied by reporting banks, who have scant concern for the quality of statistics in their anxiety to meet reporting deadlines. Too often reporting banks assign statistical tasks to temporary and junior staff. One potential channel for monitoring of monetary data would be to attach an economist to inspection and supervision teams as part of the task of evaluating the banks' balance sheets and financial statements in the macroeconomic context. In addition, it is always useful to supplement monetary data with other relevant indicators (or information variables) such as unused overdraft or credit limits, inventories, housing starts, major wage and salary settlements, surveys of business conditions and expectations, and the state of orders. Eventually developing countries too would need to work their way towards using a more inclusive monetary conditions index (MCI) as in Canada, which includes both the short-term interest rate and the exchange rate (Freedman, 1994, pp. 466–76). It is now recognized that 'a range of indicators is preferable because no single indicator can adequately summarize the monetary stance, and because each of the indicators is subject to influences other than monetary policy so that it will be easier to identify the nature of the economic disturbances by observing several indicators' (Alexander and Caramazza, 1994, p. 408).

But even the most skillfully designed and implemented monetary policy cannot function as a stand-alone instrument, particularly when large fiscal imbalances are likely to constrain structural adjustments and any move towards market-determined interest rates. Monetary policy can compensate fiscal imbalances only up to a point and an effective monetary policy presupposes an appropriate supportive fiscal policy. It is unrealistic to expect an effective monetary policy if the government needs and demands more credit than the economy can supply and accommodate. It is not merely the magnitude of fiscal consolidation that is crucial, but also 'the quality of fiscal adjustment – specifically how the structure and level of revenues and spending might affect prospects for investment and growth' that merits attention (IMF, September 1995).

# 4 Exchange Arrangements and Policies

'. . . the "good old days" of fixed exchange rates all round are gone, perhaps forever . . . concerns about exchange rates, the composition of reserves and forward cover have become part of the job description of central bank presidents all over the world, even in countries with exemplary domestic financial policies.' — *J. J. Polak*

## 4.1 POLICY RESPONSIBILITIES

The conduct of foreign exchange policy involves six areas of interdependent responsibility:

(1) the choice of the exchange rate regime (that is, fixed exchange rate, independent float, managed float);
(2) the choice of parities in the regime;
(3) specific directives to manage the float;
(4) daily decisions on exchange rate interventions;
(5) execution of intervention policy; and
(6) management of the country's foreign reserves.

Typically, while the execution of intervention decisions and reserves management are vested in the central bank, the other responsibilities are usually divided under four basic patterns (Cottarelli, 1994, pp. 332–3). It is only in a few countries (for example, Sweden, Switzerland and Croatia) that the central bank is responsible for all aspects of foreign exchange policy. The others conform to one of the following models.

- *The British–Japanese model* – the government controls all aspects of exchange rate policy, including daily intervention.
- *The Maastricht Treaty model* – the government is responsible for choice of the exchange rate regime and also formulates exchange rate policy directives, and the central bank conducts intervention policy according to government directives.

- *The German model* – the government determines the regime and parities but the Bundesbank is in charge of intervention and implementation.

As in other areas of central banking, it is neither possible nor feasible to prescribe a universal model. Nevertheless, the question remains: what are the respective implications for the developing countries of assigning all foreign exchange responsibilities to the central bank or sharing it with the government? This question pertains to the division of formal and legal responsibilities, since political and economic realities can differ from formal provisions and the most important foreign exchange and monetary policy decisions are usually made after consultations between the central bank and the government. But the formal division of responsibilities is important because of possible conflicts between the two authorities. By and large central banks in developing countries seem to be responsible for the major segments of foreign exchange policy. This is in accordance with the policy guideline that the money supply and the exchange rate are not independent instruments in the long run, and, in most cases, in the short run too, which, in turn, reflects the more basic argument that the central bank should have jurisdiction over instruments affecting the long-term nominal variables, while the government should be responsible for instruments targeted to real variables. These principles provide a rationale for assigning integrated control over monetary and exchange rate policies and capital movements to the central bank, which otherwise will not be truly independent in either the scope or timing of its decisions.

The latter aspect is often overlooked by proponents of independence who, while conceding that an independent central bank should handle monetary policy as an instrument to achieve price stability, do not seem to recognize that foreign exchange policy, which has a bearing on external stability, should also be the responsibility of a central bank. Monetary and exchange rate policies necessarily have to be assigned to the same policy authority as they represent two sides of the same instrument, although in so far as the 'portfolio effect' is empirically valid and relevant, there is some scope for separation of monetary and exchange rate policies. But is exchange rate policy too serious a matter to be left to central bankers, particularly in a democracy, as argued by eminent central bankers and as embodied in the Maastricht Treaty that assigns control of foreign exchange policy to the European Council? An influential view is that, 'Governments will not – practically they cannot – divorce themselves from decisions on appropriate exchange rate regimes or, beyond some limits, actual exchange rates levels . . . there are points at which central bank policy intersects with vital considerations of public policy generally, and I think the exchange rate is a prime case in point . . . I don't think we can escape that in a democracy' (Volcker, 1990, pp. 17 and 21). In the same vein, Tietmeyer also argues that 'decisions on the exchange rate regime, including the fixing of parties and central rates and their changes, will have to remain in the hands of the political authorities' (in Downes and Vaez-Zadeh, 1991, p. 184). It is indeed ironical that central bankers of standing should be so wholly on the side of the angels in endorsing government control of exchange rate policy. This is, however, not to say that the contrary case is without merit – particularly because economic theory does not provide definitive guidance on the choice of an exchange rate regime, which implies that this decision has inevitably to be based on political grounds, albeit in consultation with the central bank.

## 4.2 THE EXCHANGE RATE REGIME

More importantly, ever since the breakdown of the Bretton Woods par value system, and, notwithstanding the amended Article IV, Section 2(b) of the International Monetary Fund under which each member can adopt the exchange arrangement 'of a member's choice,' each country's freedom of choice is constrained in part by the choices of other countries. Its preferred choice would not be among the available options.[1] Consequently, the authorities have to

> worry continuously whether they [have] made the optimum second-best choice; whether to keep reserves in dollars or in yen; whether to cover foreign exchange positions in the forward market . . . worries that did not occupy much [of their time] as long as the par value system gave them the automatic benefit of fixed rates on the two most important currencies. (Polak, 1988, p. 134)

There is today a variety of exchange rate regimes, but no substantive taxonomy of the system can be given under a simple, single rubric. The classification used by the International Monetary Fund and published in its Annual Reports (1995, pp. 180–1) uses a table with columns listing countries under each regime (Table 4.1), which has been characterized by its former Economic Counsellor, as only a first approximation. 'It does not do full justice to the many variations in the present system' because 'an exchange rate is by definition an attribute not of a single country, but of a set of countries' and 'therefore, the world exchange rate regime cannot be described country-by-country, but only by sets of countries; not in

*Table* 4.1 Exchange arrangements of developing countries, 1975–95

| | *Mid-1975* *(1)* | End-1983 (2) | *Mid-1987* *(3)* | *31 Mar. 1995* *(4)* |
|---|---|---|---|---|
| *Pegged to a single currency* | 78 | 60 | 57 | 45 |
| US dollar[a] | 52 | 42 | 38 | 23 |
| French franc | 13 | 13 | 14 | 14 |
| Other currency[b] | 12 | 5 | 5 | 8 |
| *Pegged to a basket* | 15 | 35 | 33 | 23 |
| SDR | 6 | 12 | 10 | 3 |
| Other basket | 9 | 23 | 23 | 20 |
| *More flexible arrangements*[c] | 14 | 23 | 40 | 85 |
| Based on indicators | 4 | 5 | 5 | 3 |
| Managed floating | 9 | 22 | 22 | 34 |
| Independent floating | 1 | 3 | 13 | 48 |
| *Total*[d] | 107 | 125 | 130 | 153 |

*Notes*: [a] Including currencies maintained with relatively narrow margins to the US dollar.
[b] Including eight countries pegging on the pound sterling in 1975, one in 1983 and none in 1987.
[c] Does not include four countries (in 1995) which had limited flexibility *vis-à-vis* a single currency (U.S. dollar).
[d] The totals are affected by the increases in the membership of the IMF in the respective years.

*Sources*: J.J. Polak, 1988, p. 138 for columns (1), (2), and (3); International Monetary Fund, *Annual Report*, 1995, pp. 188–9.

terms of an arrangement, but in terms of 1/2n ($N$–1) country-pair arrangements' (Polak, 1988, p. 134).[2] The Polak critique of the Fund's classification of exchange arrangements overlooks the inherent and intractable difficulties of economic classifications in general, which are best regarded as fuzzy sets – accepted even in mathematical logic – rather than a watertight logical classification like the Linnean taxonomies of systematic botany. The Fund's classification of exchange arrangements too should be accepted as an informative and serviceable fuzzy set taxonomy. Likewise, the standard econometric techniques, such as multiple regression, are not helpful in analysing the simultaneous influence of a large number of independent variables on the choice of an exchange rate regime because 'the basic reason is that the exchange rate system is of a qualitative nature' as concluded by Heller (1977, p. 23) who used the non-parametric statistical technique of discriminant analysis to identify the independent variables that influence the choice of an exchange rate regime. The country characteristics used as independent variables were:

(1) the degree of openness as measured by the ratio of imports to the GNP;
(2) the size of a country given by its GDP;
(3) the degree of commodity concentration as approximated by the percentage of exports falling into the largest '2-digit' Standard International Trade Classification category;
(4) the rate of inflation; and
(5) the degree of financial integration as measured by the ratio of commercial banks' foreign assets to the money supply.

The analysis showed that countries which peg are characterized by:

- a high import to GNP ratio;
- a small country size;
- a high degree of commodity concentration;
- a low inflation rate; and
- a small ratio of foreign assets to the money supply.

Countries which float have the opposite characteristics (ibid., p. 25).

Since there is no harking back to the halcyon age of fixed exchange rates and the Bretton Woods par value system, despite the reasoned enthusiasm of the G-24 Report for the only exchange rate regime that could bring about greater stability to the major currencies of the developed countries (G-10) – the target zone proposal – how have the developing countries responded to the challenge forced on them by the adoption of floating rates among the world's major trading, invoicing and reserve currencies? The clear resounding answer is the spectacular rise over the past decade in the number of developing countries, including the small countries, which have adopted a genuinely floating rate (Table 4.1) in standing refutation of the once conventional wisdom that 'independent floating is either not feasible or undesirable for most developing countries, due to factors such as limited capital markets, restriction on capital flows, thin forward exchange markets, and a prevalence of real shocks that should be financed from reserves (Williamson, 1982, p. 39). The widespread adoption of floating exchange rates by developing countries is a phenomenon that has to be carefully appraised. Contrary to popular perception, most of the countries that have adopted floating rates, including even countries as small as The Gambia, with only a few banks, relied on an interbank market and, typically, they had extensive parallel markets, legal or illegal, where brokers had presumably gained experience in active foreign exchange trading (Quirk *et al.*, 1987, pp. 4–14). Alternatively, in a few other countries, the central banks resorted to auctioning to the highest bidder the foreign exchange surrendered by exporters, retaining powers likely to affect the exchange rate such as the reserve price, amount of foreign exchange put into each auction, and the eligibility criteria for bidding at the auctions. Countries have used different types of foreign exchange auctions which broadly divide into discriminatory price, including Dutch auctions (Bolivia, Ghana, Jamaica, and Zambia) and uniform price auctions (Guinea, Nigeria, and Uganda), whose experience has been reviewed in depth by Quirk *et al.* (1987). Their analysis shows up the drawbacks and limitations of foreign exchange auctions. For instance, discriminatory price auctions may discourage potential bidders from entering the auction or hamper more aggressive bidding because of the winner's curse, although it is also argued that this outcome could also be beneficial in deterring speculators 'or at best in ensuring that they pay the full price for their bids' (Feldman and Mehra, 1993, p. 507). They also pose other problems like the choice of an appropriate exchange rate for non-auction transactions (for example, government and customs). Some of these drawbacks could be resolved by uniform pricing which would better approximate the working of private foreign exchange markets. However, country experience points to the merits of the interbank market approach because it involves less government control over the availability of foreign exchange to the private sector in contrast to auctions where the government specifies the quantity available, sometimes after meeting its own requirements first. The double auction (for example, as in Romania) is more market-orientated, as it brings in the private sector on both the supply and demand sides, which, of course, is important in an interbank market where brokers match demand and supply offers. But a double auction is not a continuous market like the interbank market, since it operates at discrete points in time like a fixing session. It may be appropriate only when there is inadequate institutional capacity or experience to sustain an interbank market, which offers the most flexibility. But in so far as floating of exchange rates has been adopted to divest the central bank's responsibility for allocating and pricing foreign exchange, auctions are essentially a halfway house to the ultimate objective of floating rates.

A significant finding confirmed by before-and-after empirical tests made by the International Monetary Fund is that 'exchange rate variability (measured in various ways) has been lower since the introduction of floating rates than it had been before' (Polak, 1988, p. 140). But this finding has to be appropriately qualified to allow for two considerations. First, the adoption of the floating rate system after years of sharp variability in nominal and/or real exchange rates and the reduction of variability, 'while qualifying does not constitute a very demanding test for a floating rate' (ibid., p. 140). Second, the introduction of the float 'was in almost all cases part of a Fund-supported stabilization program, and other elements of that program (assuming it succeeded) might deserve part of the credit for the improved variability' (ibid., p. 140). But, in sum, there is no doubt that floating rates 'have proved themselves a viable option for developing countries in situations virtually unmanageable by other means', such as a pegged rate, a managed float, or by permitting fluctuations in foreign reserves. Above all, floating rates, apart from being in consonance with the philosophy of financial liberalization, have enabled countries 'to shed political responsibility for the adjustment of the exchange rate' (Quirk *et al.*, 1987, p. 4). This is no small advantage in countries where the politicization of economies and the pressures of populism on unstable governments have consistently hamstrung economic management. Nevertheless, countries which have not yet adopted a float 'would probably want to reserve judgement on whether to plunge into a floating regime without compelling necessity' (Polak, 1988, p. 141). The single-currency basket could also be a satisfactory option for small, stable, developing countries: it would also offer other advantages of using the same currency for intervention and for holding reserves and give transactors in the country effective access to the use of forward foreign exchange markets in the reserve centre. Additionally, it would make foreign exchange policy transparent, which even a disclosed basket cannot achieve. Undisclosed baskets or managed floats do give much more freedom of manoeuvre to the authorities (for example, in India and Korea) but at the cost of discarding a clear policy anchor. 'There thus remains a strong case for countries that are financially strong enough to peg, and that have a wide distribution of trade shares, to peg on a small basket of currencies without the pretence of a sophisticated system of weights. Such a basket should include the US dollar, the yen and a few European currencies' (ibid., p. 146).

## 4.3 FOREIGN RESERVES MANAGEMENT

The management of foreign reserves is one of the primary responsibilities of a central bank even if it is not in charge of the other major areas of foreign exchange policy. Yet it also happens to be the most arcane area of central bank operations on which central banks traditionally maintain a self-serving reticence and even their occasional public pronouncements are long on general principles of reserve management and short on the specifics of their portfolios.[3] Likewise, the financial statements and annual accounts and reports of central bank refer only to the broad movements of reserves and their distribution between gold and foreign exchange assets. Some reserve managers (for example, Abu Dhabi, Kuwait) do not even reveal the extent of their gold holdings and Singapore's Government Investment Corporation, which is headed by the prime minister, also cloaks its foreign reserves operations in complete secrecy. Consequently, outside analysts do not have the necessary evidence to comment on central bank portfolio behaviour, although there are some useful surveys of the basic principles of reserve management (for example, Downes, 1989) and a few country or group-specific studies (such as Blackman, 1981; Kulkarni, 1990).

The criteria of reserve management have to be evaluated in light of their objectives: namely, maintenance of liquidity and of the external value of the reserves and optimization of the income consistently with safety and liquidity. Any developing country needs to maintain an adequate level of reserves over a period of time which, first, helps to protect and enhance the credit rating of the country and facilitates its borrowing in overseas market while fostering investor confidence, and second, is required to maintain stable exchange rates. Low and fluctuating reserves compound the foreign exchange position since they create expectations of import restrictions leading to excessive buildup of inventories. The level of reserves has to be commensurate with the projected levels of imports and debt-service payments, but it is not possible to prescribe the precise level. Generally, 'the maintenance of reserves equivalent to at least three months imports seems to [provide] a good rule of thumb for countries with pegged exchange rates' (Frenkel, 1990, p. 152).[4] For instance, Korea accepted Article VIII statutes (current account convertibility) in the International Monetary Fund in 1988 when its reserves amounted to three months' imports, whereas Thailand adopted Article VIII in 1990 when it had five months' imports. Poland's currency was made virtually convertible on current account (1990) when its reserves and external lines of credit amounted to four and a half months' imports. But it is not merely the overall level of reserves which matters. Equally important is their composition in terms of currencies, instruments and maturities, which makes reserve management an exceedingly complex and sophisticated function given the volatility of fluctuating exchange and interest rates. It is interesting to note from Indian experience 'that the key factor from the angle of the rate of return is the currency composition of the reserves portfolio and not so much the maturity distribution within each currency' (Kulkarni, 1990, p. 300).

Since there is an implicit opportunity cost in holding reserves, measured in terms of return on their alternative domestic uses, reserve management techniques must also aim at compensating this cost as well as providing a hedge against inflationary erosion of the capital value of the reserve portfolio, which therefore points to the search for managing the portfolio as profitably as is prudently possible. Have central banks concerned themselves with this objective? One view is that 'an income maximization strategy involves serious risks which a central bank had best avoid' (Tarapore, 1994, p. 1486). Therefore the typical portfolio mix of central bank reserves confines them 'essentially to government paper and deposits with commercial banks and the Bank for International Settlements' (Tarapore, 1994, p. 1485). Surprisingly, after the pioneering essay of Charles Kennedy (1965, pp. 245–51) there has been no attempt to explore the potentialities of equities as part of official foreign reserves. Kennedy bifurcates the investment strategy of official reserve management into the 'defense case', that is, risk avoidance, and the 'adventurous case for a country investing in the ordinary shares of one of the reserve currency countries on the consideration that the equities of many economically-advanced countries are not merely a suitable hedge against inflation in those countries but also very worthwhile investments in their own right' (ibid., p. 248). A former Governor of the Central Bank of Barbados also took the position 'that income from investment of reserves should be maximized as long as other critical constraints are satisfied' (Blackman, 1981, p. 168). This view appears less heterodox if one considers that prudent trusts the world over invest social security and insurance funds in suitable tranches of first-class equities. In fact even the conservative Indian Trusts Act as amended over the years permits trustee investments in first-class variable dividend common shares subject to appropriate performance criteria. Why then do developing country central banks hesitate to adopt a bolder investment strategy to maximize income, since an uncritical conservatism only serves to increase the opportunity costs of a reserve portfolio? The same argument would also pose the question: is it justifiable to impound valuable foreign assets to serve as backing for the domestic currency, whether under the proportional reserve or fixed fiduciary currency systems, which also adds to the opportunity costs of foreign reserves? Gold, while not a barbarous relic, is still the most unconstitutional of monarchs in the reserves of several developing countries. Among them, thirty-seven central banks have no gold reserves but twenty-eight others (including Syria, Cameroon, Côte d'Ivoire, Lebanon, Uruguay, Algeria, Qatar, Pakistan, Kuwait, Libya, Saudi Arabia, India, and Nigeria) have more than 10 per cent of their reserves in gold (*Central Banking*, 1995, pp. 73–6). But, by and large, developing countries do not seem to have given much thought to activating dormant gold by amending any legal restrictions on activation, as in the Reserve Bank of India Act. India had no doubt activated gold as a pledge for overseas credit during the acute foreign exchange crisis of 1991, but there is scope, as well as risk, in the increasingly varied menu of derivative physical instruments and also paper instruments involving gold deposits, leases, swaps, options, futures, and forwards in the world gold market (Kulkarni, 1992). The contrary view against activation of gold is that aside from the riskiness of derivatives, its role as an iron ration should be left undisturbed because decisions about gold 'cannot be made on purely economic grounds' and 'the political economy of a country often determines whether gold is secured in vaults or whether it is actively invested in the financial markets' (Kulkarni, 1990, p. 306).

It may also be noted in passing that foreign exchange auctions have not been very common or prolonged among developing countries because in most cases exchange rate flexibility has been achieved in the framework of an interbank market. Experience (for example, in Ghana, Jamaica, Lithuania, Moldova, Nigeria, Sierra Leone, Uganda, and Zambia) shows that they have rarely been sustainable over long periods of time and have been replaced by a fixed rate or interbank regimes. There are significant disadvantages associated with them. They have slowed down the development of genuine interbank markets without absorbing the parallel market and have 'contributed little of lasting value to the efficiency of foreign exchange allocation' (Kovanen, 1994, p. 25).

Central banks have also to consider the impact of foreign reserves valuation changes on their domestic accounts and balance sheets, particularly when the domestic currency is strong, which makes its local currency balance sheet weaker, and conversely when it is weaker externally, the stronger is the local currency balance sheet. Consequently, central banks have to make appropriate modifications in their accounting norms and practices to protect their balance sheets, as in the case of the Reserve Bank of India, which has instituted the following procedures (Tarapore, 1994, p. 1486). First, provision is made for losses on the entire portfolio, which is affected by a valuation change and not merely on a cash basis. Second, while securities are 'marked to market' depreciation provisions are made on a monthly basis from current income and any subsequent recovery of prices does not allow for a claw-back of the losses. Third, following a movement of the reserves from a weaker to a stronger currency, the conversion loss, over the holding rate for the month, is immediately recorded as a valuation change and not treated as current income.

Apart from accounting reforms, central banks also need to address some relevant questions of the appropriate institutional arrangements for prudent and profitable investment of foreign reserves. First, is it desirable to bifurcate this function so as to entrust the income and profit maximization operations to a separate entity like Singapore's Government Investment Corporation, while the central bank (like the Monetary Authority of Singapore) retains control over the liquidity and intervention segment of the portfolio. Singapore's successful management of reserves under a dual authority is very much of a special case deriving from the sheer size of its reserves and the role of Singapore as an international financial centre. As such its experience, although of considerable interest, is not really replicable in the typical developing country. A second practical issue is how central banks can best use the services of professional asset managers, since it is not advisable to rely on in-house expertise for such a highly specialized market-orientated function. For this purpose it is important not only to draw up detailed agreements containing guidelines and directives but also to develop the requisite in-house capability to evaluate the performance of the portfolio manager on a risk-adjusted return basis, bearing in mind that the evaluation has to take account of the portfolio manager's contribution to the overall portfolio performance as distinct from the contribution of the market. In addition to the proper selection of portfolio managers and the ongoing training of staff analysts, reserve management calls for an appropriate organizational structure for strategic and tactical decision-making and implementation.[5]

A more basic issue which merits greater attention than it has received so far is that central banks have been too exclusively preoccupied with reserve asset management to the exclusion of the equally important aspect of external liability management and funding, which is usually vested in the ministries of finance. It would be more economical and efficient to centralize both asset and liability management in the central bank, with due provision for policy inputs from the ministry of finance, in order to evolve a coherent strategy, which would also help make central bank autonomy more meaningful.

## 4.4 CAPITAL ACCOUNT CONVERTIBILITY

The steadily increasing number of developing countries which have introduced current account convertibility by accepting Article VIII of the International Monetary Fund's Articles of Agreement poses the more difficult question of the rationale and timing of convertibility on capital account defined as the absence of cross-border controls, or the equivalent taxes and subsidies, on international capital transactions (Quirk, 1994, p. 373). In recent years several developing countries – Indonesia, Costa Rica, El Salvador, Guyana, Jamaica, Trinidad and Tobago, and Venezuela – have fully liberalized their capital account by abolishing exchange controls with no untoward economic consequences. In fact, the result in each case has been a pronounced strengthening of the balance of payments position on current and capital account, which reflects not only the catalytic role of Fund-financed stabilization programmes but also autonomous inflows of private capital (Ibid., pp. 386–87). In some cases Fund members have had implicit capital convertibility through using another country's currency (the US dollar in Liberia and Panama and the Australian dollar in Kiribati). Yet another group of countries with full convertibility includes the smaller intrinsically open island economies such as those in the Eastern Caribbean, Maldives, the Seychelles and Lebanon where the daunting security problems left no administrative alternative. Countries with currency boards offer an interesting combination of fixed exchange rates and convertibility (Argentina, Estonia, Hong Kong, Lithuania). In only two other groups has capital convertibility existed alongside fixed or semi-fixed exchange rate regimes – namely Indonesia, Malaysia, and Singapore, which have closely integrated financial markets; and the major oil-exporters (Bahrain, Kuwait, Oman, Qatar, Saudi Arabia, the United Arab Emirates, and the Yemen Arab Republic).

The issue then is whether other developing countries should opt for capital account convertibility and if so what are the considerations governing its timing and sequence. Admittedly, even the Fund's Articles of Agreement (VI, Section 3) permit members to maintain capital controls that are necessary, a concept which requires reappraisal now that the Fund's surveillance procedures provide for changes in capital controls and for monitoring of abnormal movements in capital. This leads to an examination of the pros and cons of capital account controls, which are usually justified on two grounds: first, the optimality argument for permanent retention either continuously activated or on a stand-by basis to cope with recurrent balance of payments crises; the second, commonly referred to as the sequencing argument, relates to the temporary recourse to capital controls in the transitional stages of economic and financial liberalization. The classic presentation of the optimality case for permanent controls by Cairncross (1973) is based on variations of the misuse of resources argument. The loss and misuse of resources through capital outflows can occur for several reasons:

(1) because of the importance of domestic investment in economic growth;
(2) because capital exports are associated with adverse terms of trade when a sharp rise in import prices reduces real wages and puts the bulk of the burden of terms of trade movements on wage earners;
(3) because of the effect of overlending on the balance of payments; and
(4) because of the tax revenues on investment income which accrues to the investing country (which is more an argument for tax reform).

Each argument, except for (4), depends, as noted by Cairncross, on market imperfections because of the inability of exchange and interest rates to equilibrate the balance of payments. This listing, however, excludes the frequent flight of capital from developing countries for personal or political reasons quite unconnected with economic factors like interest rates, exchange rates and taxes. The other major arguments supportive of capital controls relate to the questionable efficacy of full liberalization, the benefits of insulating the economy through dual or multiple exchange rates; the advantages of imposing a ceiling on speculative transactions and maintenance of a fixed exchange rate regime. But monetary independence is arguably an illusory concept because capital will tend to seek out the point of highest return and nor is maintaining a particular exchange rate regime an objective in itself.

The sequencing argument maintains that the order of liberalization is important and that temporary maintenance of capital controls should be viewed as part of a scheme of liberalizing and opening the economy. There has been an extensive debate on whether monetary reform and trade liberalization should occur prior to capital convertibility, even though the successful experience of Indonesia demonstrated the feasibility of capital liberalization which preceded the financial reforms of 1983–5 including the abolition of credit and interest rate controls. In fact Indonesian experience is critical as offering 'strong evidence and the only one of a long-term nature that developing countries have the capacity to maintain capital convertibility in spite of balance of payments weakness' (Quirk, 1994, p. 386). Two East European countries, Hungary and Poland, have simultaneously been able to liberalize both trade and capital accounts. There is also growing evidence that commodity convertibility rather than financial convertibility is of the greatest welfare significance.

The experience shows that policies adopted by the industrial countries of financial liberalization and international integration offer the best approach also for developing countries but for this to be fruitful appropriate fiscal policies coupled with the introduction of market interest rates and exchange rates are crucial. Even so it would be in order to strike a note of caution: while not questioning the ultimate economic merits of capital convertibility, developing countries would also need to have an armoury of instruments to cope with unwanted capital inflows and outflows. It would not be amiss to invoke in this context Polak's earlier cautionary note to developing countries 'to reserve judgement on whether to plunge into a floating regime [capital convertibility] without compelling necessity' (1988, p. 141).

It is therefore instructive to review the experiences of five developing countries – Chile, Colombia, Egypt, Mexico, and Thailand – that received massive and sudden inflows of capital in the past five to ten years in order to assess the role of central banks in limiting the risks of destabilizing effects of such 'net inflows, which rose from a relatively small share of GDP to twice or three times starting amounts within the space of one or two years' (Schadler 1994, p. 358). Sterilization of these inflows initially took a wide range of monetary actions such as open market operations, increases in reserve requirements on all or selected parts of bank deposits, various forms of central bank borrowing from commercial banks, restricting access to rediscount facilities, enlarging the band within which exchange rates could move, and limiting banks' open foreign exchange positions. Significantly, 'as the persistence of the inflows became obvious, a tightening of fiscal policy proved to be the only means of containing inflation and avoiding a real appreciation [of the exchange rate]' (ibid., p. 364). An important reason why fiscal policy could not be more wide ranging and stringent was the difficulty of garnering public support for a tightening of fiscal policy, when economic conditions are perceived as favourable 'coupled with the need in some countries [for example, Thailand] for investment in infrastructure to accommodate higher investment stemming from the inflows' (ibid., p. 365). Monetary policy was the single most widely used instrument to counter the effects of capital inflows in the 1990s, judging by the fact that eight out of the nine countries resorted to sterilized intervention through open market operations, variations of reserve requirements, and management of government deposits, while there was a more varied mix of other policy instruments. The IMF Survey (1995b) of capital markets 'illustrates how individual policies interact to either magnify or reduce the volume of inflows, affect their composition, or alter their macroeconomic consequences' (p. 93) but does not assess the relative contribution of different instruments in the policy mix. But it does concede the possibility that 'sterilized intervention in conjunction with controls on inflows and large government borrowing requirements will undermine the "individual effectiveness" of these policies' (ibid., p. 94).

# 5 Regulation and Supervision

> '. . . a central bank really needs considerable supervisory authority over the banking system. More often than not the central bank is in the strongest political position, in a sense, to exercise effective supervision.'
> — *Paul Volcker*

Even the most unreconstructed monetary libertarian would be hard put to it to controvert the rationale for at least a basic regulatory and supervisory framework for the banking and financial system, a position which, however, leaves room for legitimate debate on the extent, nature, scope, and forms of regulation. This is an area which raises a whole cluster of critical interrelated issues. What, in fact, is the case for regulation, or re-regulation, now that liberalization and deregulation of the financial system are an accepted policy objective and most developing countries are well-set on the path to substantial liberalization? Is the central bank necessarily the most appropriate agency for supervision? What are the typical problems encountered in supervision, and what measures are necessary and desirable to enhance the efficiency of the supervisory process in developing countries? What is the appropriate role for the central bank as a lender of last resort? Is deposit insurance a necessary adjunct to the prudential framework of the banking system?

## 5.1 PRUDENTIAL REGULATION

There is a useful distinction between prudential regulation and supervision. Prudential regulation is concerned with formulating prudential rules for banks and financial institutions, which include licensing or authorization, ownership rules, adequacy of capital, reserves and liquidity ratios, rules on foreign currency and other risk exposures, and deposit insurance. Supervision, on the other hand, is the inspection and monitoring process to ensure the implementation and effectiveness of these rules and is targeted toward ensuring the financial soundness and safety of banks.

Although supervision is sometimes classified as microeconomic, this is not strictly accurate because it has also a wider macroeconomic aspect and interest in the market and systemic level. The objectives of prudential regulation and supervision, however, are the same; they are both concerned essentially with the safety of banks and the protection of depositors and investors as part of the financial safety net, which also includes the role and functions of the central bank as the lender of last resort. It is, however, not possible to formulate a tidy target and instrument approach in regulation and supervision because a single instrument may have multiple objectives, as, for instance, in the case of reserve ratios which have a prudential component as well as another component for variation in keeping with the requirements of monetary policy.

The liberalization of financial systems, if anything, further strengthens the case for effective regulation and supervision of a prudential character to guard against the greater degree of risk in an increasingly competitive system. The standard arguments in support of prudential regulation based on the externalities such as systemic risk and the contagion effect are further strengthened in the context of developing countries because of the more pronounced informational deficiencies and asymmetries between lender and borrower as well as the greater probability of client risk.

The emphasis of bank regulation and supervision is primarily on preventive measures, notably the enforcement of internationally accepted standards of accounting and audit, adequate transparency of accounts, mandating provisions for bad and doubtful loans and write-downs or write-offs of irrecoverable credits. Compliance with financial ratios and requirements is comparatively easy and in fact several developing countries have had no problems in measuring up to the Basle Committee's 8 per cent benchmark. Malaysia, for instance, had such requirements in place at a higher level even before the Basle Accord, 1988. Admittedly, even the Basle Accord has its own anomalies such as non-recognition of offsetting risks, treatment of all government bonds as equally riskless, and insufficient cognizance of off-balance sheet liabilities, which are a growing item in developing countries. Moreover, the Basle Accord criteria are primarily geared to international banks whereas developing countries need to evolve more country-specific criteria. For instance, a two-tier system of minimum capital requirements could be adopted: the first tier comprising an absolute amount of paid-up capital (for example, in Sri Lanka) and the second tier a ratio of capital-to-risk assets with appropriate modifications to suit the country's financial structure. More importantly, as a notable central banker has perceptively remarked, 'meeting the minimum capital requirement to establish a bank should not by itself be enough to obtain a banking license' because 'the human capital, that is to say, the moral and professional quality of the bank's prospective management, is in fact more important than its capital; no deposit-taking institution should be allowed to be established when the prospective management is not entirely satisfactory to the licensing authorities' (Mancera, 1991, p. 53). The quality and background of the sponsors and board of directors is no less important. The crucial nature of these requirements is well exemplified by the Bank of Credit and Commerce International episode (*c.* 1991).

Developing countries are also particularly prone to the perils of what Goodhart calls 'unnecessary dirigisme' which often leads to a failure to take account of the real and financial costs of regulation and its compliance as well as its undesirable externalities such as lessening competition and hindering financial management. 'As in other areas of economic development policy, central banks in developing countries have an unfortunate tendency to mistake bank legislation and regulation on advanced- country lines for financial development itself' (Johnson, 1973, p. 71). Paradoxically, this tendency does not extend to the need for appropriate amendment to outdated legislation such as the law of negotiable instruments and trusts which in many Commonwealth countries has not kept pace with changing requirements. The perils of regulatory overkill are only too well-exemplified by the Reserve Bank of India (RBI), which, as remarked by a former economic advisor to the Government of India, 'receives far more information than it can ever use for regulation' (Desai, 1994, p. 129). This plethora of information certainly did not save the RBI from some egregious regulatory failures in the Indian securities scam (*c.* 1992) for which it was roundly criticized by the Joint Parliamentary Commission in its report (22 June 1993).

## 5.2 LOCATION OF SUPERVISORY AUTHORITY: OPTIONS

The available data on the location of supervisory authority (Table 5.1) clearly show that in most Asian, African and Middle Eastern

*Table* 5.1 Supervisory authorities for banks

| *Region* | *Central bank* | *Department of ministry of finance* | *Other agency* |
|---|---|---|---|
| Africa | 41 | 0 | 1[d] |
| Asia | 25 | 3[a] | 2[e] |
| Europe | 36 | 1[b] | 7[f] |
| Middle East | 16 | 0 | 1[g] |
| Western Hemisphere | 17 | 3[c] | 15[h] |

*Notes*:
[a] Japan, Kiribati, Korea
[b] Austria
[c] Dominica, Mexico, St Lucia
[d] Madagascar
[e] Hong Kong, Marshall Islands
[f] Belgium, Denmark, Germany, Hungary, Norway, Sweden, Switzerland
[g] Lebanon
[h] Antigua and Barbuda, Bolivia, Canada, Chile, Colombia, Dominican Republic, Ecuador, El Salvador, Grenada, Guatemala, Nicaragua, Panama, Peru, USA, Venezuela

*Source*: Adapted from José Tuya and Lorena Zamalloa (1994, Table 1 and Appendix 1). The data are derived from an IMF survey.

countries banking supervision is vested with the central bank and it is only in the Western Hemisphere that this authority is about evenly divided between the central bank and a separate authority, which is either the ministry of finance or a specialized agency (the superintendencia). This configuration is a reflection of historical and traditional factors rather than a reasoned choice based on careful evaluation of the merits of alternative options. Nor does economic doctrine suggest any a priori criteria for the appropriate distribution of supervisory authority. There has, however, been an extensive debate in recent years on whether the central bank is necessarily the most appropriate supervisory agency, taking account of both macroeconomic and microeconomic arguments for and against, or whether supervisory and regulatory functions are best delegated to a separate specialized agency.

On the macroeconomic level, the available evidence based on a limited sample of mostly developed countries (Table 5.2) does suggest 'that central banks without supervisory responsibilities were more successful in attaining a low inflation rate than central banks with shared or full supervisory responsibility' (Heller, 1991, p. 65). This seems to support the notion that central banks that concen-

*Table* 5.2 The supervisory responsibility of central banks and inflation performance[a]

| | | |
|---|---|---|
| *Central banks without supervisory authority* | | |
| Canada | 5.0 | |
| Germany | 2.9 | |
| Japan | 1.4 | 4.9 (3.3 excluding Venezuela) |
| Switzerland | 3.9 | |
| Venezuela | 11.4 | |
| *Central banks share supervisory authority* | | |
| France | 7.7 | |
| Italy | 11.5 | |
| Netherlands | 2.3 | 6.5 |
| USA | 4.3 | |
| *Central banks with supervisory authority* | | |
| Argentina | 298.7 | |
| Australia | 7.8 | |
| Brazil | 116.3 | |
| Ireland | 10.2 | 66.2 (excluding Argentina/Brazil) |
| South Africa | 13.8 | |
| Spain | 10.7 | |
| UK | 5.7 | |

*Note*: [a] Inflation rates are average annual rates for 1980–87 in per cent.

*Source*: H.R. Heller, 1991, table 1, p. 65.

trate wholly on monetary policy tend to be more successful in achieving the target of price stability, now increasingly recognized as the prime objective of central banks, than central banks that have major supervisory responsibilities. Such a conjuncture suggests, prima facie, a conflict of interest between the monetary policy and supervisory functions of the central bank. Heller's findings are further supported by Goodhart's results (1995, p. 371), which also included the developing countries. Both also agree that although there may be some correlation between the responsibility of the central bank for monetary policy and its supervisory role, the operative factor may well be the former, which determines the overall inflation performance. The apparent association between achieving price stability and the absence of supervisory responsibilities may well be caused by a number of other influences, not captured in this test. Therefore one is led to the conclusion that a central bank's involvement in supervision does not necessarily weaken its stance on monetary policy, and a central bank's inflation performance and its supervisory role are more or less separate issues. The structure of a country's banking and financial system is more important for the conduct of monetary policy and its inflation performance (Goodhart, 1995, p. 372).

At the micromanagement level, there are broadly four types of alternative supervisory arrangements: entrusting bank regulation and supervision to

- a department of the central bank;
- a department of the ministry of finance;
- an independent agency like the superintendency of banks in a number of Latin American countries; and
- a hybrid entity that combines any of the preceding options, as, for instance, elevating the function of banking supervision in a central bank to semi-independent status.

Of these options, the ministry of finance option seems clearly the least desirable, in so far as narrow fiscal criteria of revenue or expenditure may well override the more substantial supervisory considerations. For instance, the ministry may be tempted to thwart any increase in loan loss reserves or write-offs of non-performing loans, or to postpone closure of failed institutions for fear of any adverse budgetary impact of bail-outs or restructuring. Moreover, a supervisory department within the ministry of finance is hardly likely to command the same degree of autonomy and insulation from political and budgetary pressures as the central bank. In view of this the effective choice would seem to be between placing supervision with the central bank or an independent agency, or else exercising the hybrid option. These issues have been well researched in several studies (Heller, 1991; Tuya and Zamalloa, 1994; Goodhart, 1995). This extensive debate points to the following broad conclusions, which together establish a consensus in favour of vesting the supervisory function with the central bank. A basic argument is the commonality of the objectives and institutional requirements of banking supervision and monetary policy, notably insulation from political pressures, ease of data collection and coordination and the economies of staff and resources. Supervisory and monetary concerns overlap and can be often in conflict. For instance, supervisory recommendations at both the domestic and international levels in a recession, which may require banks to increase loan loss reserves and restrict credit to weed out weaker borrowers, may run counter to monetary policy requirements, to lower interest rates and enhanced availability of credit to stimulate economic recovery.

An increasingly decisive and influential argument for vesting supervisory powers with the central bank is the growing globalization of financial institutions and markets and the liberalization of the current accounts of a large number of developing countries, who have opted for Article VIII status of the International Monetary Fund's Articles of Agreement, which ensures freedom of payments and transfers on current account. Central banks have constant and intensive international contacts with other central banks as well as with international markets and agencies; which enables timely recognition of impending adverse developments in regard to international banks, as in the case of the Bank for Credit and Commerce International.[1] Mutual consultations among central banks as part of the prudential network of financial intelligence are natural and feasible and with inter-central bank entities like the Bank for International Settlements of an extent that can hardly be matched by an independent supervisory agency which lacks such contacts and necessarily tends to be more inward-looking. It may well be below the salt in the international financial community relative to a central bank. The resolution of inter-agency conflicts is much more difficult and developing countries would do well to heed, in this sphere, as in other spheres of economics, the wisdom of Occam's razor – that entities should not be multiplied needlessly.

Those who support the role of the central bank as the lead supervisor also invoke several other weighty arguments, notably that the critical role of the central bank as a lender of last resort in resolving financial system makes it imperative for it to have close and continuous knowledge of banks that can only be acquired by its hand-on supervision. There are also 'important synergies for the formulation of monetary policy because the central bank will be more sensitive to key financial sector developments' (International Monetary Fund, 1994, p. 14). For the management of liquidity shocks, which can occur under even the most efficient monetary management, the central bank needs first-hand and up-to-date knowledge of the entire financial system, of the linkages and exposures of financial institutions and close contacts with other central banks. Without such knowledge and contacts, the central bank will find it more difficult to distinguish illiquidity from insolvency and determine in time the most appropriate mode of functioning as a lender of last resort.

The arguments against placing bank supervision in the central bank are both doctrinal and institutional, and foremost in the latter category is the contention that 'banking supervision inevitably takes too much time away from what should be the main task of the central bank, namely the design and implementation of monetary policy' (ibid., p. 14). This point is not without merit in so far as the supervisory function is arguably the most demanding and time-consuming task in any central bank, and the supervision department is often the largest.[2] However, this is more a matter of efficient reorganization which can be resolved by wise delegation and greater autonomy for the department within the central bank. There is greater substance in the argument that a lead role in supervision might hamper the central bank in the implementation of monetary policy. The quasi-legal objection that 'the need to close banks often involves an element of expropriation of private property, which is best left to a democratically elected body' (ibid., p. 14) would, however, be valid even if an agency other than the central bank exercised supervisory functions.[3]

Although the case for the central bank's supervisory role is, on balance, stronger, this does not imply that there is necessarily a case for merger of existing autonomous supervisory agencies with central banks, which can continue, provided there is effective co-ordination between the agency and the central bank. Some countries – for example, Argentina, Costa Rica, Finland, Lebanon, and Uruguay – have opted for an alternative hybrid approach in which banking supervision is accorded semi-independent status within the central bank. The Reserve Bank of India's proposed new Supervisory Board also exemplifies the hybrid option attempts to elevate the supervisory tasks of the central bank to a much higher status, but it still remains to be seen whether it 'will not be just a department of the bank with staff drawn mainly from the bank itself' (Patel, 1994, p. 50) or whether it will be autonomous and representative.[4]

## 5.3 MARKET FORCES AS A SUPERVISORY TOOL

The evaluation of the various institutional alternatives for supervision authority finally leads to the question: is there any role for market forces and market discipline in the regulatory and supervisory process – which involves substantial costs of compliance – in the developing countries: say, on the lines proposed by the Reserve Bank of New Zealand, which has taken the position that bank supervision should rely more on market forces with a correspondingly reduced role for the central bank or any other supervisory authority (International Monetary Fund, 1994, p. 14)? In the market approach envisaged by the Reserve Bank of New Zealand, prudential requirements (for example, limits on risk exposures and open currency positions) would be abolished, with the exception of capital adequacy requirements, in favour of public disclosure and market discipline. There would be a more active and responsible role for the directors of the bank in the sound management of their banks. Public disclosure requirements (such as risk concentration, capital, credit rating) would be increased concomitantly with the strengthening of the financial infrastructure (for example, by moving to a real time gross settlement system) so as to reduce the systemic consequences of bank failure.[5] Developing countries too should attempt to complement their non-market supervisory mechanisms by strengthening the forces of market disciplining. In fact the scope for market forces as a macroeconomic regulatory mechanism for banks in developing countries has not yet been explored systematically on the lines of its potential in the USA (Jordan, 1994). The efficacy of market forces as a regulatory tool is of course contingent on the development of all the elements of market discipline, notably adequate transparency of bank accounts and the responsiveness of banks to market signals. There is one other crucial element of market discipline – that no bail-out be anticipated – which may be hard to satisfy, for it is inconceivable that a central bank in a developing country will announce the abdication of its role as a lender of last resort. Moreover, market discipline requires a legal basis in the form of legislation like Truth-in-Lending and Truth-in-Investment and even this offers no assurance that the average depositor, borrower, or investor has the necessary knowledge and awareness to protect himself. Even in the US few depositors seem to be aware of the Law of Dormant Accounts which debars access to inactive accounts after a lapse of a specified period of years. The Law of Dormant Accounts is, however, extremely fuzzy and banks hardly publicize it. For instance, it is not clear what constitutes activity and what is its minimum level. Admittedly, the doctrine of '*caveat emptor*' (buyer beware) has to come into play at some point but it has its limitations even in the most sophisticated countries.

## 5.4 SCOPE AND EFFICIENCY OF SUPERVISION

Far more important than the institutional location of supervisory authority are the issues relating to the scope and efficiency of the supervisory process. One basic issue is the scope of coverage – how far should the central bank's supervisory jurisdiction and its lender of last resort facilities extend? Generally, central banks confine themselves to the clearing banks, given their uniqueness attributable to their joint generation of liquid liabilities, which are media of payment and of non-marketable illiquid business loans. The central bank's concern is to protect the money creation process and the clearing/payments system. There are exceptional cases like the Monetary Authority of Singapore, which has wide-ranging powers to regulate and supervise the whole financial system. But given the trend for deregulation and the breaking up of the Chinese walls between banking and non-banking business, the case for the central bank to act as the unitary supervisory authority becomes increasingly stronger. There are real risks in fragmentation of supervisory authority, which can lead to both regulatory overkill and regulatory arbitrage by the supervised institutions, and possibly even 'somewhat lighter supervision than otherwise would be the case', as in the United States (Volcker, 1990, p. 51)

The really critical issue is the quality and adequacy of supervision and many studies have shown that inadequate supervision, particularly in the wake of financial liberalization and reforms, has been a major contributor to the spread of financial crises (Sundararajan and Baliño, 1991). Even in the United States, 'lax supervision' has been cited as a contributory factor in the savings and loan industry debacle (Volcker, 1990, p. 51). Bank supervision is a highly specialized occupation and 'even banking and finance majors are usually unable to conduct bank examination work without further training' or prior banking experience, in recognition of which the Central Bank of the Philippines has organized a Supervision and Examination Institute (Laya, 1980, pp. 201–2). But the quality of the supervisory staff would be contingent on the payment of competitive rates of remuneration, considering that most qualified and competent bank supervisors have attractive alternative openings in banks, legal and auditing firms. Would central banks be able and willing to maintain the requisite differential *vis-à-vis* the competing private sector? To the extent that they are able to accomplish this, as in the case of the Monetary Authority of Singapore, the quality of bank supervision would be equal to the challenges facing it.

One significant reform which would enable central banks to finance the higher remuneration to supervisors is the levy of fees and assessments on the institutions which it supervises, which could be based, say, on the supervisory hours spent on an institution or expressed as a percentage of the balance sheet total. Such a measure would make the supervisory process more cost-effective and for the supervised institutions it would be a legitimate expense no different in principle from the fees paid to external auditors.

The core of the supervisory process is the right balance between document-based off-site supervision and on-site examinations based on a specified time cycle relying on manuals which use criteria like the US Federal Reserve's 'CAMEL Test': C for capital adequacy; A for asset quality; M for quality of management; E for earnings and L for liquidity. The most difficult components of bank examination are the appraisal of bank management and the quality of bank assets (Sirisena, 1990, pp. 471–5). The experience of Sri Lanka, which has had no bank failures, shows that, 'although on-site examinations are both time-consuming and costly, the supervisory process in Sri Lanka places substantial reliance upon this method' (ibid., p. 470). Moral suasion too can be an effective tool of supervision, particularly in oligopolistic banking systems, provided that the supervisory staff has the requisite professionalism and credibility. A comparatively neglected source of information is market intelligence on the position of individual banks, which has been effectively tapped by resourceful central banks like the Monetary Authority of Singapore. But in general central banks in developing countries are much too insulated from the hurly-burly of the market place to exploit such information.

Since the pace of financial reform and liberalization is rightly said to be determined by the efficacy of supervision, it is interesting to note from Indonesian experience that 'the philosophy (to protect the interest of depositors) and objectives of bank supervision in the regulation era or in the deregulation (liberalization) era are basically unchanged (Binhadi, 1992, p. 589). In the final analysis, the accent of supervision would necessarily have to be on institutions rather than on their functions, since it is institutions which ultimately fail or succeed. But even the most effective supervision is no safeguard of financial stability because, as Walter

Bagehot was never tired of reminding his readers, good banking is more a matter of good bankers rather than of good banks and good laws.

## 5.5 LENDER OF LAST RESORT

The term 'lender of last resort' (LLR) describes the functions and responsibilities of a central bank to meet the demands for high-powered money (through open market operations or emergency loans through the discount window) arising from illiquidity and insolvency of financial institutions. The normal obligations of the central bank to provide liquidity are well understood and accepted but its precise role in conditions of banking crises and directives has been the subject of much debate, particularly on grounds of adverse selection and moral hazard.

The doctrine of the lender of last resort, as originated by Sir Francis Baring (1797) and subsequently refined and developed by Henry Thornton (1802) and Walter Bagehot (1873), and also as exemplified by the role of the Bank of England in the nineteenth century, emphasizes that the LLR's responsibility is macroeconomic, rather than microeconomic (to individual institutions), to protect the aggregate money stock and overall financial stability by minimizing the contagion or spillover effects of crises on the financial system (Hirsch, 1977; Humphrey, 1989). Bagehot's enunciation of the doctrine contributed several original elements, particularly the pre- announced commitment to provide liquidity at a penalty rate to the market during crisis situations against widely acceptable collateral assets valued at market prices, to temporarily illiquid but solvent borrowers. Even under free banking, random shocks such as political instability, civil disturbances or the failure of a large enterprise, may trigger massive switches of cash balances from inside (bank-created) money to outside (high-powered) money, which competitive banks are inherently incapable of providing. Under a fiat money standard, which is now universal, only the central bank (LLR) can provide outside money. Thus, the capability of the central bank as the sole source of high-powered (outside) money constitutes the economic rationale of the LLR doctrine.

There are, however, practical problems in implementing central bank's responsibilities as a LLR. First, there is the question raised by the traditional omission in most central bank statutes to spell out its LLR obligation and for central banks to rely on an implicit doctrine of constructive ambiguity which in practice permits them to exercise discretionary powers in this as in other respects. The absence of specific location of the lender of last resort authority can also raise unsuspected operational problems as in the case of the two strongest Saudi Arabian commercial banks in 1985 and 1986 (National Commercial Bank and Saudi American Bank), who had to 'wait more than 18 embarrassing' months before they could open a branch in London, because 'the Bank of England reportedly questioned the Saudi Arabian Monetary Agency's status as the lender of last resort' (Wilson, 1991, p. 48). This is an area where central banks in developing countries should take the necessary initiatives in setting out the duties and powers of the lender of last resort in their statutes without fear of the usually exaggerated risks of moral hazard – the propensity of individuals and institutions to increase the probability or magnitude of risk against which they are formally insured or protected. For instance, recourse to open market operations rather than discount window loans to meet emergency demands for high-powered money would obviate any risks of channelling assistance to individual institutions. The researches of Bordo (1989) offer impressive historical evidence to support the classical Baring–Thornton–Bagehot doctrine of the LLR as a preventive and corrective of banking crisis and panics without the need to render assistance to insolvent or weak banks. In sum an adequate and efficient LLR is a necessary part of the financial infrastructure of any functioning fractional reserve banking system and its absence or failure can be disastrous for aggregate output and employment, as proved by the Federal Reserve's failure to act as an LLR in the Great Depression of the 1930s (Friedman and Schwartz, 1963).

In the light of this analysis it would be useful to examine the practical applications of the doctrine of LLR in some typical developing countries. To begin with, the following review (based on Sundararajan and Baliño, 1991, pp. 29–35) sets out the scope and limitations of the central bank's role as an LLR in the crisis episodes considered, where the underlying problem was insolvency rather than illiquidity, of such a scale that in many instances the normal LLR facilities were just inadequate and special credit facilities had to be set up. An unexpected and certainly undesirable feature in most instances was the replacement of emergency lending at market or penalty rates by concessional long-term lending. Consequently, either the central bank or the government ended up actively subsidizing many financial institutions. In some cases emergency legislation was enacted to broaden the institutional range of the LLR through special *ad hoc* funds (Thailand) or arrangements to onlend funds through stronger institutions (Philippines). The central bank also intervened in the management of sick institutions (Argentina, Chile, and Malaysia). In Thailand soft loans from the central bank were extended to troubled banks and finance companies but no bank was liquidated, whereas a variety of disposition decisions were employed for finance companies including liquidations, mergers, restructuring and recapitalization. In the Philippines, the preferred method for the larger commercial banks was takeover by a government institution or acquisition by the government with central bank support and intervention.

What are the typical crises which warrant invocation of the LLR functions? The term 'financial or banking crisis' is widely used and often the definitions vary with the specific symptoms of the crisis being analysed. An acceptable definition is to use it to refer to a situation in which a significant group of financial institutions have liabilities exceeding the market value of their assets, causing runs and other portfolio shifts, and the collapse of some financial institutions, necessitating government intervention leading to liquidation, mergers, or restructuring. Typically, such crises are caused by an increase in the share of non-performing loans, an increase in losses (because of mismatches of interest rates, instruments, maturities and currencies and off-balance sheet liabilities) and a decline in investment values. The specific role of central banks in coping with and resolving banking crises may be illustrated with reference to the experience of a selected group of countries in Asia and Latin America.[6] The policy packages were aimed, first, at arresting the spread of the crises, restoration of depositors' confidence, and safeguarding the payment and settlement systems; and, second, at rehabilitation of problem banks through orderly restructuring and recapitalization. The various measures undertaken in these countries – reflecting the differences in the institutional framework and the political and economic constraints – covered, in addition to emergency measures, specific actions to assist borrowers and failing banks, as well as reforms of banking laws and regulations (see Table 5.3 for a stylized framework).

*Table* 5.3 A stylized framework for resolving banking crises

| *Objectives* | *Constraints* |
|---|---|
| Restore depositors' confidence and protect some or all depositors | Legislation |
| | Limits on budgetary resources |
| Prevent hasty liquidation of assets | External imbalances and constraints on foreign borrowing |
| Avoid undue monetary fluctuations<br>Prevent moral hazard<br>Protect solvent banks and debtors | Political considerations in distributing the losses between government, the central bank, bank-owners, depositors, and borrowers |
| Protect the payment system | Public interest and employment considerations, for example, effect on competition and banking concentration |
| Minimize budgetary costs (or costs to the insurance agency) | |
| Ensure equitable distribution of losses | |

| | | *Instruments* | |
|---|---|---|---|
| *Emergency* | *Long-term* | *to deal with failing banks* | *to deal with borrowers* |
| Financial support and other lender-of-last resort actions | New institution(s)<br>New legislation | Liquidation<br>Merger | Assistance to reschedule domestic debt |
| Guarantees on deposits<br>Disclosure of information to dispel rumours or to revive confidence | Strengthened supervision | Sale<br>Recapitalization<br>Restructuring | Technical assistance<br>Subsidies and assistance to foreign currency debtors<br>Negative real interest rates |
| Central bank intervention in management of weak banks | | | |

*Source*: V. Sundararajan and T. J. T. Baliño, 1991, p. 52.

The recapitalizing of banks typically involved various forms of subsidization by the central bank (or a separate government agency). The analysis of various country experiences strongly suggests that: central banks usually lack the expertise in administration of a commercial bank or a specialized agency and 'are ill equipped to assume the administration of bad loans of banks being recapitalized or restructured'. Even more importantly, central bank losses on account of bad loans, which are also less transparent, compromise and hamper monetary control. The above findings of the IMF research study are also broadly supported by the survey of bank failures in both developed and developing countries (Goodhart, 1995, pp. 372–410), which also shows that, barring liquidity support and an occasional role as lead organizer, the central bank's role in resolving bank crisis is much less than that of the government and government-sponsored agencies.

The emergence of crises has also had the salutary effect of triggering substantive regulatory and supervisory reforms in the sample countries. Thus, in Thailand central bank supervision was extended to finance companies and the central bank's powers of intervention and enforcement options were broadened, while strengthening regulations to limit concentration of ownership and portfolios. In Malaysia the central bank has expanded its powers to intervene in all deposit-taking institutions, establishing the Board Audit and Examination Committees to strengthen to oversight of bank management and tightening lending limits per borrower. Chile put through major legislative reforms beginning in 1986 which, among others, provided for tighter capital requirements; public disclosure of information on the nature and quality of the assets of financial institutions; more precise definition of credit limits to a single borrower; and a formal rating system for financial institutions.

In sum, while timely support from the central bank and the government during a crisis can prevent major and prolonged disruptions to the payments system and the economy at large, the effective restructuring and recapitalization of the banking system requires significant fiscal adjustment, structural reforms of the non financial sector and maintenance of macroeconomic stability. Equally, central banks must balance their legitimate concern for financial stability against the need to promote market-driven efficiency. But in most decisions of regulatory and prudential issues, the emphasis has been on stability and efficiency with virtually no regard for equity concerns like the interests of users of financial services, who have begun to question whether liberalization in oligopolistic financial systems has resulted in lower bank fees and charges and improved services.

## 5.6 DEPOSIT PROTECTION SCHEMES

The protection of the nominal value and liquidity of bank deposits up to defined limits per account and per customer through explicit deposit insurance schemes, funded with premiums paid by the institutions, is often regarded as a part of the prudential machinery. The insurer is generally, but not always, a government-owned institution like the central bank or an autonomous corporation. Deposit protection may also be implicit (Table 5.4).

*Table* 5.4 Comparison of implicit and explicit deposit insurance schemes

| *Feature* | Implicit schemes | *Explicit schemes* |
|---|---|---|
| Rules and procedures governing deposit protection | No | Yes |
| Obligation to protect depositors | At discretion of government | Legal obligation up to insurance limits; discretion to protect uninsured depositors |
| Extent of protection | Can vary from no protection to total protection | Can vary from limited to total protection |
| Prior funding | None | Initial capitalization and possibly regular payments by government. Premium payments by banks. |
| Funding in event of bank failure | Government | From insurance fund; shortfalls may be covered by special levies on banks or by loans or additional capital from government. |

*Source*: Adapted from Table 2 in Talley and Mas, 1990, p. 14.

The rationale of deposit insurance schemes is basically twofold; to protect small depositors from losses in the event of bank failures and to insulate the banking system against possible unrestrained panic withdrawals in cash by depositors, that can cripple the financial intermediation process, disrupt the settlement and payment systems, and above all cause severe macroeconomic contagion effects. Explicit deposit insurance is essentially a scheme to protect small depositors; hence the ceilings on accounts and customers. Insured deposits by their very nature constitute a relatively small proportion of total deposits of any insured banks. Consequently, deposit insurance by itself does not create a moral hazard, as is so often mistakenly stressed in discussions of deposit insurance.The moral hazard could be more rightly attributed to the banking community's presumption that the central bank will ultimately provide full protection through lender of last resort and associated measures. Sometimes a third justification is also adduced: to provide a formal and consistent mechanism for resolving failing bank situations. This reason is, however, not integral to the overall justification for deposit insurance schemes since the mechanisms for resolving bank failures and financial distress have to be in place regardless of whether a country has deposit insurance schemes. Moreover, these mechanisms really appertain to the lender of last resort functions of a central bank. This is a major argument for vesting the ownership and management of a deposit insurance system in a separate autonomous corporation since it thereby avoids a conflict of interest for the central bank.

Several developing countries have established explicit deposit insurance schemes. Among these are Argentina, Bolivia, Chile, Colombia, Honduras, Kenya, India, Nigeria, the Philippines, Trinidad and Tobago, and Turkey. Some developing countries (Taiwan, Equatorial Guinea, Israel, Solomon Islands, Thailand, and the Yemen People's Democratic Republic) have enabling provisions in their current banking laws, for establishment of deposit insurance. In Afghanistan, the People's Republic of China, and Pakistan (for nationalized banks) the state fully guarantees all bank deposits, thereby obviating the need for formal insurance, which also shows the redundancy of deposit insurance for public sector banks in countries like India where nationalized banks account for the bulk of bank deposits (Mas and Talley, 1990, p. 43). Most developing countries do not have explicit formal systems whereas almost all the major developed countries, including France, the Federal Republic of Germany, Japan, the United Kingdom, and the United States, have deposit insurance schemes.

This, however, has not precluded the governments of most developing countries from undertaking various policy actions which are described as implicit protection of depositors. Such measures have usually been brought into play in the case of impending failures of public banks or large private banks. Both explicit and implicit deposit protection schemes have the same set of objectives – protection of small depositors and stability of the banking system. This therefore poses the question: in what way is a formal deposit insurance system more efficient and desirable than an implicit protection scheme? The main advantage of a properly functioning formal insurance system is that the extent of protection offered, the types of financial institutions and instruments that would be eligible, the financing of the system and the operative rules of the game are predetermined. They are designed specifically to allay fears of systemic contagion among banks. In contrast, an implicit system is inherently discretionary and *ad hoc*, which covers the option of extending no protection at all in the cases where there is no perceived threat to the stability of the banking system. Formal insurance has the advantage that it provides a convenient mechanism for shifting the costs of deposit protection to the insured banks in the form of required payments of premiums which can be actuarially graduated. This also seems appropriate because deposit insurance benefits banks by lowering their cost of funds, whereas in an implicit system banks derive benefits but do not incur any costs, which are ultimately borne entirely by the central bank or the government budget (tax-payers). Formal insurance also offers small depositors more effective protection because it is designed expressly, in large part, to fulfil this objective. Arguably, formal insurance is likely to be more effective in forestalling and stemming bank runs than an implicit scheme, since it involves a legal obligation to protect depositors (up to a specified limit) whereas the magnitude of protection under any implicit system is wholly at the discretion of the authorities and, consequently, less assured. The problems of moral hazard arise in both presumptive and explicit deposit insurance schemes and must be anticipated through effective supervision and inspection of the adequacy and quality of capital and the asset portfolio. The moral hazard is accentuated under systems that offer 100 per cent coverage of depositors, as in Norway and the former Yugoslavia – the only two countries to offer such coverage. But

Norwegian experience certainly does not point to any untoward problems arising solely because of full coverage of deposits. The United Kingdom device of co-insurance (that is, insurance of only 75 per cent of each deposit up to a prescribed maximum amount) implies that all depositors share the risk and therefore have an incentive to monitor the financial condition of individual banks. But the creation of incentives does not ensure that depositors will have the necessary expertise and resources to be able to evaluate the condition of their banks.

The perceived benefits of explicit deposit insurance are, however, contingent on adequate financing and efficient management of such systems, as is well borne out by the experience of the Philippines' Deposit Corporation, which because of its low capital base and inadequate contributions found it increasingly difficult to settle the growing claims of depositors of the failed thrift and rural banks (approximately 140 rural banks) representing 6 per cent of total deposits (*c.*1988). The shortfall had to be made up by borrowing and a rise in premiums, which further reduced the profits of an already ailing banking system. Currently, only about a dozen developing countries have formal deposit insurance systems, but it is not self-evident that such a system would be desirable in all countries. Rapid growth of innovations in financial institutions and instruments also poses the question whether deposit insurance should be extended to non-bank financial intermediaries – an issue which has not been addressed sufficiently by central banks and policy-makers. Moreover, the introduction of such systems in steady state economies with a proven record of banking stability may even have unintended adverse announcement effects. A viable deposit insurance system presupposes not only adequate funding with uniform premiums, because of the difficulties of actuarial assessment of bank risk, but also compulsory membership. Initial government contributions to the capital of the insurance fund, as in India, Nigeria, and the Philippines, or periodic contributions as in Spain, help to strengthen the credibility of the system. The insurance limits and premiums, however, need to be kept under constant review to make adjustments for inflation and any structural changes in the banking system. It is equally important to ensure that an autonomous deposit insurance corporation, separate from the central bank, is not saddled with other unrelated functions such as credit guarantees – as in India, where the Deposit Insurance Corporation was merged (1978) in a singularly ill-conceived move, with the Credit Guarantee Corporation. But even the most efficient deposit insurance is no substitute for timely and effective inspection and supervision of banks by the central bank or an autonomous supervisory agency. A viable and well-designed deposit insurance system is at best a useful but not a wholly necessary adjunct to the prudential machinery. As such there has to be close and effective liaison and co-ordination between the supervisory agency and the deposit insurance agency, particularly in the event of prospective mergers and restructuring of failed banks.

In view of the universal privatization vogue it is pertinent to ask whether the private insurance industry in developing countries has the resources and capability to shoulder a larger proportion of the burden of deposit insurance burden now borne almost entirely by the public sector (government or central bank). This is highly problematic considering that in most developing countries insurance – life and general – is the least developed and weakest sector of the financial system. Even in the USA an authoritative study by the Federal Deposit Insurance Corporation (FDIC) concluded that private deposit insurance coverage will continue to remain fairly narrow in scope and focused on individual customers or selected institutions (FDIC, *Deposit Insurance for the Nineties: Meeting the Challenge*, 1983, p. xvii). The FDIC found, after discussion with representatives from a selected group of companies, 'little reason to believe that comprehensive insurance programs can be made available from the private sector' (ibid., p. xvii).

Deposit insurance schemes are inherently complex mechanisms which have to be in the public sector in the developing countries, with provision for compulsory membership, partial coverage, subject to review for inflation, and with adequate funding with some assurance of government back-up in a crisis; and for the insurer to have varied and flexible options to resolve bank failures. More importantly, deposit insurance should be vested in the fully autonomous, unsubsidized public corporations distinct from the central bank, to avoid conflict of interest, but with adequate representation for the central bank on their boards of directors. The mutualization of deposit insurance with due safeguards is also a possibility which merits consideration as a device to minimize moral hazard, on the lines of the mutualization of the credit guarantee scheme in Malaysia.

# 6 Developmental Role

'. . . in the early stages of central banking . . . the emphasis must be on the development of a banking system to control. This is not only a logical order; it is also the historical order of events in the underdeveloped country I have most studied; the England of earlier centuries.' — *R.S. Sayers*

'. . . the monetary authority, wherever placed, should be composed of people who have no official interest in the allocation of central or commercial bank credit . . . the chief task of a central bank should be to create or extinguish money and not to assume the tasks of a development bank.'— *Lauchlin Currie*

## 6.1 ISSUES AND CHALLENGES

A major issue in both the historical and contemporary debate on the objectives and functions of central banks in developing countries is whether they should also undertake promotional and developmental activities. Accordingly, this chapter addresses the following main interlinked issues in order to assess 'the contribution that central banking may make towards the healthy and speedy development of the economy' (Sayers, 1961, p. 33):

(a) Should the central bank in a developing economy . . . confine itself to the negative function of ensuring that no monetary sickness impedes the progress of industrial and commercial development?
(b) Or should it strive itself to make some positive contribution, stimulating enterprise in particularly important directions?
(c) And what should be the scope, in terms of institutions, of its activities?

In the early days of a central bank the accent has necessarily to be on the development of a banking system to control because this is not only a logical order but also the typical historical sequence in underdeveloped countries. However, the issue is not simply that 'once stabilization has been achieved, should it perhaps be the aim of the central banks to keep out of the way, merely ensuring that no financial crisis impedes the efforts of the enterprising builders of the country's industry and trade?' (Sayers, 1957, p. 34). Once the banking system has attained a certain critical threshold of development, the stabilization and developmental objectives and policies of a central bank tend to be necessarily concurrent rather than sequential. Consequently they pose problems of harmonization in so far as the two basic objectives may conflict. Even in the developmental sphere the role of a central bank should be viewed as not merely one of passively adapting the techniques of central banking to 'suit the changing economic structure' (Sayers), but of actively changing and modifying the financial structure itself to promote development. There is now a sufficient body of experience to be able to assess whether central banks in developing countries have responded to the following challenges (Brimmer, 1971, pp. 781–82). Have they:

(1) 'while not ignoring their traditional tasks – taken innovative steps to encourage economic development?'
(2) 'been able to alter the flow of credit in favor of development needs?'
(3) 'assisted in creating institutions specifically designed to provide development finance?'
(4) 'succeeded in efforts to encourage the mobilization of savings by private financial institutions?'
(5) 'used their proximity to the centers of political power to advise their governments as to the importance of monetary and fiscal stability in creating a climate conducive to investment and limit growth?'
(6) 'Finally, what is the record of success, and of disappointment, harvested by those central banks in the struggle for economic development?'

The conjunctural objectives are spelt out in all central bank statutes, whereas the promotional and developmental objectives are stated explicitly – usually in the case of the developing countries and exceptionally in developed countries. For instance, in the USA, the Federal Reserve Act enjoins the Board of Governors and the Federal Open Market Committee to 'maintain long run growth of the monetary and credit aggregates commensurate with the economy's long run potential to increase production so as to promote effectively the goal of maximum employment, stable prices, and moderate long-term interest rates' (Section 2A.1). The Federal Reserve Act also specifies that the Board of Governors should act 'in furtherance of the purposes of the Full Employment and

Balanced Growth Act of 1948'. Although 'the Federal Reserve has often been asked to provide credit on particularly favourable terms to sectors of the economy that either have special problems or are deemed to have special potential . . . those requests are resisted, usually successfully' because 'if you begin using . . . the central bank to support one area of the economy or another, it will be practically and psychologically impossible to, at the same time, restrain the creation of money generally' (Volcker, 1990, p. 17). Nevertheless, the absence of reference to promotional objectives has not inhibited central banks in developed countries from using monetary policies to implement basic national economic goals. For instance, central banks in Italy, Japan, the Netherlands, Sweden and West Germany have used various techniques such as asset reserve requirements and government borrowing and relending to preferred sectors (with or without interest subsidies) such as housing, agriculture, exports, small business and underdeveloped regions. Such promotional techniques are sought to be justified on the grounds that these are typically the sectors which tend to suffer disproportionately from credit restrictions in deflationary policies (US Committee on Banking and Currency 92nd Congress, 1972). The Swedish Riksbank is an outstanding example of a central bank which has always played an active role in promoting various economic and social programmes for preferred and priority sectors, such as housing, principally through asset reserve requirements. In the 1920s and 1930s the Bank of England played a leading role in the restructuring of the cotton and textile industry in Britain. 'In the mind of the Governor himself [Montague Norman], these problems of economic organization had more attention than the narrower field of monetary policy with which central banks are conventionally concerned' (Sayers, 1976, p. 502). The Bank of England took bold initiatives in establishing specialized institutions like the Reconstruction Finance Corporation for the supply of long-term capital for rehabilitation of depressed industries. Admittedly, central bankers are no less prone to fallacies of 'misplaced concreteness' than other economic practitioners but it is much too cavalier to say that 'as in other cases of economic development policy, central banks in developing countries have an unfortunate tendency to mistake bank legislation and regulation on advanced-country lines for financial development itself' (Johnson, 1973). It is interesting to recall that the Bank of England's report on the desirability and practicality of establishing a Central Bank in

Nigeria for promoting the economic development of the country concluded: 'it is hard to see how a central bank could function as an instrument to promote the economic development of the country' (Fisher, 1953, p. 18). This scepticism has subsequently given place to a more positive approach to central banking.

The statutes of the newer central banks and monetary authorities established in the 1970s and 1980s, with the technical assistance of the IMF, have specific provisions for promotional roles (for example, in Bhutan, Botswana, Fiji, Maldives, Solomon Islands, Swaziland, Vanuatu). In assessing their promotional role the central banks of developing countries have to be judged by their revealed practice rather than by the scope of their statutes. Their promotional practices have usually been ahead of the letter of their laws which suggests that central banks, given the will and commitment, usually have adequate implicit discretionary power to fulfil promotional objectives. Despite the adequacy of enabling powers, central banks seem to be subject to prolonged lags between perception and implementation. For instance, the Statutory Report of the Reserve Bank of India (under Section 55 (1)(G), 1938) observed: 'During a period of financial development such as exists in India today, it may be desirable for Central Bank credit to be made available in a larger number of ways and with less restrictions than when the financial structure is more complete' (p. 35). But it was not until the 1950s that the Reserve Bank of India embarked on its promotional and developmental activities. More than statutes and formal powers it is the central bank's status, expertise, and influence, in relation to the government, developmental agencies and the financial community, which defines its promotional opportunity-set as a regulator, innovator, participant, guarantor and catalyst of financial development.

## 6.2 RATIONALE AND MODALITIES

Paradoxically, the rationale of central banking has been argued too exclusively on grounds of monetary and regulatory policy and the role of a central bank as a lender of last resort even though historically development precedes control and regulation. But central bank developmental activities are much too diversified to be analysed through a unitary paradigm. The primary rationale of the promotional and developmental role was first clearly enunciated by Keynes in his classic pioneering work on Indian Currency and Finance (1913) and in his Memorandum on Proposals for the Establishment of a State Bank in India (6 October 1913) to the Royal (Chamberlain) Commission on Indian Currency and Finance) which contained a detailed blueprint of a scheme for a State Bank of India in 1913 long before the recommendation of the Brussels Conference (1920) for establishing a central bank in countries where there was no central bank (Chandavarkar, 1985a). Significantly, Keynes based the rationale of his state bank not only on its monetary and regulatory role but even more on its developmental role as an agency to promote industry and agriculture as well as the banking system. Keynes rejected the Bank of England as an unsuitable model for India because, being essentially a product of history, it had a strictly conventional role as the government's banker, bank of issue and a lender of last resort. In a magisterial exhortation to 'the formers of the new bank's constitution' [for India] he advised them to 'put far from their minds all thoughts of the Bank of England . . . It is in the state banks of Europe, especially in that of Germany, or in those perhaps of Holland or Russia that the proper model is to be found (1971, p. 168). Keynes commended the examples of the European state banks, which were based on conscious design, had more flexible currency issue systems than the Bank of England, and developmental objectives, such as the provision of direct credit and rediscount facilities to promote industry and agriculture. For instance, the revised Statute of the Bank of Russia (1894) provided for direct funding of industry, commerce and agriculture by authorizing it to extend credit up to three years and to make loans against bills secured by hypothecation or guarantee, or any other securities deemed adequate by the ministry of finance. Its rediscount facilities (up to eight months) for commercial paper was extended to private banks on loans on securities which were not acceptable directly by the State Bank with the risk of being divided between the two institutions. Keynes also referred to the facilities of the German Reichsbank for quick transfers of deposits at no charge from any one of its 486 branches to another without recourse to checks or clearing systems. Thereby the Reichsbank economized the use of specie – an important consideration for a developing country – which fell from about 40 per cent of the total monetary circulation (1876) to about 17 per cent (1900). Keynes suggested that the proposed State Bank of India (*c.* 1913) too should open branches as rapidly as possible at most places with a district treasury without, however, jeopardizing the Bank's profitability, and also create appropriate rediscount facilities to Indian banks on the most desirable lines of European experience. Subsequently, in his evidence to the Royal (Hilton Young) Commission (1926) Keynes reaffirmed that 'a central bank would be helpful in expanding the commercial banking organization' (Keynes, 1981a, p. 524). Keynes was, however, acutely concerned that 'although the growth of banking in India was of utmost importance, a startling series of failures will do much to retard it' (1971, p. 159). Hence he was equally conscious of the need to regulate commercial banks in India, many of which suffered from undercapitalization, mismanagement, and conduct of nonbanking activities. He was thus cognizant of the regulatory and prudential aspects of central banking at a time when it hardly figured in public policy even in the European countries. It is, however, a revealing commentary on the long time-lag between ideas and implementation in India's monetary history that it was not until the late 1940s that the Reserve Bank of India (1935) established Departments of Inspection and Development, and not until the late 1960s and 1970s that the State Bank of India (the former Imperial Bank of India) and the nationalized commercial banks embarked on a planned expansion of branches in under-banked areas. It is, however, noteworthy that for all his innovativeness in other respects, Keynes did not address the policy issue of a productive use of seigniorage (currency) and central bank profits and in fact hoped that the Government of India's decision to divert half of future coinage profits to capital expenditure on railways 'will be reconsidered before the time comes' (1971, p. 275). This was also an implicit recognition of the limits to the developmental role of a central bank. A latter-day Keynes would not have been supportive of the use of central bank profits to capitalize development finance institutions.

But one of the many puzzles in the history of central banking doctrine is the total absence of any systematic attempt to formulate the developmental role of central banks following the pioneering venture of Keynes in this field. The literature on central banking has been narrowly focused on problems of monetary policy and exchange rate regimes. Even the pioneering study of Sen on *Central Banking in Underdeveloped Money Markets* (1952) did not analyse the developmental role of central banks until its fourth revised edition (1967). This theme has been further developed subsequently by Sayers (1957, 1961), Asseily (1967), Chandler (1962), Brimmer (1971), and Chandavarkar (1987a, 1988).

The promotional and developmental role of central banks derives from a combination of factors. First, even in developed economies, it has been noticed that passivity on the part of the central bank does not ensure the neutrality of monetary policy. The absence of credit priority programs does not mean that priorities will not be created. The large corporate business sector is effectively the preferred sector in all industrialized countries for loans from financial institutions and it is this sector which suffers least even when it is the primary target of credit restrictions. It is the other sectors which therefore 'suffer disproportionately from policies designed to deflate the economy' (Staff Report of US Committee on Banking and Currency, 1972, p. iii). There are no comparable studies of sectoral incidence of credit policy in developing countries but a similar presumption would not be unjustified. This explains why central banks in developing countries 'tend to trust to the subsidization of credit for purposes deemed socially worthy – in this case development projects – to achieve the desired results' (Johnson, 1973, p. 71). Typically, central bank credit subsidies are targeted toward the so-called priority sectors like housing, export finance, rural credit, cottage industries, small businesses, and co-operatives.

Regional imbalances in the distribution of credit are a manifestation of the wider 'regional problem of different regions growing at uneven rates' (Kaldor, 1970, p. 337), which results from the principle of 'circular and cumulative causation (Myrdal, 1957), increasing returns to scale, and 'the strong positive association between the growth of productivity and efficiency and the rate of growth in the scale of activities – the so-called Verdoorn Law (Kaldor, 1970, p. 340). 'In many countries . . . the banking system, if not regulated to act differently easily becomes an instrument for siphoning off the savings from the poorer regions to the richer and more progressive ones where rates of return on capital are high and secure' (Myrdal, 1965, p. 29). The regional distribution of credit is not merely an issue of efficiency but one which involves equity considerations as well recognized by authoritative central bankers. 'This is not an idle question. In any event, in a federal state, the regional distribution of credit will always remain an issue of contention, and can't be dismissed simply by reference to the virtues of competition' (Patel, 1994, p. 43). But regional imbalances also occur in unitary states as well as in developed countries like the Mezzogiorno in Italy and the

Appalachian region of the United States. There is in fact a pronounced urban bias in the financial systems of developing countries, although it is difficult to present systematic evidence since such data, even if available, are not published for fear of generating feelings of internal colonialism (Chandavarkar, 1985c). A classic example is Thailand, where the Bangkok Thon Buri metropolitan area is a net user of credit whereas the rest of the economy, which is predominantly rural, is a net source of deposits (Table 6.1). In the Philippines the level of utilization of deposits in Metro Manila

*Table* 6.1 Thailand: ratio of commercial bank loans to deposits, 1967–77 (weighted mean by region)

| | *Bangkok Thon Buri* | All changwads (provinces)[a] | *Central* | *North-east* | *Northern* | *Southern* |
|---|---|---|---|---|---|---|
| 1967 | 0.927 | 0.420 | 0.366 | 0.426 | 0.436 | 0.468 |
| 1968 | 0.887 | 0.443 | 0.363 | 0.434 | 0.532 | 0.480 |
| 1969 | 0.954 | 0.459 | 0.377 | 0.440 | 0.599 | 0.464 |
| 1970 | 1.054 | 0.451 | 0.407 | 0.417 | 0.513 | 0.493 |
| 1971 | 0.990 | 0.442 | 0.427 | 0.357 | 0.487 | 0.496 |
| 1972 | 0.861 | 0.410 | 0.372 | 0.359 | 0.462 | 0.480 |
| 1973 | 1.013 | 0.454 | 0.415 | 0.415 | 0.496 | 0.522 |
| 1974 | 1.114 | 0.424 | 0.401 | 0.410 | 0.459 | 0.445 |
| 1975 | 1.154 | 0.476 | 0.444 | 0.487 | 0.525 | 0.477 |
| 1976 | 1.142 | 0.512 | 0.487 | 0.512 | 0.566 | 0.506 |
| 1977 | 1.118 | 0.633 | 0.615 | 0.651 | 0.713 | 0.565 |

*Note:* [a] Excluding Bangkok Thon Buri.

*Source*: K. Meesook, 1978, cited in Chandavarkar, 1985c, p. 25.

is 90 per cent of total deposits while the deposit utilization rate in the rural hinterland is only 48 per cent; the loans granted in Manila constitute 79 per cent of total loans and investment while loans funnelled to the rural areas constitute only 21 per cent (Vicente, 1993, p. 28). This is also characteristic of many other developing countries like Indonesia, where there is concentration of credit in the more urbanized regions of Jakarta Raya and Central-East Java; Malaysia (Kuala Lumpur and Penang); Jamaica (Corporate Area of Kingston, Mandeville and Montego Bay), and India, where the four largest cities, Bombay, Calcutta, Delhi and Madras, account for 85 per cent of total credit. Even in the United States because of 'redlining' by commercial banks who restrict credit to high-risk customer areas, the Community Reinvestment Act 1978 was enacted to require financial institutions 'to demonstrate that their deposit facilities serve the convenience and needs of the communities in which they are chartered to do business'. The flows of rural savings into urban credit outlets reflect the more basic economic disparities within less developed countries between the developed 'centre' (urban areas) and 'the periphery' (rural hinterland), a dichotomy which prevails in the international sphere, although, ironically, the developing countries seem to be more conscious of international disparities than of regional disparities within their own boundaries. But the onus of redressing regional imbalances should more properly rest on the government – operating through tax and other related incentives – rather than the central bank, which can at best prescribe credit to deposit ratio targets. Such *dirigiste* measures (for example, in Thailand, India, Mali) are often difficult to enforce and have even proved counterproductive. It is also easy to overlook that in a market-orientated economy such imbalances may reflect the lack of suitable lending outlets. A central bank could, however, encourage the expansion of rural banking through 'liberal licensing and provision of training facilities as in the Philippines where the Central Bank Institute trains prospective employees of the new rural banks free of charge' (Vicente, 1993, p. 27).

In sum, the basic issue is not financial urban bias *per se*, which may only reflect the greater credit-intensity of urban economic activity and its larger contribution to national net value added, but whether it is excessively regressive, and if so, what is an appropriate concerted strategy for the central bank and government to redress it. A reduction of the disparities in regional credit to deposit ratios has to be achieved not so much by reducing transfers of savings to urban areas as by more vigorous mobilization of rural savings and by improving the credit absorption capacity of rural areas. Such corrective programmes, however, must also be based on the nature and pattern of the underlying rural-urban flows of savings and credit in relation to policy objectives and, above all, on the development of efficient rural financial markets.

More generally, official credit programmes, whether under the aegis of the central bank or the government, are claimed to be necessary to correct market failures in private capital markets, which are presumed to exist whenever potential borrowers cannot access credit at reasonable cost. This may be due to:

- inadequate and asymmetric information, rendering risk assessment difficult and inaccurate;
- monopolistic elements in the intermediation process;
- absence of secondary markets for specific security instruments like residential mortgages; and
- absence or inadequacy of financial institutions or services in rural areas.

Allied to these considerations are those related to exploitation of economic externalities, implementation of social objectives, or correcting the market-determined distribution of income, which are thought to be particularly relevant to planned development in developing countries. Governments intervene to direct credit into sectors where they are presumed to generate more backward and forward linkages, or in cases where there is a divergence between private and social costs and return. For instance, the role of the Reserve Bank of India in planned development was recognized at an early stage. The First Five-Year Plan stated that

> Central Banking in a planned economy can hardly be confined to the regulation of overall supply of credit or to a somewhat negative regulation of the flow of bank credit. It would have to take on a direct and active role, firstly in creating or helping to create the machinery needed for financing developmental activities all over the country and secondly ensuring that the finance available flows in the directions intended. (Rangarajan, 1988, p. 645)

Central banks in developing countries have used a variety of techniques to discharge their developmental role, a typical sample of which is presented in Table 6.2.

## 6.3 THE CASE FOR DIVESTITURE

Regrettably, there are no data, even on a selective basis, to answer the basic question: whether a central bank's assumption of a developmental role has been productive and justified. No central bank, as far as is known from published sources, has even

*Table* 6.2 Developmental techniques of selected central banks

| *Instruments* | *Bangladesh* | *China* | *India* | *Indonesia* | *Korea* | *Malaysia* | *Nepal* | *Pakistan* | *Philippines* | *Sri Lanka* | *Thailand* |
|---|---|---|---|---|---|---|---|---|---|---|---|
| Credit guarantee and insurance schemes | × | | × | × | | × | × | | × | × | |
| Participation in capital and management of development institutions | × | | × | × | × | × | | × | × | × | × |
| Portfolio targets for priority sectors | | × | × | × | × | × | | | | × | |
| Differential interest rates | × | × | × | | | × | × | | | × | |
| Preferential rediscount rates and facilities | × | | × | × | | | × | × | × | × | × |
| Allocation of central bank profits | × | | × | | × | | × | × | × | × | |
| Target credit – deposit ratios for rural branches | | | × | | | | × | | × | × | × |

*Note*: The country information in this table is incomplete. It covers instruments that have been in use at one time or another.

*Source*: Author's compilation from central bank publications.

attempted to appraise the costs and benefits of undertaking a developmental role. Any effective evaluation of the developmental role of central banks raises the following points which together strongly suggest its speedy divestiture because of conflicts with the central bank's primary function of achieving price stability through appropriate monetary and exchange rate policies as well as its prudential responsibilities.

First, whatever the historical justification for the developmental role the rationale for its continuance is dubious. Such a role is justified, if at all, only in the very early stages of central banking. But with the general development of the banking and financial system, there is an inevitable conflict with monetary policy objectives, which exists both in the short and long run, despite the assertion that 'in the longer run, they are very much mutually compatible' (Rangarajan, 1988, p. 648). Nor can monetary policy be assigned a secondary role 'of a countervailing power keeping monetary expansion under reasonable control to ensure . . . reasonable price stability' if 'the compulsion to expand development expenditures necessarily leads to an expansionary fiscal policy' (ibid., p. 648).

The subsidy-based quasi-fiscal activities of central banks through refinance and other channels enlarge the monetary base (reserve money) and the credit multiplier and complicate monetary management. They also undermine market-related interest rate policies since they do not reflect the true cost of credit and capital and could lead to misallocation of resources. Participation in development finance carries the risk of operating losses, which eventually get monetized and lead to loss of control of the money supply as evidenced by the experiences of central banks in Latin America, Ghana, Jamaica, the Philippines, and Uganda.

The World Bank too concluded that 'while individual sectors have benefitted from directed credit, the real effect on growth and whether those who received such credit used their resources more productively is difficult to ascertain' (World Bank, 1993, p. 22). The available evidence, however, does strongly suggest that subsidized credit, whatever its modality, reinforces existing distortions, particularly in countries with protectionist trade policies and macroeconomic instability. Directed and subsidized credit schemes are difficult to target, and even within the priority sectors the more influential and affluent borrowers benefit disproportionately and such credit adds more to profits than to increased productivity. They do not necessarily favour the poor, as shown, for instance, by World Bank studies in Costa Rica where the agricultural credit disbursed by the Banco National was actually more skewed than the distribution of income and land (ibid., p. 22). They often crowd out firms which were not the beneficiaries of such preferential treatment and in many cases are a prolific source of non-performing loans. Subsidized credit can also be highly regressive if revenues are derived from labour and sales taxes and spent on those with higher incomes. Subsidy schemes tend to lose their effectiveness over time and 'have not corrected the inadequacies of the financial market' and 'have tended to constrain the financial sector's flexibility to adjust resource flows to changing economic conditions' (ibid., p. 23). Credit subsidies and similar quasi-fiscal activities have also been a potent source of operating losses for central banks (discussed in Chapter 11), 'often reaching magnitudes that are larger than the regular budget deficits' which 'come very generally from the performance of functions that an independent CB's charter should not include' (Bruno – former Governor, Bank of Israel – 1994, p. 10). Governments often find central banks a politically convenient channel of preferential credit immune from parliamentary review. 'But it results in a loss of transparency, and no less important, in the loss of central bank independence from fiscal (and political) pressures and the inability of a CB to take care of its primary obligation to price stability and the health of the financial system' (ibid., pp. 10–11). The case for divestiture of quasi-fiscal activities is valid even if such losses have not occurred because the quasi-fiscal developmental role conflicts with both monetary and prudential obligations of a central bank. The experience of the Bank of Israel (founded in 1954) offers an instructive case study of phased divestiture of directed and preferential credit. In its early stages the Bank of Israel was heavily involved in direct allocation of credit to agriculture through the main co-operative settlement organizations, but this function was later transferred to specialized agencies (such as the Bank of Agriculture) and later on to the regular commercial banks. Likewise the large-scale mortgage lending for immigrant housing is now being done through retail banks. Israel's export subsidies too have also been gradually eliminated completely.

Colombian experience in the 1970s – when the Banco de la Republica acted as both a central bank to control money supply and as a development bank – also confirms the validity of divestiture:

> The Junta Monetaria emphasized the role of the central bank as a development bank and urged selective credit controls and productive credit for working capital, but the President of the Republic, on February 18 1974, frankly admitted the mistakes that had led to serious inflation, that there was a need to distinguish between the roles of a central bank and a development bank. (Sandilands, 1990, pp. 254–5)

Thereafter, he 'took much more decisive action, overruling the Junta Monetaria, to control the money supply and fiscal deficit', and 'as a result, inflation fell to a very low level in the final months of his administration' (ibid., pp. 254–5).

The Bank of Mexico, which had a very active policy of selective credit channelling to priority sectors like agriculture over several decades, found that this 'is not necessarily conducive to the most efficient allocation of resources' and that central bank policy should legitimately focus on 'the control of the monetary base, and through it of aggregate demand' rather 'than on the allocation of credit' (Mancera, 1990, pp. 39–40). Accordingly, credit to priority sectors was transferred to development banks, namely, Banrural (agriculture), Nafin (industry) and Bancomext (export financing). But the Bank of Mexico's selective credit measures 'also played a useful role in showing commercial banks that it was possible to provide financing to certain priority activities such as agriculture and, if carefully managed, less risky than believed' (ibid., p. 39).

In some cases although the central bank's agency functions may be financially neutral, like the management of the Employees' Provident Fund (covering the organized sector of the economy) by the Central Bank of Sri Lanka, it is a responsibility which 'is outside the purview of a central bank, and should be transferred to another body or government agency' (Presidential Commission on Finance and Banking, Sri Lanka, 1992, p. 102). The Commission made this forthright recommendation despite the unanimous appreciation of the central bank's efficient management by the government and representatives of organized labour. The Central Bank of Sri Lanka has already hived off its profitable gold sales outlets at the airport to commercial banks. The Presidential Commission has also recommended that the Credit Information Bureau (CIB), in which the Central Bank of Sri Lanka has a 51 per cent share of the capital, should eventually be divested 'when the CIB becomes a self-supporting fee-based institution' (ibid., p. 84).

In contrast, the Reserve Bank of India (RBI) has displayed a curiously hesitant and ambivalent approach to divestiture of its manifold developmental activities. On the one hand, it has shed its role as an apex institution of long-term industrial finance to the Industrial Development Bank of India, but it still owns the National Bank for Agriculture and Rural Development (NABARD), the apex institution for agricultural finance. As a former Governor of the RBI has categorically stated:

> Among the existing responsibilities of RBI, it is worth considering whether NABARD should not be detached from it. The arguments that all matters relating to monetary policy should be centralized in one place wears rather thin when one is talking of rural or cooperative banking; and, at any rate, I am talking of separating the developmental role that NABARD plays. The central bank should be left free to concentrate on sound monetary and exchange rate policy which is going to be a difficult business in any case. Even the developmental role of NABARD might gain by separation. (Patel, 1994, p. 50)

The case for divestiture is equally strong in regard to the participation (ownership and/or management) of central banks in credit guarantee schemes which have been set up in several developing countries to cover some portion of the losses incurred by financial institutions, in particular commercial banks, in their loans to small and medium businesses with viable projects and good prospects of success but without adequate collateral or evidence of creditworthiness (for a comparative survey and evaluation see Levitsky and Prasad, 1987). Such schemes are operated wholly by central banks (for example, in India, Ghana, Barbados, Jamaica, Sri Lanka) or partly as in Malaysia, Nepal. It is no part of this analysis to pronounce on the merits or drawbacks of such schemes. Rather, it suggests divestiture of the central bank's ownership to independent entities as in Thailand or the Cameroons. Central bank guarantees are a species of indirect or contingent credit subsidy and are open to the same objections as direct subsidies.

There is no doubt a growing consensus that directed and subsidized credit is not only inefficient but pervasively inequitable and that 'in the longer term it needs to be reduced or phased out' (World Bank, 1993, p. 123). Curiously, such well-justified diagnosis is also followed by uncritical ritualistic prescriptions by international agencies to member countries that any remaining subsidies; 'should be identified and treated as an explicit government subsidy in public sector budgets' (ibid., p. 23). Transfers of central bank subsidies to the government budget are usually sought to be justified on grounds of greater transparency of fiscal accounts. This is not in fact the case, as has been shown by a pioneering analysis by Wattleworth (1983) which clearly established that since interest paid and interest received on subsidies both appear above the line in the unified cash budget, the annual cost of these subsidies is reflected in the observed fiscal balance, but it is nowhere identified overtly: 'because the subsidies are spread over the entire lifetime of loans, their total magnitude is easily overlooked and usually grossly underestimated (ibid., 1993, p. 147). The fact that interest income and payments are also tax deductible enhances the implicit value of credit subsidies. Such 'subsidies' also contribute to the creation of long-term structural deficits that restrict the short-term flexibility of fiscal policy. The only country in which calculations of the financial cost of subsidies is 'regularly done (although very roughly) is the United States' (Wattleworth, 1983, p. 6). The only quantitative estimate of the cost of subsidies for a developing country (Korea, 1970–9) showed that expenditure on subsidies was the fastest growing item in the budget and by 1979 was greater than the entire budget of the consolidated Central Government (ibid., p. 6), which excludes the cash value of loan guarantees. Conceptually, the estimation of subsidies is difficult because it depends on the borrowers' opportunity costs over the period of the loan and the subsidy. Indirect subsidies and the cash values of loan guarantees are also not reflected in the budget. The concealed value of credit subsidies means that 'they are more difficult to control than other expenditures because they may escape scrutiny when austerity forces budget cuts to be made' (Wattleworth, 1993, p. 171). Ideally, 'the true magnitude of subsidies, that is the present discounted value of the subsidy stream should be entered explicitly in the budget in the originating year as an expenditure item' and this magnitude is not to be found in any of the government budgets of developing countries. Even among the developed countries, only the budgets of the United States, Germany and Netherlands show the subsidy element of direct government loans and guarantees (Premchand, 1993, p. 155). In fact it would be easier to estimate and present the cost of credit subsidies in central bank accounts. Therefore, the relative merits, if any, of central bank and government subsidies do not hinge on the degree of transparency. In fact, as one central bank governor has rightly argued:

> One has to . . . do away with concessional rates altogether. The major advantage from this would be greater availability of credit for all purposes and due regard to the productivity of investment financed. In fact, I would advise against any interest subsidy from the exchequer as well for the same reasons . . . I know from my experience with the Aga Khan Rural Support Program that small borrowers are happy to pay rates of interest much higher than the current minimum, if money is made available without much harassment and bribes . . . All concessional lending tends to be looked upon as a gift . . . and the borrower too gets into a frame of mind where willful non-payment of interest and capital seems warranted. This vicious circle can only be broken by a total departure from the present policy. (Patel, 1994, p. 46)

This clearly establishes that more than the modality and transparency of credit subsidies the real issue is the dubious economic rationale of subsidies *per se*. It also points to the responsibility of the central bank, following diverstiture, to ensure through moral suasion that budgetary subsidies too follow suit. Divestiture, however, does not imply a diminution in the developmental bailiwick of the central bank. Rather it points to a shift in its thrust and emphasis from quasi-fiscal activities involving ownership in part or whole and management of development finance institutions and disbursement of credit subsidies to financially neutral activities that generate externalities and reduce transaction and information costs.

## 6.4 FINANCIAL INFRASTRUCTURE

Effective central banking policies require an adequate and efficient financial infrastructure that encompasses several critical ingredients:

(1) a properly designed and enforced legal framework;
(2) timely, accurate and transparent accounts and information on the status of the financial sector using internationally accepted accounting and auditing standards;
(3) efficient and effective systems of payments, clearing and settlements;
(4) and, above all, an adequate supply of trained financial manpower.

In turn, these desiderata imply the adoption of appropriate internal management and credit policies and procedures in all financial institutions. Among these, the central bank can play a direct role in developing an efficient payments system which is an essential component of a smoothly functioning market economy supported by an efficient and complex financial system. Its specific role consists in: (1) 'establishing public policy to govern the structure of clearing and settlement arrangements; (2) supervising the payment system through the clearing organizations and banking institutions that play key roles in risk management; (3) in providing settlements across its books; and in operating large-value payment mechanisms' (Summers, 1991, p. 44). Although there is scope and much gain by allowing private enterprise to compete in the function of payment services to the public, in the case of large-value payments, given their critical nature and safety net attributes, the operation of such mechanisms alone or in tandem with privately operated entities is properly the role of central banks who must also take due care in controlling daylight credit (intra-day liquidity) 'they provide to the financial system and the payment system risk they absorb' (ibid., p. 44).

Although most central banks 'are not directly involved in the clearing functions of payment system, it is appropriate that they be given oversight and rule-making responsibility for controlling risk and unintended credit expansion during the clearing process' which 'concerns the responsibility to minimize, eliminate or collateralize daylight and overnight overdrafts that can occur during the clearing process and unintentionally expand the money supply creating systemic risk' (D. B. Humphrey, 1994, p. 28). These observations may be empirically verified by reference to the fragmentary available evidence which is nevertheless sufficiently representative. For instance, in most countries covered by a Bank of England survey questionnaire (BoE Group), the central bank directly runs the clearing system and even 'when it does not it is almost always intimately involved as a participant and supervisor' and 'in almost all . . . countries the net payments are settled by transfers between commercial bank deposits held with the central bank' (Bank of England, 1995, pp. 36–7; and Table 6.3). It is noteworthy that twenty-two out of the thirty-five central banks who responded to this questionnaire reported major reforms to the payments systems since 1975 and in these the central bank had initiated them.[1] Chile was the lone outlier where the central bank was not the initiator and in Jamaica only some of the reforms were initiated by the central bank (Table 6.4).

*Table* 6.3 Payments systems – selected countries

| *Country* | *Central bank (CB) runs payments system* | *Nature of relationship between central bank and payments system* |
|---|---|---|
| Bahamas | Yes | Clearing house |
| Bangladesh | Partially | CB runs clearing houses in cities; elsewhere, Sonali Bank |
| Barbados | Yes | Clearing house |
| Belize | Yes | Supervisor and manager |
| Brunei | No | Run by the Brunei Association of Banks |
| Botswana | | Settlement through transfer between CB accounts |
| Chile | No | 'Rules' and participates |
| Cyprus | Yes | Chairs the clearing house meetings |
| Fiji | No | Settlement through transfer between CB accounts |
| Gambia, The | Yes | Chairs clearing sessions |
| Guyana | No | Hosts clearing operations and has a clearing relationship with commercial banks |
| Hong Kong | No | Advises on regulation |
| India | Partially | Runs clearing houses where it has banking offices |
| Israel | No | Member of Clearing House Committee, supervises paper-based clearing |
| Jamaica | Yes | Co-ordinates, provides facilities |
| Kuwait | Yes | Clearing house |
| Malta | Yes | Clearing house |
| Mauritius | Yes | Clearing house |
| Mexico | Yes | Regulator |
| Namibia | Yes | Provides clearing house and settlement facilities |
| Nigeria | Yes | Supervisor, clearing house |
| Pakistan | Partially | Runs clearing houses where it has banking offices |
| St Lucia | Yes | Clearing house |
| Saudi Arabia | Yes | Operates and controls |
| Sierra Leone | Yes | Clearing house |
| Singapore | No | Chairman of the Singapore Clearing House Association |
| Solomon Islands | | Settlement through transfer between CB accounts |
| South Africa | No | Participates and runs settlement |
| Sri Lanka | Yes | Clearing house |
| Swaziland | Yes | Clearing house |
| Trinidad & Tobago | Yes | Clearing house |
| Uganda | No | Provides logistical support and ensures adherence to regulations |
| United Arab Emirates | Yes | Clearing house |
| Zambia | Yes | Paid for services by participating institutions |

*Source*: Bank of England, 1995, p. 38.

*Table* 6.4 Reforms to payments systems since 1975

| *Country* | Reforms | *Central bank (CB) initiated reforms* | *Nature of reform* |
|---|---|---|---|
| Bahamas | No | | |
| Bangladesh | No | | |
| Barbados | No | | |
| Belize | Yes | Yes | Facilitate and expedite presentation and settlement of financial instruments |
| Brunei | No | | |
| Botswana | No | | SWIFT system is in use as of 1993 |
| Chile | Yes | No | Electronic transfer of funds system |
| Cyprus | Yes | Yes | Automation of clearing |
| Fiji | No | | |
| Gambia, The | No | | |
| Guyana | No | | |
| Hong Kong | Yes | Yes | Reforms of payments system under way |
| India | Yes | | Automatic clearing, MICR technology |
| Israel | Yes | Yes | Encoding of cheques, automated clearing house |
| Jamaica | Yes | Some | |
| Jordan | Yes | Yes | Automation of settlement system |
| Kuwait | Yes | Yes | Occasional procedural changes |
| Malta | Yes | Yes | SWIFT, Direct Credit, automated clearing |
| Mauritius | No | | Automated Clearing and Payments System under consideration |
| Mexico | Yes | Yes | |
| Namibia | No | | |
| Nigeria | Yes | Yes | Automated system for sorting cheques in 1990 |
| Pakistan | Yes | | |
| St Lucia | Yes | | Clearing system |
| Saudi Arabia | Yes | Yes | |
| Sierra Leone | No | | |
| Singapore | Yes | Yes | Automated Clearing System, Interbank GIRO, SHIFT |
| Solomon Islands | Yes | | Current system started 1992 |
| South Africa | Yes | Yes | National Payment System Strategy |
| Sri Lanka | Yes | Yes | Automated cheque clearing, interbank funds transfer |

*Table* 6.4 *Continued*

| | | | |
|---|---|---|---|
| Swaziland | No | | |
| Trinidad & Tobago | Yes | Yes | Special clearing items |
| Uganda | Yes | Yes | Automated clearing, local settlement, inter-town clearing |
| United Arab Emirates | Yes | | |
| Zambia | No | | |

*Source*: Bank of England, 1995, p. 39.

The typical pattern of payments systems in lesser developed countries is a clearing house for paper-based check clearing, whereas in the more developed members of the BoE Group (for example, Israel, Hong Kong, Singapore and Sri Lanka) this is supplemented by automated and electronic interbank transfer systems. There is, however, no consistent pattern of non-cash payment use in developing countries, some of whom (for example, Thailand) show an extraordinarily high recourse to credit cards compared even with developed countries like Australia (Table 6.5).

*Table* 6.5 Cashless payment instruments (as % of total transactions)

| *Country* | *Cheques* | *Credit cards* | *Debit cards* | *Paper credits* | *Paperless credits* | *Direct debits* | *Period* |
|---|---|---|---|---|---|---|---|
| Australia | 60.1 | 10.4 | 5.0 | n.a. | 20.1 | 4.4 | Sep. 91 |
| India | 99.0 | 1.0 | — | — | * | * | Mar. 93 |
| Iran | n.a. | n.a. | — | n.a. | — | — | — |
| Korea | 74.4 | 5.1 | — | 12.9 | 2.8 | 4.8 | 1992 |
| South Africa | 60.0 | 19.0 | — | — | 6.0 | 15.0 | 1992 |
| Sri Lanka | n.a. | n.a. | — | n.a. | — | n.a. | — |
| Thailand | 25.37 | 5.27 | 60.0 | 7.12 | n.a. | 2.23 | End 91 |

*Note*: *Paperless credits and direct debits have only recently been initiated in India.

*Source*: Dott and Shanmugham, 1994, p. 22.

The main concern of a central bank in regard to the reform of the payments system is to provide a cost-effective system to speed up clearing and settlement and to eliminate the troublesome phenomenon of check float which can go up to as long as thirty days in China (D. B. Humphrey, 1994, p. 29). Regardless of the type of payment system, it is important to ensure that the user prices fully reflect all the costs involved so that the user who prefers one instrument over another is charged the relevant price. Currently, even in developed countries (for example, the USA, France) payers by cheque do not pay the full operating and float costs of using a cheque (as in Canada) with the consequence that cheques are overused, creating a float which wastes resources from the national point of view. Another avenue of payments reform in developing countries is the development of giro systems (the dominant mode of non-cash payment in Western Europe) which, unlike cheques, have low cost and generate no float benefits for the payers because of the certainty of settlement (no return items). The post office money order systems prevalent in many developing countries could easily serve as the nucleus of an up-to-date giro system. But it is useful to be reminded 'that a payments system functions, to a large degree, on trust and that new innovations in the payments area, while technologically feasible, . . . are not necessarily cost-effective' and 'are not always enhanced in the market place' (D. B. Humphrey, 1994, p. 29). Hence the sage advice: 'Thus an evolutionary approach is best when it comes to altering the payment arrangements of the general public' (ibid., p. 29).

There is, however, a more basic constraint on improving the outreach of the payments systems in developing countries, namely, the comparatively high ratio of currency to money supply. One study found that a classification of forty-five countries into four groups according to per caput GNP was found to be significant in explaining differences in the degree of development and effectiveness of financial infrastructure (Bhattacharyay, 1988, p. 317; and Tables 6.6 and 6.8). This study found the intergroup differences of currency to money supply to be significant at the 5 per cent level of significance. However, to date there has been no systematic analytic and empirical study of the currency ratio in developing countries following the pioneering monograph of Khazzoom (1966). The high currency–money supply ratio – a good indicator of financial shallowness – and the low monetization ratio in developing countries constrain the credit creation potential of the banking system through the dampening of the credit multiplier which occurs through leakages into currency instead of a reverse flow from circulation into the banking system. The efficacy of credit policies depends on the depth of the financial system and the width of the transmission channels, as measured by a combination of criteria such as:

(1) monetization ratio;
(2) currency to money supply ratio (Table 6.6);
(3) number of bank offices per unit of population census (thousand, million);
(4) number of customers (account holders) per branch;
(5) range and efficiency of banking services and payments system, as measured by time and costs of bank transactions (withdrawals, clearing, processing, and so on), convenience of hours of service, etc.
(6) average size and duration of cheque float.

Central bank actions and policies cannot directly influence several of these indicators, which reflect non-monetary influences like underdevelopment, poverty, illiteracy, tax evasion, and degree of urbanization. But central banks can take initiatives in creating and fostering money markets, like the Reserve Bank of India's lead in establishing the Discount and Finance House of India, mainly with the object of creating a secondary market in treasury bills and commercial bills. There is historical precedence for such concrete initiatives in developed countries like Canada, where there was no organized short-term money market before 1953, when the Bank of Canada took a series of promotional measures (1953–8) to create a short-term money market (Crow – former Governor, Bank of Canada – 1990, pp. 19–20) which included short-term financing – line purchase and resale agreements – to investment dealers, reserve averaging, and countrywide wire facilities for transfer of government securities. This experience would suggest that the central bank can make a useful contribution to structural change in the financial sector. In the right environment, such as Canada's money market in the 1950s, a few key policy actions can propel rapid modernization. In turn, a well-functioning money market has proved of great value in improving the competitive efficiency of financial markets and in the implementation and transmission of monetary policy (ibid., p. 20).

In the final analysis, the efficiency of financial infrastructure depends on the availability of properly trained financial personnel, and yet the role of human capital in financial systems is still the most neglected area in the otherwise prolific literature on finance

*Table* 6.6 Currency ratios for selected countries, 1985–6

| *Country* | *GNP per caput (dollars 1985)* | Ratios of currency to money supply |
|---|---|---|
| *Low income* | | |
| Ethiopia | 110 | 0.36 |
| Bangladesh | 150 | 0.12 |
| Nepal | 160 | 0.54 |
| India | 270 | 0.36 |
| Kenya | 290 | 0.33 |
| Tanzania | 290 | 0.45 |
| Ghana | 370 | 0.48 |
| Pakistan | 380 | 0.37 |
| Sri Lanka | 380 | 0.59 |
| *Middle income* | | |
| Indonesia | 530 | 0.05 |
| Philippines | 580 | 0.27 |
| Egypt, Arab Republic | 610 | 0.27 |
| Thailand | 800 | 0.18 |
| Brazil | 1640 | 0.12 |
| Hungary | 1950 | 0.06 |
| Portugal | 1970 | 0.29 |
| Malaysia | 2000 | 0.14 |
| Mexico | 2080 | 0.15 |
| South Africa | 2010 | 0.02 |
| Poland | 2050 | 0.09 |
| Argentina | 2130 | 0.24 |
| Republic of Korea | 2150 | 0.07 |
| Algeria | 2550 | 0.34 |
| Greece | 3550 | 0.25 |
| Singapore | 7420 | 0.17 |
| *Oil-exporters* | | |
| Libya | 7170 | 0.19 |
| Saudi Arabia | 8850 | 0.24 |
| Kuwait | 14480 | 0.07 |
| *Industrial countries* | | |
| Italy | 6526 | 0.09 |
| New Zealand | 7010 | 0.24 |
| UK | 8460 | 0.08 |
| France | 9540 | 0.10 |
| Australia | 10830 | 0.07 |
| Japan | 11300 | 0.04 |
| Canada | 13680 | 0.07 |
| Switzerland | 16370 | 0.01 |
| USA | 16690 | 0.08 |

*Source*: Excerpted from Bhattacharyay, 1988, pp. 314–15.

and financial reforms. The World Bank's Development Report (1989) recognized the importance of 'good compensation and career prospects' (p. 94) but inexplicably did not address the problems of financial personnel. Hence its candid acknowledgement that 'it has treated in a perfunctory way the human and political dimensions of the subject, both in discussing the origins of the financial problem and in offering prescriptions for change' (ibid., p. 132). Typically, developing countries find 'it much easier to staff a central planning commission [central and commercial banks] with the handful of PhDs [MBAs] which most countries can supply, than to acquire the mass of persons with intermediate skills, technical and administrative competence and so on without whom any modern economy risks grinding into inefficiency' (Hobsbawm, 1969, pp. 61–2). This, of course, is only another symptom of the wider syndrome of uncritical credentialism in developing countries, so aptly described by Thomas Balogh as 'Oxbridge Rampant'. The key to economic efficiency and development lies in the creation of a society and an economy based on mass competence rather than pyramidal elitism as so well exemplified by the economic history and performance of the US economy. Keynes in a little known pronouncement remarked: 'In the ultimate analysis, economic prosperity depends on how large a scale you are able to produce competent people in all walks of life' (Chandavarkar, 1989, p. 142). This, in the financial sphere, easily translates into the proposition that adequate and financial personnel implies not only the higher echelons of executives, managers, economists, financial analysts, and accountants but also the intermediate subalterns of supervisors and inspectors and the foot soldiers of clerks, tellers and machine operators.

The training and development of financial personnel could therefore be regarded as a special responsibility of central banks, considering that this is by far the most critical bottleneck in the widening and deepening of financial intermediation, much more so than funds, premises and equipment. The training programmes and institutions run by central banks merit constant review to ensure that basic skills of financial personnel keep pace with financial and technological innovation and deregulation, as distinct from on-the-job skills which are best left to individual banks and institutions. Given the externalities of such training and education, individual banks do not find it worth their while to offer basic training to financial personnel. Central bank training facilities for personnel in the financial sector are an apt example of the macroeconomic benefits of investment in human capital. There is scope for setting up autonomous training institutions under the aegis of the central bank like the Bahrain Institute of Banking and Finance (BIBF) which provides training and education in the financial sector. The institute meets the selective training needs of levy-paying financial institutions with programmes and services that are responsive, cost-effective and adhere to standards of excellence. It provides training and assistance in support of Bahrain's economic growth and establishment as a regional financial centre. It offers courses in different aspects of banking and insurance, which range from basic and introductory courses to more advanced studies dealing with specialized subjects such as credit analysis, investment banking, management development, microcomputers, and so on. Equally, judicious financial personnel planning might also help forestall the opposite predicament of the industrial countries, who 'are throwing more and more resources, including the cream of our youth, into financial activities, remote from the production of goods and services, into activities that generate high private rewards disproportionate to their social productivity' (Tobin, 1984, p. 14).

To conclude, there is a meaningful distinction between, on the one hand, the divestible developmental role of a central bank which involves financial participation and divestiture techniques, and its legitimate, financially neutral, promotional role. The promotional role of the central bank is crucial in financial development in terms of filling the gaps in the financial structure in respect of instruments, institutions, markets and personnel. It should be envisaged in terms of active 'supply-leading' initiatives rather than passive 'demand-following' response considering that the financial system, which is a special species of public utility, is predicated on the dictum that 'facilities create traffic'. Then again, on the analogy of efficient public utilities, financial institutions need a certain cushion of 'excess capacity' to cope with not only seasonal peaks – seasonality of monetary aggregates is a feature of developing countries – but also to ease the adjustment to the long-term structural growth of the real sector. A central bank's promotional strategy has to be flexible and innovative in identifying current and prospective market failures and gaps, as well as in matching the flow of savings from the predominant household sector to the investment demands of the corporate and government sectors. In other words, a central bank has to be both an innovator and a catalyst in its promotional role.

## 6.5 FINANCIAL LIBERALIZATION AND REFORM

Financial liberalization and reform are the core issues of formal finance, but the discussion has been overly aggregative considering that it involves three distinct constituents, each with different policy implications. There is, first, the negative aspect of eliminating financial repression and restructuring of institutions with substantial nonperforming assets; second, the positive element of reform in the regulatory and institutional framework; and, third, the post-liberalization agenda of how to maintain and monitor a viable competitive financial system and cope with the problems generated by liberalization. Reform and liberalization are emphatically not a once-over exercise but a continuing essay in flexible and responsive public policy, in which the central bank has an important but not an exclusive role.

A congenial financial and monetary climate is an essential prerequisite for the effective discharge of the monetary, prudential and promotional roles of a central bank. This implies the elimination of 'financial repression' defined as the cumulative repressive effects of microeconomic and macroeconomic factors such as usury laws, administered interest rates, bank reserve requirements, credit controls, credit subsidies, discounting privileges and inflation, which interact to reduce and misallocate scarce capital. (McKinnon, 1984, p. 3) More generally, financial repression connotes 'indiscriminate distortions of financial prices, including interest rates and exchange rates, which reduce the real rate of growth and the real size of the financial systems relative to nonfinancial magnitudes' (Shaw, 1973, pp. 3–4). But the analysis of both financial repression and of liberalization as its corrective have been overly aggregative.

For instance, the McKinnon definition of financial repression does not allow for the prevalence of restrictions on the entry and licensing of new banking units and financial institutions which is customarily the case in most developing countries. The banking industry does not enjoy the freedom of 'contestable' markets – that is, of entry and exit – which is a necessary condition of a liberal system. Even if licensing of domestic entrants into the banking industry is comparatively liberal, there are usually severe restrictions, if not an outright bar, on the entry of foreign units into the financial services sector, a matter which has now come up before GATT at the instance of the developed countries who would like to extend free trade to all types of cross-border services. But are the developing countries ready for free international trade in financial services?

*Table* 6.7 Scope of financial reforms in selected countries

| *Objectives* | *Instruments* | *Countries* |
|---|---|---|
| Improvement of monetary controls | Improvements in framework of financial programming | Algeria, China, Egypt |
| | Switch from direct to indirect market-based controls | Botswana, China, Costa Rica, Hungary, Indonesia, Mauritius, Philippines, Sri Lanka |
| To improve the mobilization and allocation of domestic savings | Development of money and government securities markets | Indonesia, Malaysia, Oman, Sri Lanka, Yemen Arab Republic, Zaire |
| | Reduction of selective credit policies, development of capital markets, and term finance, integration of unregulated financial institutions | Costa Rica, Dominican Republic, Indonesia, Malaysia, Papua New Guinea |
| | Improvement in supervision of financial institutions, creation of deposit insurance schemes | Chile, Dominican Republic, Panama, Trinidad & Tobago |
| | New financial institutions and instruments and adequacy of bank regulation and legislation | Aruba, Bolivia, Hungary, Kenya, Nepal |
| Market-orientation of interest rates | Reduction of interest rate subsidies and of bad debts, liberalization of interest rates, introduction of prime rate or base lending rate system | Bangladesh, Chile, Malaysia, Mauritania, Senegal, Uruguay, Bolivia, Burundi, The Gambia, Haiti, Indonesia, Malaysia, Philippines, Sierra Leone |

*Source*: Adapted from Villanueva, 1988, p. 15.

Central banks have played an active role in financial liberalization through comprehensive reform packages (Table 6.7). There is now a consensus that the scope, modality, design and sequencing of financial reform and liberalization in an increasingly globalized financial system are the really critical issues. Full liberalization does not appear to be the first-best policy until the macroeconomic climate is relatively stable and an effective regulatory and prudential framework is in place.

> Latin American experience suggests the undesirability of simultaneous liberalization of exchange and trade controls suggest the undesirability of simultaneous liberalization of exchange and trade controls and capital movements, although in the end internal and external liberalization will be complementary. The latter should await internal reform and establishment of domestic macroeconomic stability. (World Bank, 1989, p. 128)

A more recent comprehensive evaluation of the theory and experience of financial reform (Caprio, Atiyas and Hanson, 1994) 'suggests that the following criteria be satisfied before complete deregulation:

- macroeconomic conditions are reasonably stable
- the financial condition of banks and their borrowers is sound
- at least a minimal base of financial skills has been attained
- some checks are in place to limit collusive behaviour among banks in the determination of interest rates.

To this one must also add the critical precondition of adequacy of the regulatory and prudential framework. The authors also note that New Zealand, Indonesia and Malaysia had at the commencement of reforms 'highly capable central banks, suggesting the building of the research and implementation sides of central banks is a critical precondition for successful reform' (ibid., p. 426).

It is noteworthy that this study cautions that 'when these conditions are not satisfied, interest rates may rise to exorbitant heights in real terms, threatening the net worth of borrowers and ultimately the soundness of the financial system, as was seen in Chile and, to a lesser extent, in Turkey in the early 1980s' (ibid., pp. 434–5). But as an analysis of real interest rates in a sample of twenty-eight developing countries concludes, it is necessary 'to understand the causes and consequences of high real interest rates in the particular setting of each country before any remedies are applied if and when necessary' (Galbis, 1993, p. 71).

Perhaps it is a symptom of both the complexity of financial liberalization and of the predictable dialectic of intellectual analysis that there is now an emerging revisionist interpretation of financial reform in a significant study of Korean policies by the World Bank. This study concludes that

> the Korean policy makers may have followed a nonmarket approach [since 1974] to the financial reform but it was reinforced, though indirectly, by the competitive forces, normally generated by the markets and it is only 'when the conditions were rife Korea took the bold step as in 1993 to divest its financial policy of its dirigistic elements and finally discarded it. (Dalla, Khatkhate *et al.*, 1995, p. 29)

More importantly, the study argues that 'Korea's approach to regulated financial reform was rooted in its institutions, history, and its peculiar genius to devise nonmarket institutions as complementary and supportive to the market system', but also adds 'that the Korean model is not possible to replicate in other developing countries' (ibid., p. vi).

There is, however, still a conspicuous lacuna in the literature, which has yet to focus on some major post-liberalization issues and problems, both structural and institutional. It does not address the most challenging problem for central banks in the wake of liberalization: how to ensure effective competition in oligopolistic financial systems with high degrees of concentration which are so characteristic of developing counties (Table 6.8). Oligopolistic competition is no doubt a complex phenomenon, which is 'part competitive, part collusive' and 'to define an oligopoly in terms of the number of firms in the market, concentration ratios, or any other such measure is of dubious relevance' (Nicholson, 1972, p. 203). But 'the number, however, becomes one of many other factors and we would, prima facie, expect little relationship between numbers in the market and collusive activity' (ibid., p. 204). While this reasoning is basically valid, it is equally true that concentration ratios are used because of lack of a better mechanism, which also explains why tests of oligopolies are still widely based on concentration ratios. More importantly, central banks have to be alert to the emergence of collusive interest rate cartels even in apparently liberalized markets, a situation which can be at least partially corrected by maintaining the contestability of the banking industry

*Table* 6.8 Selected banking system concentration ratios (total assets)

| *Economy* | *Year* | *3Bank* | *4Bank* | *5Bank* | *Herfindahl index*[a] |
|---|---|---|---|---|---|
| *East Asia* | | | | | |
| Hong Kong[b] | 1985 | 75 | 77 | 78 | 0.429 |
| Indonesia | 1988–9 | 48 | 59 | 69 | 0.100 |
| Japan | 1989 | 23 | 30 | 37 | 0.044*a* |
| Korea, Rep. of | 1989 | 41 | 50 | 58 | 0.098[a] |
| Malaysia | 1989 | 42 | 56 | 61 | 0.102[a] |
| Singapore | 1989 | 60 | 69 | 71 | 0.132[a] |
| Taiwan, China | 1989 | 32 | 41 | 50 | 0.079[a] |
| Thailand | 1988 | 56 | 66 | 72 | 0.138 |
| *Other Asia* | | | | | |
| Bangladesh | 1986–8 | n.a. | 74 | n.a. | 0.200 |
| Pakistan | 1986–8 | n.a. | n.a. | 84 (1991) | 0.260 |
| Philippines | 1986–8 | n.a. | 40 | n.a. | 0.060 |
| *Africa* | | | | | |
| Algeria | 1986–8 | n.a. | 100 | n.a. | 0.290 |
| Botswana | 1986–8 | n.a. | 100 | n.a. | 0.450 |
| Cameroon | 1986–8 | n.a. | 82 | n.a. | 0.180 |
| Côte d'Ivoire | 1986–8 | n.a. | 67 | n.a. | 0.140 |
| Morocco | 1986–8 | n.a. | 70 | n.a. | 0.180 |
| Nigeria | 1986–8 | n.a. | 52 | n.a. | 0.090 |
| Senegal | 1986–8 | n.a. | 78 | n.a. | 0.160 |
| Tunisia | 1986–8 | n.a. | 80 | n.a. | 0.190 |
| *Other* | | | | | |
| Chile | 1986–8 | n.a. | 54 | 88 | 0.090 |
| Turkey | 1986–8 | n.a. | 52 | 76 | 0.040 |
| *OECD* | | | | | |
| Canada | 1989 | 54 | 69 | 43 | 0.140[a] |
| France | 1989 | 49 | 49 | 89 | 0.119[a] |
| Germany | 1983 | 43 | n.a. | 75 | n.a. |
| UK | 1989 | 29 | 34 | n.a. | 0.036[a] |

*Notes*:

[a] The Herfindahl index is a measure of concentration derived by summing the squares of the share of firms. A high Herfindahl indicates high concentration. The Herfindahl is underestimated for the following economies as it is derived from truncated samples: Australia (9 largest banks); Canada (8 largest banks); France (15 largest banks); Japan (20 largest banks); Korea (19 largest banks); Malaysia (6 largest banks); Singapore (5 largest banks); Taiwan, China (19 largest banks); United Kingdom (15 largest banks).

[b] The data for Hong Kong include commercial banks only.

*Source*: Excerpted from the *East Asian Miracle*, World Bank Policy Research Report, 1993, p. 252.

through liberal licensing of new banks, domestic and foreign, and branch offices.

Financial competition, however, is also an ambiguous concept, since bank credit is a vector of both price and non-price elements such as lending constraints and criteria, availability and collateral. Even fully competitive positive market rates of interest may fall short of market-clearing levels, or may rise to risky levels with adverse consequences for financial institutions and the economy at large. This means that there will always be credit rationing whose genesis is the Keynesian 'fringe of unsatisfied borrowers', that is, those 'who are not considered to have first claims on a bank's funds but to whom the bank would be quite ready to lend if it were to find itself in a position to lend more' (Keynes, 1971, pp. 326–7). Moreover, even in regard to price competition it is often overlooked that the effective lending rates of bankers are higher than the nominal quoted rates of interest because of other factors such as compensatory balances, commission charges, collateral margins, and so on, which vary from bank to bank and customer to customer. A more readily identifiable related issue is the feasibility of maintaining effective competition in predominantly government-owned banking systems as in India. Such competition is not meaningful unless government-owned banks are debarred by law from access to the government budget to meet operating losses. A possible solution, if full privatization is not practical politics, is at least partially to privatize them with full autonomy, entrusting the management to a private group (Patel, 1994, p. 48) and possibly subjecting them to market discipline through listing on the stock exchange. A corollary of this is full freedom for banks to charge for bank services which may run into the awkward question: whether banks have used competition to appropriate higher profits without necessarily improving or lowering the cost of bank services, a point forcefully made in the evidence to the Presidential Commission on Banking and Finance in Sri Lanka, 1992.

Financial liberalization is incomplete and ineffective unless governments become 'alert enough not to borrow at too high rates of interest or to corner too large a slice of private savings by granting tax and other incentives for its own borrowing' (Patel, 1994, p. 45). Turkey's limited progress in financial deepening is attributed to 'continued demands placed on financial institutions to absorb government paper' (Caprio, Atiyas and Hanson, 1994, p. 427) with reserve and liquidity requirements at 35 per cent of deposits, 'a higher proportion than any of the other countries in the sample'. Central banks too will need to be alert to any hysteresis in the form of lingering elements of administered interest rates, as in India, and constantly to review the legal framework of banking and finance to maintain competition and accommodate the emergence of new financial instruments and services. For instance, in many British Commonwealth countries the laws governing negotiable instruments and trusts are outdated. But the more thorny problem is the penchant of the judiciary 'to be guardians not just of law but also of equity or morality, as each judge sees it' which is 'not compatible with economic liberalism and should be firmly discouraged, if need be, by explicit provision in banking and other laws' (Patel, 1994, p. 46). The message is that the mind-set 'not just of politicians, and bureaucrats and bankers, but of the whole community, including ordinary citizens and judges, needs to change radically if economic and financial liberalization is to have a real chance of enduring' (ibid., p. 46). In sum, the post-liberalization role of a central bank should be to act as 'the Curator of Financial Organization' (Sayers, 1976, p. 501) as well as a catalyst of financial development.

# 7 Informal Finance

'. . . such islands of conscious power in an ocean of unconscious cooperation.' — *Sir Dennis Robertson*

Although the developmental and promotional role of central banks in relation to the formal financial sector is well recognized and established, the attitudes of central banks to the substantial sector of informal and semi-informal finance in developing countries present a curious amalgam of ignorance, prejudice, and even hostility or at best a grudging benign neglect, which stem from a mistaken association of informal finance with the illegal or underground economy of evasion of controls and taxes. Even legal informal finance is regarded as outside the sphere of a central bank either because of a perception that it is not of much macroeconomic significance, or else that it cannot be regulated or controlled, a stance which should not, however, preclude a constructive role. Such attitudes explain, among others, why central banks in developing countries hardly seem to command any knowledge, much less any links with the informal sector or even care to comment on informal finance in their annual reports and publications. There is virtually no central bank which has a special unit or cell dealing with informal finance, with the possible exception of the Special Assignment Division of the Department of Supervision and Examination of Financial Institutions in the Bank of Thailand and even this office is concerned primarily with the surveillance and control of illegal and fraudulent practices by the non-bank financial intermediaries rather than fostering and assisting the informal sector in any positive way. The Bank of Thailand has a Financial System and Development Section, which, in addition to the development of financial infrastructure, markets and instruments, deals with current policy issues including the unorganized money market, but there is no unit responsible solely for informal finance.[1] Paradoxically, the significance of informal finance seems better recognized by international institutions (World Bank, 1989, pp. 112–21; Asian Development Bank, 1990, pp. 187–211) than by national central banks. An example in point is the failure of the Reserve Bank of India since its inception (1935) to develop links with indigenous bankers (Reserve Bank of India, 1970, pp. 488–89).[2] Economists too, while emphasizing the fungibility of finance, tend to regard formal and informal finance as non-competing groups, overlooking the close lending and borrowing links between formal and informal finance through concurrent participation of economic agents in both sectors. For instance, the McKinnon–Shaw doctrine tends to ignore the ramifications of informal finance and wealth effects in the determination of macroeconomic scenarios. On the other hand, the validity of the neo-structuralist critique of the McKinnon–Shaw analysis regarding the effects of an increase in formal deposit rates in drawing funds from informal markets is a matter for empirical determination. Generally, the literature has tended to concentrate more on the microeconomic and sectoral aspects of informal finance than on its macroeconomic implications, which, however, have begun to attract growing attention in recent years (Chandavarkar, 1985b, 1987b; Montiel *et al.*, 1993; Agenor and Haque, 1994).

## 7.1 CHARACTERISTICS AND SIZE

It is evident from the typology of the informal sector (Table 7.1) that it provides a remarkably extensive range of financial intermediation covering, borrowing, lending, custodial, insurance and conglomerate services, which fill the deficiencies of formal finance. It is difficult to give a logically clearcut and comprehensive definition of informal finance, which is often better identified by its basic characteristics such as ease of entry and exit, freedom from official regulation, multiple interest relationships between transactors, small scale of operations, informality of procedures, nominal information and transaction costs and, above all, the informality of its procedures. In fact these features constitute its intrinsic economic rationale and account for its comparative advantage over the formal financial sector. The substantial informal financial sector is outside the purview of all the customary controls applied to organized banking like reserve requirements, interest and portfolio ceilings, selective credit controls, rediscount facilities, and even moral suasion, which consequently, exempts it from the stricture that 'financial repression is the rule rather than the exception in less developed countries' (McKinnon, 1984, p. 3).

*Table* 7.1 Typology of informal and semi-formal finance

| *Semi-formal* [a] | *Informal and autonomous* [b] |
|---|---|
| *(a) Autonomous* | *(c) Mutual* |
| Co-operative credit societies | Communal clubs |
| Credit unions | Mutual aid associations [c] |
| Banques populaires | ROSCAs[d] (social, commercial, financial) and non-rotating associations |
| Village banks | *(d) Proprietary* |
| Cereal banks | Moneylenders |
| | Indigenous bankers |
| Pawnshops (state or municipal) | |
| *(b) Reactive* | Pawnshops |
| Finance companies | Trader-lenders) Tied credit |
| Curb market brokers | Farmer-lenders) |
| Parallel currency markets | Relatives and friends |

*Notes*:

[a] The semi-formal financial system includes a variety of arrangements, often involving groups of persons as members of an organization. These are usually outside the purview of the formal monetary and banking authorities, but are sometimes licensed and supervised by other governmental agencies.

[b] A heterogeneous set of autonomous individual and group financial arrangements that generally fall outside the scope of central bank control, taxation, and regulation.

[c] These provide insurance for sickness, weddings, funerals, for example, Igbo clubs in Nigeria, Iddir in Ethiopia.

[d] Rotating and non-rotating savings and credit associations are generally based on affinity groups (family, neighbourhood ethnic, occupational) and are variously named as *susus* and *tontines* in West Africa; *chilembas* in East Africa; *chit* funds and *kuries* (India); *arisan* (Indonesia); partner system (Jamaica); *mujin* and *kye* (Korea); *hui* and *kuthu* (Malaysia and Singapore); committees (Pakistan); *paluwagan* (Philippines); *cheetu* (Sri Lanka); *piua huey* (Thailand).

There is, however, a distinct and meaningful dichotomy of informal finance between its autonomous and reactive sectors which has different implications for analysis and policy (Chandavarkar, 1987b). It consists of an autonomous sector comprising mutual entities, money lenders, indigenous banks and pawnshops, which has developed independently and in many ways even precedes the formal sector. The constituents of the autonomous sector are apt examples of an intermediate financial technology and the Economic Theory of Clubs: that is, of voluntary economic entities, which are intermediate between the purely private good and the purely public good. But, surprisingly, the economic theory of clubs has not yet been extended to a rigorous analysis of voluntary savings and credit clubs despite the impressive developments in the analytical framework. The other segment is the reactive part of the sector (for example, urban curb markets and finance companies) that is primarily a response to the deficiencies in and controls over formal finance. The reactive segment well exemplifies the operation of Goodhart's Law (Goodhart, 1984, p. 96): that central bank attempts to control specific monetary aggregates and banking institutions promptly breed near-money assets and competing entities like fringe banks. It is the reactive component of informal finance that is more directly affected by credit policy and the level of financial repression and therefore interacts with macroeconomic factors in the formal economy. For instance, an increase in the rate of inflation can increase both the supply of funds to and the demand for credit from the informal sector by reducing the real deposit interest rate in the formal sector and raising the demand for alternative assets such as real estate, durable goods or foreign exchange. Consequently, the reactive component is the most responsive to any changes in regulation or the degree of liberalization of the formal sector. The reactive sector expands and contracts contra-cyclically to repression and liberalization of formal finance and serves as a conduit for financial disintermediation, as well substantiated by the post-war experience of South Korea (Cole and Park, 1983). Because of the linkages between formal and informal finance,[3] monetary policy, as shown by Indian experience, also affects informal finance, albeit with varying time lags, and consequently the overall cost and availability of credit, with the exception that informal finance is not amenable to selective credit controls (Acharya and Srinivasa, 1983, 1984). Indian experience also shows that the effects of monetary and credit policy are attenuated but not completely frustrated because the predominance of currency transactions and the leakages of currency from the banking sector to the informal sector dampen the credit multiplier.

The macroeconomic significance of informal finance has to be viewed in the light of its size and impact on the transmission channels of monetary policy such as interest rates. The available data on informal credit markets, although based on anecdotal information and occasional surveys and disparate sources, suggest a broad consensus that the size and share of such markets in many developing economies, is significant, ranging from about a third to almost three-quarters (Table 7.2). Even in a sophisticated economy like Taiwan, the ratio of credit to private enterprises from informal markets to those from the regulated market averaged nearly 30 per cent during the period 1971–88 (Huang *et al.*, 1992). There is,

*Table* 7.2 Size of informal finance

| *Country* | *Rural credit* | *Urban credit* |
|---|---|---|
| Bangladesh | 63% | — |
| China | 33–67% of all borrowings from informal sources, mid-1980s | — |
| India | 39% of rural households debt, 1982 | 40% of urban household debt, 1982 |
| Indonesia | 83% of agricultural households received no formal credit | 93% of capital of households with informal business activities |
| Korea | 51% of average liabilities of farm households | — |
| | 50% of average outstanding loans of farm households | Urban informal credit was 15% of deposit money bank loans, 1978 |
| Malaysia | 70% of rural borrowing | — |
| | 62% of all farm loans | — |
| Nepal | 76% of farm family credit | — |
| Nigeria | 95% of farm loans | — |
| Pakistan | 69% of rural credit | — |
| Philippines | 78% | Less than 10% of small businesses received formal credit 45% of urban credit, in 1987 |
| Sri Lanka | 45% of credit to paddy farmers | — |
| Thailand | 45% of outstanding credit in 1987 | — |
| | 52% of rural credit | 17% of total deposits and 20% of total loans |

*Sources*: Asian Development Bank, 1990, Table 3.1.

however, also evidence to show that the informal sector tends to shrink with financial liberalization, deepening, increased monetization, improved information flows, and lowering of transaction costs. For instance, the All-India Rural Credit Surveys indicate that the informal sector has declined in the last two decades from about 85 per cent of outstanding rural debt (1962) to about 40 per cent by 1982 because of the rapid expansion of organized banking in the rural sector. A similar decline is noticeable in other countries like Sri Lanka and Thailand (Montiel *et al.*, 1993, pp. 17–18 and 42).

Although there is no systematic contemporary evidence, it is common knowledge that interest rates in the informal sector are substantially higher than those prevailing in formal markets and are also often higher than the ceilings prescribed in anti-usury laws. The high interest rates in informal markets reflect a combination of factors, such as monopoly rents, high transaction and administrative costs, risk premia, and the opportunity costs as measured by rates of return in alternative outlets. But there are no consistent time series data, except for Korea, on interest rates in informal markets that would enable trend hypotheses to be fully tested. In the case of Korea, a clear decline in informal interest rates from 50 per cent (1975) to 25 per cent (1989) is discernible as a sequel to financial liberalization in 1980 (based on a Bank of Korea sample survey, cited in Montiel *et al.*, 1993). Econometric results indicate that arbitrage relationships with foreign financial variables such as expected devaluation premia are even more influential than domestic money market conditions in determining the level of interest rates in informal markets in a large number of developing countries (Montiel *et al.*, 1993, p. 25 and Appendix B). This suggests that informal credit markets are quite efficient in mediating between domestic and foreign financial conditions and are even forward-looking in anticipating future policies (Agenor and Haque, 1994, p. 13).

## 7.2 PARALLEL MARKETS FOR FOREIGN EXCHANGE

Alongside domestic informal finance, parallel markets for foreign exchange in developing countries have emerged primarily as a result of exchange controls, unrealistic official exchange rates, foreign trade restrictions, high inflation, political and social instability, which together lead to exchange rates substantially more depreciated than the official rate. In so far as parallel markets emerge in response to the imposition of exchange and trade controls, they are analogous to the reactive sector of domestic informal finance. The resultant parallel market premium, that is, the proportion by which the parallel market exchange rate exceeds the official rate, may vary substantially over time and across countries (Table 7.3). The analysis and evidence provided by Montiel *et al.* (1994), which integrates both the domestic informal credit markets and parallel markets for foreign exchange in a systematic and consistent framework, suggests that informal interest rates are influenced not only by domestic money market conditions but also by arbitrage relationships with foreign financial variables.

The welfare implications of parallel currency markets are unclear, except when they are associated with illegal activities. But they do create a variety of distortions and affect the transmission mechanism of short-term macroeconomic policies. They impair the effectiveness of capital controls imposed by the central bank and since parallel exchange rates are more volatile than official rates they tend to accentuate the instability of domestic prices (Table 7.3).

*Table* 7.3 Variability in exchange rates and prices in developing countries, 1975–86[a]

| *Country* | *Exchange rates* | | *Consumer prices* |
|---|---|---|---|
| | *Official* | *Parallel* | |
| Bangladesh | 0.301 | 0.519 | 0.370 |
| Bolivia | 2.689 | 2.577 | 2.745 |
| Chile | 0.893 | 0.930 | 0.754 |
| Colombia | 0.693 | 0.732 | 0.672 |
| Greece | 0.578 | 0.593 | 0.620 |
| India | 0.173 | 0.178 | 0.280 |
| Indonesia | 0.438 | 0.459 | 0.348 |
| Korea | 0.243 | 0.231 | 0.373 |
| Malawi | 0.324 | 0.413 | 0.304 |
| Malaysia | 0.058 | 0.061 | 0.165 |
| Mexico | 1.604 | 1.637 | 1.446 |
| Morocco | 0.371 | 0.356 | 0.321 |
| Nigeria | 0.214 | 0.458 | 0.539 |
| Pakistan | 0.216 | 0.147 | 0.260 |
| Singapore | 0.061 | 0.064 | 0.137 |
| Tunisia | 0.306 | 0.320 | 0.291 |
| Zambia | 0.437 | 0.481 | 0.675 |

*Note*: [a] Standard deviation of the quarter-to-quarter rate of change of the relevant variable, divided by the sample mean.

*Sources*: *International Financial Statistics* (IMF), and *World Currency Yearbook*, various issues, cited in Montiel *et al.* (1993), p. 37.

The most effective solution is to eliminate these controls and let prices reflect the real scarcity of foreign exchange. But full liberalization, more particularly of the capital account, has a variety of costs, which are not yet fully understood.

## 7.3 TRANSMISSION CHANNELS

Informal credit and foreign exchange markets play an important role in transmitting the effects of macroeconomic policy instruments to aggregate demand through a number of channels, which, following the model developed by Montiel *et al.* (1993), may be broadly divided into general and partial equilibrium interactions. The general equilibrium effects operate through the impact of policy changes on the expected rate of inflation, the parallel market premium, and the economy's stock of foreign assets. The partial equilibrium channels include interest rate effects through the informal credit market, changes in household wealth and the government budget. In so far as monetary policy changes also affect the profits of the central bank, the fiscal effects of these changes constitute a separate channel through which the effects of policy on demand are transmitted. Besides the monetary policy implications, informal markets pose prudential risks in so far as the failure of one or more finance company can start a contagion effect in the formal sector, as happened in Thailand in the 1980s. It is also often overlooked that the semi-formal co-operative credit sector, which is usually beyond the purview of the central bank, is a source of leakage in credit controls and can impair credit policy, as in India, Malaysia, and Pakistan.

The informal sector also poses serious fiscal problems in so far as it frustrates tax collection because the bulk of informal transactions are unrecorded. Attempts to increase taxes on formal sector transactions, say on the interest income can induce a switch of activity to the informal sector. Consequently, the tax base becomes smaller and more unstable as informal markets expand. The tax evaded income and wealth tends to create an excess demand for assets which can be easily concealed, such as real assets and foreign exchange, which further impairs the efficiency of macroeconomic demand management.

## 7.4 THE ROLE OF CENTRAL BANKS

Central banks, however, also need to recognize that even with the utmost feasible liberalization of formal finance, a hard core of autonomous informal finance will always remain at one end of the financial continuum, because of its low transaction costs, ease of access, asymmetric information advantages and, above all, as a lender of last resort to the poor and underprivileged. But autonomous informal finance has also some inherent limitations which stem from its small average size and operating characteristics which preclude efficient financial intermediation beyond a recognizably low-scale threshold. It is therefore primarily a vehicle of small-scale savings and small-scale credit, which also suggests that 'the organized sector is more efficient as an intermediator than is the unorganized sector if we believe that the market evolves toward the more efficient system' (Cho, 1990, p. 480). If anything, the informal sector acts as a vehicle of disintermediation – that is, borrowing or lending outside the institutional sector – which may be reflected in one or more of the following channels:

(1) intercompany borrowing or lending;
(2) sale by banks of assets on repurchase agreements to the private, non-banking sector;
(3) increase in the utilization of acceptance facilities and the rediscounting of such acceptances outside the institutional sector by companies seeking to reinvest their liquid funds; and
(4) discounting of bank endorsed trade bills with large depositors rather than by banks for their own accounts.

The disintermediation caused by such factors erodes the efficacy of monetary policy, fragments the money and capital markets and impedes the efficient mobilization and allocation of savings.

What then are the main elements of a positive central bank policy toward informal finance, which while preserving its advantages does not hamper monetary policy? First and foremost, central banks in developing countries should accord high priority to the creation of properly designed and staffed special units or cells to research, monitor, promote and refinance the informal and semiformal finance sector. Such a step would also send positive signals to the participants in this sector. These units would need to work in close collaboration with the legal and supervision departments and credit information bureau of the central bank as well as the ministries of agriculture and co-operatives. In the case of countries who are members of multinational central banks such cells will have to be necessarily located in the national agencies of the respective countries. The proposed special units for informal and semi-formal finance in central banks will, however, need to develop an adequate ongoing interdisciplinary data base through their own or contracted research, using universities or the non-governmental type of research institutes like the African Development Institute and the Center for African Monetary Studies in Dakar, SEACEN (South East Asian Central Banks) Centre (Malaysia), and CEMLA (Centre for Latin American Monetary Studies) (Mexico). The thrust of research should be as much on ascertaining attitudes and aspirations as on investigating operations and reviewing developments. It is perfectly feasible to collect and analyse relevant data on informal finance and make meaningful policy recommendations under the aegis of central banks as exemplified by the experience of South East Asian central banks as reviewed in a seminar organized by SEACEN Centre in 1986. A good example of productive research on informal finance is the very exhaustive paper presented by the Bank of Thailand at this seminar based on the findings of a special task force (1989) to study personal and business ROSCA operations, trade credit and check discounting practices, which helped to provide a basis for policy recommendations. In addition to the creation of special cells, central banks should also consider setting up an inter-central bank machinery to serve as a clearing house of information and policies on informal and semi-formal finance in the region. Hitherto the scope of regional co-operation in regard to matters of informal and semi-formal finance has not been explored in the forums of inter-central bank co-operation among developing countries.

Central banks can also facilitate graduation of semi-formal institutions to formal status as in the Cameroon (Haggblade, 1978, pp. 35–6) and foster market-orientated linkages between the informal and formal sectors based on an intermediate financial technology within an appropriate legal framework. The question of linkages has been discussed mostly in the context of linkages with commercial banks, without, however, identifying the role of central banks (Germidis *et al.*, 1991, pp. 214–40; Ghate, 1992). The efficacy of the central bank efforts to foster linkages would be contingent, among others, on the promotion of group borrowing and lending units in commercial banks specially equipped to deal with informal non-rotating entities which are permanent groups, unlike ROSCAS which are temporary, and the creation of entities organized on the group lending principle like the Grameen Bank in Bangladesh. An instructive example in this context are the initiatives of the Nepal Rastra Bank (1988) in organizing the first National Consultation on Self-Help Groups in Nepal and working out a plan for the linkage of such groups with banks on the following lines:

(1) it is limited to pre-existing non-rotating financial groups because they possess permanent loan funds and carry out both saving and lending activities;
(2) external credit is contingent upon the amount of savings deposited as collateral;
(3) under the lead bank programme (1988) additional technical and other support services may be offered by line agencies to the groups whose internal structure and functioning will remain untouched.

Concomitantly, central banks should create market-orientated rediscount and refinance facilities (that is, without any element of subsidy) for promissory notes or other credit paper originating from the informal sector such as *hundis* (India), *chekputi* (Indonesia) and *kalata* (Malawi) which could be made conditional on a guarantee by authorized banks or brokers like the *tontineers* in West Africa, *mboni* in Malawi, and the *compradores* in Southeast Asia. Such rediscount and refinance facilities could also be extended to apex organizations of credit unions and co-operative societies. This would, in turn, necessitate central bank inspection and supervision procedures for semi-formal finance in collaboration with the respective ministries of agriculture and co-operatives. Such promotional activities would not involve any direct financing and management by central banks, whose primary function as controllers of money supply and prudential supervisors of the financial system would therefore remain unimpaired. But the main stumbling blocks in bringing the informal sector within the ambit of the central bank seem to be not so much any institutional factors as the mind-sets of monetary authorities, with their adherence to obsolete dogmas like the real bills doctrine and theories of productive credit which inhibit rediscounting of informal sector paper on the ground that it may not represent genuine credit but accommodation paper, or that the banking and non-banking business in the informal sector be legally separated. The Reserve Bank of India's masterly inactivity in this sphere is an apt cautionary tale of doctrinal orthodoxy as the main constraint on integrating informal and formal finance.[4]

# 8 Research and Advisory Role

'I look upon the bank as having the unique right to offer advice and to press such advice even to the point of nagging; but always, of course, subject to the supreme authority of the government.' —*Montague Norman*

'. . . advisers ADVISE, ministers decide policy.' — *Margaret Thatcher*

## 8.1 THE SCOPE

It is too little known that Montagu Norman's classic statement on the advisory role of a central bank was a studied response, to a lead question by the Royal Commission on Indian Currency and Finance 1926 (Minutes of Evidence, vol. V, non-Parliamentary Question, 14597). Its timing is significant for this was an age when the advisory role of a central bank hardly figured in public consciousness, which no doubt explains its omission from the statutes of central banks of the older industrial countries and those established in Europe under the aegis of the League of Nations in the 1920s and the early 1930s as well as those set up in Latin America around the same time (Kisch and Elkin, 1932). In contrast, the statutes of new central banks in the developing countries after the Second World War spell out explicitly their advisory role based on their economic research functions, as, for instance, the Monetary Law Act of Sri Lanka which assigns specific advisory responsibilities to the central bank and spells out the specific channels of exercising these responsibilities.[1] A particularly interesting example of the advisory role is the Bank of Israel Law, under which the Governor 'does not only govern his own institution' which is assumed to look after a 'stable currency' as well as 'employment and growth' but he (or she) is also the Senior Economic Adviser to the Government', which implies his presence as an 'observer at cabinet meetings whenever economic issues are brought up' (Bruno, 1994, p. 16). This provision is noteworthy not only for defining explicitly the central bank's advisory role but for according the governor (and the bank) the prime status of 'Senior Economic Adviser'. In the event that the law does not specify the advisory role of the central bank it should be at least a matter of established convention, for no central bank would relish the invidious role of a *kibitzer* dispensing profound but unwanted advice.[2] But regardless of whether the advisory role of the central bank is defined by statute or convention, we have to address the question: what is the rationale and scope of such a role and how well are central banks equipped to discharge it? The rationale derives from the unique strategic situation of central banks as sources of independent expertise underlying their monetary policy role as an integral part of macroeconomic management.

Central banks have considerable comparative advantages as technocratic economic think tanks – of which there are not too many in the developing countries – by virtue of their specialised expertise and direct contacts with financial markets, which, if coupled with their necessary autonomy, makes them a valuable source of objective macroeconomic advice to governments. In a good many countries, central banks 'have long been an important center for independent policy analysis and professional training, sometimes reaching beyond their immediate operational responsibilities [like] the role played for decades by the Bank of Italy or the Bank of Mexico in developing talent and in fostering a high degree of intellectual independence' and 'their performance could well provide an alternative model for other nations at an early stage of development or undertaking the transition to a market economy' (Volcker, 1990, p. 7). Other central banks too have played a comparable role in their countries, notably, the Reserve Banks of Australia and New Zealand, the Central Banks of Finland, Israel, Indonesia, Netherlands, Spain, and Thailand. Central banks play a key role as 'a minister of financial health' and provide 'not only intellectual leadership in the economic sphere but constitute islands of sanity and moral authority' in an arbitrary or turbulent environment' (Bruno, 1994, p. 17).[3] An independent professional central bank fulfills the role of 'both a compass and a conscience,' as so memorably phrased by David Horowitz, the founder of the Bank of Israel and its governor for its first seventeen years (Ibid., 1994, p. 13). The achievements and performance of many central banks refute the contrarian view that 'not often have important ideas on economics entered a government by way of its central bank. Nor should anyone be disturbed. There is not the slightest indication that it will ever happen again' (Galbraith, 1975, pp. 36–7). One has only to recall the impressive innovative intellectual output of the perenially maverick Federal Reserve Bank of St Louis; the pioneering contributions of the Central Bank of the Netherlands to techniques of monetary analysis and programming; and the varied initiatives of the Bank of Israel in setting up the national accounts, pioneering input–output tables, growth studies, designing five-year plans, and in formulating a comprehensive programme for the absorption of mass-migration from the former Soviet Union (Bruno, 1994, p. 16). Similarly, the Central Bank of Argentina, at the initiative of Raul Prebisch, originated the issue of its own securities to overcome the shortage of government securities for open market operations. The chief economist of the Commonwealth Bank of Australia, Leslie Melville, suggested (1941) to the Australian Government the novel technique first known as Special Deposits, 'which became for many years the chief instrument of central bank control over the Australian banking system' (Arndt, 1978, p. 1).

## 8.2 THE LIMITS

It is, however, not always possible to evaluate the performance of a central bank as an advisor since such advice is generally given in confidence without publicity but there are a few publicly known cases of disgreement on major policy issues between the central bank and the government as in Sri Lanka in 1953, when the Central Bank 'questioned the wisdom of increasing the budget deficit to meet the additional costs of food subsidies . . . and opposed the continuance of excessive food subsidies at the expense of development expenditure' (Presidential Commission, 1992, p. 58, para.). This Commission, in an unusually candid analysis, noted that in the early years the Central Bank of Sri Lanka 'conducted its advisory roles with some degree of transparency', but 'in recent years the Annual Reports have contained less analysis and discussion of policy issues which have therefore been shielded from public debate'. The Bank's Annual Reports, the Commission noted, 'have been replete with statistics on various sectors of the economy but have been selectively thin on data interpretation and analysis that would help the reader make an informed judgement on vital economic policy issues' (ibid., para. 9, p. 58). The Commission was unequivocal in recording that 'the evidence placed before it suggests that the Central Bank of Sri Lanka has not always exercised this right' of offering 'nagging' advice to the government (para. 11, p. 59), a salutary reminder that a central bank's statutory right and professional competence are by themselves no guarantee that it will be an effective and influential advisor to the government. On the other hand, disagreement with and rejection by the government of a central bank's advice should not be a matter of 'amour propre.' If a central bank is 'well equipped for its technical tasks . . . it can focus opinion, and yet defer, without loss of diginity, to the judgement of the nation through its central political machine' (Sayers, 1961, p. 45). The advisory role of the central bank is therefore always and necessarily subject to 'the supreme authority of the government'. In the same vein, Keynes, too, rightly stressed that the economist's 'advice . . . should not have the last word or the power, but must be a necessary ingredient in the decisions of those who have been entrusted with the last word and with the power' (1981, p. 27). More controversial is Margaret Thatcher's overly sharp dichotomy between advisers, who only 'advise' and ministers who 'decide policy' (1993, p. 715). A central bank may be an advisor in one role (exchange rate arrangements) to the government but it is also a policy-maker in monetary matters. The critical question then is: are central banks fully equipped to discharge effectively their advisory role within the accepted policy framework?

## 8.3 REDEFINING THE ADVISORY ROLE

Central banks, for their part, will need to reappraise carefully the apparatus of their advisory role, which, to begin with, implies a wider mandate in regard to extending the jurisdiction to cover not only the central government but also state governments and even the municipal authorities in some instances, as when they decide to borrow in the capital market. Thus in federations it is equally important for the central bank to monitor and be in close and constant touch with state governments, whose budgetary policies can pose difficult problems like the persistent overdrafts of the state governments with the Reserve Bank of India. As a minimum, a central bank should have formal and informal channels of communication and representation on joint organs of decision-making involving the central government, the state governments, development banks, and development agencies. Similarly, the advisory mandate of a central bank should be deemed to comprehend not only conventional monetary policy but also exchange rates, financial development and related issues. Monetary and fiscal targets can conflict as shown by the 'unpleasant monetarist arithmetic' of Sargent and Wallace (1981), as well as the related problem of co-ordinating the monetary and exchange rate targets (exchange rate policy if the central bank does not have sole responsibility for it).

There are, however, some major requirements to be fulfilled in order to safeguard and enhance the advisory role of central banks. To begin with central banks have to ask themselves: are they making the most efficacious use of their own economic research and advisory units? Or, are these treated as a 'frills' department, saddled, among others, with chores like the preparation of governor's speeches to a medley of audiences, or as an integral part of a central bank's monetary, prudential and developmental responsibilities? Does the Economic Advisor/Head of Economic Research have independent access to the Governor? Does he or she have the right to participate in the meetings of the Board of Directors as in Sri Lanka and the Philippines (where the Head of the Department of Economic Research has the 'right to be heard but not to vote' at the meetings of the Monetary Board)?[4] Such provisions safeguard the quality and independence of advice without involving advisers in sterile bureaucratic games of second-guessing the views of the chief executive and higher management. A perennial occupational hazard for the hapless central bank economic adviser is to be asked to provide the *post facto* rationale for measures and policies already decided upon by the governor and the board. Unless the economic research department of a central bank and its head have the requisite independence, in addition to expertise, the credibility and influence of the central bank, in turn, with the government and the banking community is soon eroded. A healthy but eminently feasible innovation to protect the independence of economic advisers might be for central banks to abolish tenure for economic advisers and obtain, on a rotating basis, the services for a limited period of economists in the 'prime of their powers . . . whose bent and desire is to devote their lives to scientific research and to guiding from the centre the evolution of the economic structure, rather than to administration or to politics' (Keynes, 1981b, p. 26). But in developing countries the central bank's chief economist, like his or her counterpart in government, is more often than not a permanent member of the staff and there is virtually no interchange – only unilateral transfers – of economists from academia to central banks and governments.

But these organisational changes have to be supported by an appropriate economic intelligence and research agenda. A serious lacuna in most central banks in developing countries is the woeful lack of first-hand market intelligence based on personal contacts and knowledge of financial institutions and markets, so typical of the Bank of England.[5] Typically, research departments of central banks, which tend to acquire the ambience of academic think-tanks with at best only arm's-length contacts with the market place, can hardly be expected to function as the central bank's eyes and ears in performing its wider bridging functions.

> The central bank is uniquely able to perform a multiple bridging function, between the public and private sectors, between the financial system and the real economy, and between the domestic economic community and the outside world. This function provides some of the most stimulating and rewarding work in central banking. (Hughes, 1992, p. 26)

The economic research wing, in addition to its bread and butter lines of monetary programming and preparation of policy memoranda, must strive to identify and work in areas on the cutting edge of research such as the regional aspects of monetary policy and financial development, financial innovations and their implications for financial legislation and monetary policy, links between formal and informal finance, intermediation margins, analysis of bad and doubtful debts experience of commercial banks (drawing, among others, on the records of the bank inspection and supervision departments), identifying and measuring the float in the payments system, information and transaction costs, credit rationing, problems of maintaining competition in the financial system, and implications of liberalisation for customer bank charges. The economic data and research of the central bank are in the nature of a public good and their timely publication is imperative to enhance the transparency and credibility of the central bank. These arrangements merit review and reform in the context of the recent recommendations of the Executive Board of the International Monetary Fund to the Interim Committee (September 1995) calling upon member countries to compile and publish, with technical assistance from the Fund, comprehensive, timely and good-quality core statistics as follows:

- exchange rates
- international reserves
- the central bank balance sheet
- reserve money
- broad money
- domestic credit
- interest rates
- consumer prices, producer or wholesale prices
- external trade
- current account balance
- external debt/debt service
- fiscal balance
- GDP/GNP
- industrial production
- unemployment
- wages and earnings

This list could be appropriately supplemented to suit country requirements for internal use by subsets covering items like unused bank overdrafts, inventories, and at a later stage, sample surveys of bankers' and business attitudes and expectations.

It has also been suggested whether, given the proclivity of governments both in developed and developing countries to manipulate data to yield the prognosis the government wants to see, bureaus dealing with labour and other non-monetary statistics could be 'transformed into a branch of the central bank' and by giving great [*sic*] independence to the latter, the risk of such interventions might be reduced' (Elster, 1994, p. 6).[6] While this is an alluring argument, it might also burden the central bank with the task of collecting and analysing masses of non-monetary data. A possible solution based on a more rational division of labour would be for the central bank to retain monetary, balance of payments, and financial statistics and hive off real statistics to an autonomous statutory national statistical commission, which, like the central bank, the supreme court and the auditor-general, would then be insulated from political pressures.

Whatever the specifics of organisation and research programmes the economic departments of central banks have rich potential and there is no reason why they should not replicate the achievement of the Commonwealth (later Reserve) Bank of Australia, where, under the leadership of its one-time chief economist, Leslie Melville, 'the Economist's Branch provided the leaven which in course of time leavened the whole mass of the Bank's Head Office organisation' (Giblin, cited in Arndt, 1978, p. 1). But the effectiveness of the advisory role is a function not only of the established professionalism of the central bank and its integrity, but above all of 'unbounding courage to be unpopular when need arises' (Bruno, 1994, p. 17). Equally, no central bank, however independent and professional, is exempt from the 'Limitations of the Expert' (Laski, 1968) and the caveat that economists too are fallible and can differ on the same issue. Also, as a former Governor of the Central Bank of the Solomon Islands notes perceptively: 'Any attempts to oversupply influence, like any other commodity, can easily lead to consumer resistance and a backlash against the central bank, for nothing works to excess, not even the influence of the central bank' (Hughes, 1992, p. 28). The central bank's advisory role has also to be seen in the context of the 'case for a certain diffusion of authority and responsibility for major macroeconomic policymaking' as 'otherwise the head of state is too dependent on the advice of a single minister and may not have the means to explore alternatives' (Currie, 1981, p. 182).

# 9 Islamic Central Banking

> 'The most hated sort of retail trade, and with the greatest reason, is usury, which makes a gain out of money itself, and not from the natural object of it.' —Aristotle [384–322 BC], *Politics*, trans. B. Jowett, bk. I, ch. 10, p. 1258b

> '. . . whereas Allah permitteth trading and forbiddeth usury'. —*The Glorious Koran*, Surah II, v. 275, trans Mohammed Pickthall

Aristotle's ancient castigation of usury has assumed practical shape in contemporary times with the introduction of interest- free Islamic finance wholly or in part in several Muslim countries, notably in Iran, Pakistan, Saudi Arabia, and Malaysia. The distinguishing feature of Islamic finance, in contrast to conventional banking and finance, is the absolute prohibition against the payment and receipt of all forms of interest (the Arabic term for which is *riba*) without any distinction being made between real and nominal rates of interest (Khan and Mirakhor, 1992, p. 531). However, the literature to date typically assumes that all loan contracts are necessarily fixed-rate transactions and does not seem to have addressed a pertinent related question: whether variable rates of interest, as, for instance, on housing mortgages, are compatible with Islamic finance, considering that in such loan contracts neither the lender nor the borrower knows, *ex ante*, what the future rate of interest will be during the pendency of the contract. As such the stigma of a fixed rate would not seem to attach to them. Islamic economic doctrine, which is based on the Quran and the Sunnah (teachings and traditions of the Prophet Mohammed) does not provide a detailed rationale for the prohibition of interest 'beyond asserting, axiomatically, that charging interest is an act of injustice and thus forbidden' (ibid., p. 531). But in the present context, the relevant concern is not the rationale but the implications of interest-free banking for the scope and efficiency of central banking in its primary areas of monetary policy as well as its supervisory and developmental roles. These implications are defined by all the distinguishing features of Islamic finance, besides the prohibition of interest, which have a bearing on the transmission mechanism and operational aspects of central banking.

## 9.1 ISLAMIC FINANCE

Islamic banks rely, besides their own capital and equity, on two main sources of funds: transaction deposits and investment deposits. The former correspond to interest-free demand deposits in conventional banking and being transaction balances cannot be used by banks for profitable investment. But banks can levy a service charge on account holders to meet the costs of operating this type of account whose nominal value is guaranteed. Investment deposits – termed profit and loss accounts – are akin to shares in a firm, mutual fund, or investment trust and depositors are entitled to a share of the profits or losses made by the bank in terms of a sharing ratio agreed in advance between the banks and depositors which cannot be modified during the maturity of the transaction except by mutual consent. Investment deposits are the principal source of funds for banks and carry no guarantee on their nominal value. Likewise, on the lending side banks are required under Islamic Law (*Shariah*) to use the two techniques that fully meet Islamic requirements on loans, namely, the Mudarabah and Musharakah arrangements wherein lenders share in the profits and losses of the borrowing enterprise. In Mudarabah the financier has no role in management while in Musharakah all the parties rightfully participate in management. If profit–loss accounts are infeasible there is a variety of permissible alternative instruments such as instalment sale, hire purchase, partnership, lease purchase, formal transactions, and loans for a definite period of time without interest or profit sharing (*Qard al-Haranah*).

Islamic finance has gained considerable momentum since the second half of the 1970s and is currently operative in two basic forms in about forty-five countries comprising most of the Muslim world. The first represents some type of Islamic banking or financial institution alongside conventional interest-based banking. In such cases two types of institutions have evolved: Islamic banks, mostly in Muslim countries, and Islamic investment and holding companies, which operate in some Muslim but mostly in non-Muslim countries. Generally, in both cases Islamic banks are subject to specific regulations that apply to all banks or financial institutions. Examples of Islamic banks in Muslim countries include the Fayad Islamic Bank in Bahrain, Dubai, Jordan, Qatar and Sudan. Islamic investment companies, with either a national or international charter, include the Dar al Mal al Islamic (Geneva), Albarakah

International Ltd (London), Al Rajhi Company for Islamic Investment Ltd (London), the Islamic Investment Company (Bahamas). These institutions, mostly privately owned, compete with conventional interest-paying banks and invest their interest-free deposits in profitable investment outlets.

Although Islamic banking in Malaysia began with the establishment of Bank Islam Berhad (1983), it is only with the implementation of the Interest-free Banking Scheme (IFBS) on 4 March 1993, that Malaysia has emerged as the first country to implement a dual banking system, whereby an Islamic banking system functions on a parallel basis to the conventional banking system. The second basic form that Islamic finance has taken involves the restructuring of the whole financial system in accord with Islamic doctrine as in Saudi Arabia (since the Royal Decree no. 23 of 15 December 1957), in Iran (since the Law for Usury-Interest Free Banking, August 1983) where all banks operate under Islamic law and Pakistan (since the primary circulars of 20 June and 26 November 1984) where only foreign banks are exempt from the ban on interest-based transactions.

## 9.2 MONETARY POLICY

Monetary policy in a conventional environment aims at the control of the cost, availability and supply of money but in an Islamic system the central bank lacks the capacity to set the cost of funds (financial rates of return). Consequently, it has to resort to other instruments to influence the volume and availability of money, such as variation of reserve requirements, refinance and profit-sharing ratios, selective credit controls, open market operations and moral suasion. Thus, for example, adjustments in profit-sharing ratios can be used as a substitute for bank rate variations: credit can be tightened by reducing the share accruing to the businessmen and eased by increasing it (Uzair, 1982). This proposal, however, 'may have resource allocational implications' and also involve imposition of limitations on the freedom of contracts, besides consequences for property rights, since under the Shariah 'the partners are responsible for losses to the extent of their financial involvement' (Khan, 1995, p. 24). Clearly, there is a problem of inequity if, for instance, the central bank rules require a lower return from profits than from the share in losses, and nor is it certain whether the central bank is entitled to modify existing profit-sharing contracts (ibid., p. 24). Likewise, variations in the refinance ratio (which refers to the central bank refinancing of a part of the interest-free loans provided by the commercial banks) can influence the quantum of short-term credit extended. There has also been a proposal that the central bank should acquire an equity stake in commercial banking by holding, say, 25 per cent of the capital stock of the commercial banks (Uzair, 1982). Its rationale is that it would give the central bank access to a permanent source of income so that it could effectively function as a lender of last resort. Analytic studies have shown that indirect methods employing reserve requirements changes and variation of profit-sharing ratios can achieve the objectives of monetary policy in a closed Islamic economy (Khan and Mirakhor, 1990) as well as the more realistic case of an open economy (Zaidi and Mirakhor, 1991). The latter study, using a general equilibrium model, concluded with the caveat that the model's results should not be taken too literally – that monetary policy can be used to affect output in an open Islamic economy in spite of the constraints on monetary policy imposed by substitution possibilities among domestic and foreign assets. Although the rate of return on equity shares of commercial banks is market-driven, the supply of reserves is regulated by the central bank through variations in its stock of bank equity shares, which in turn changes the cost of borrowing for the banks. But even more instructive than the results of theoretical models is the actual experience of Saudi Arabia, Iran and Pakistan in demonstrating the nature and scope of monetary policy in open Islamic economies.

The Saudi Arabian Monetary Agency's (SAMA) monetary policy relies primarily on variations of the reserve ratio requirements, since it is debarred from using the rediscount facility under Islamic law and cannot use open market operations as the Kingdom does not have any public debt in the form of government securities which can be used for such operations. A significant secondary tool is selective credit controls, which include regulation of credit ceilings, cash margins, terms and conditions of customer transactions, limits on prohibitions on specific categories of loans, and fixing the assets to be held within the Kingdom by each bank. SAMA also deploys its own accounts and government deposits with commercial banks to regulate the money supply. However, it is difficult to make a full evaluation of SAMA's monetary policy in the absence of any analysis or commentary in its annual reports, which contain only descriptive monetary statistics.

Monetary policy in Iran is aimed at achieving a targeted inflation rate for the consumer price index, which is decided by the Money and Credit Council based on the recommendations of the central bank, the Bank Markazi, which has a number of instruments for implementing monetary policy. First, it specifies the rates of return on deposits by term and the rates of profit on lending facilities by sector, except for those on credit to the trade and services sector, where rates are freely determined. At the end of 1992/93 deposit rates ranged from 7.5 per cent for less than a year to 15 per cent on five-year deposits, while the rates of profit ranged from 9 per cent (agriculture) to 12–16 per cent (housing). The second set of instruments, used particularly since the abolition of bank-specific credit ceilings at the beginning of 1991/92, comprises variation of reserve ratio requirements and the rates charged on lending of encashment facilities provided to banks. The reserve ratios are specified for each class of deposit, diminishing as their term increases (10 per cent on five-year deposits to 30 per cent on demand deposits). Specialized banks are subject to a uniform (and lower) reserve ratio of 10 per cent. The Bank Markazi has two credit facilities to banks: a rediscount window at rates of charge between 14 and 16 per cent; and an overdraft facility (used to cover reserve deficiency) at penal rates of interest of 20–34 per cent depending on the size of the overdraft. The Bank Markazi's credit to the government is subject to an overall limit specified in the Budget Law of 1993/94. But to date fiscal policy has dominated the operation of monetary policy in Iran where the oil revenues and budgetary policies to a large extent determine the monetary base and the money multiplier has been relatively stable.

Traditionally, monetary policy in Pakistan has relied on a wide range of instruments including cash reserve and liquidity requirements, ceiling on the rates of return on various forms of credit, and credit ceilings for individual banks. While bank-specific ceilings have been the primary instrument in recent years, the authorities aim to phase out these ceilings and replace them by control of bank reserves through auctions and open market operations in order to accelerate the movement toward a system of indirect market-based monetary control. In July 1992 the authorities replaced the bank-specific ceilings by a system of differential credit-deposit ratios (30 per cent of rupee deposit liabilities and 40 per cent of foreign currency deposit liabilities) with exemptions for pre-shipment export credits, credits for commodity operations, advances to public sector enterprises, and financing for the Prime Minister's Self-Employment Scheme.

One of the constraints on a comprehensive monetary policy in an Islamic system is the absence of a wide and active interbank money market. A remedy to this is now being sought by the creation of a properly designed money market, as in Malaysia where the central bank has introduced, effective 3 January 1999, an Islamic interbank money market for the trading of Islamic bankers' acceptances, and interbank investments with negotiable profit sharing ratios as between the investing and receiving institutions. The central bank of Malaysia has also set up an Islamic interbank cheque clearing system separate from the conventional cheques (Bank Negara, 1994, p. 52).

Despite the proliferation of analytic studies on the scope and effectiveness of monetary policy in Islamic economies, the potentialities and problems of open market operations in variable-dividend securities as a monetary instrument have been barely researched. A priori reasoning suggests that there are some intrinsic constraints on the scope and effectiveness of open market operations in equities for monetary policy purposes, notably the shallowness of stock markets, volatility of security prices, and the problems of adverse selection in diverse equities unlike fixed-interest securities which are a comparatively homogeneous product. More importantly, the purchase and sale of equities for monetary policy purposes might also distort the transmission of effects of economic fundamentals on equity prices. Likewise, equity prices being more volatile than bond prices, the probability of trading losses as a result of open market operations in equities can undermine the overall financial position and credibility of the central bank. It would also not be easy to disentangle the effects of central bank intervention to support stock exchange values, as at one time in Japan, as distinct from the effects of intervention for monetary policy purposes. The role of the central bank as a substantial owner of specific stocks can also pose potential problems of unwarranted and unintended intrusion in corporate governance and conflicts of interest. Islamic central banks would therefore need to rely more on variation of reserve requirements and profit–loss ratios than on open market operations.

It is always open to a central bank to exercise moral suasion as an instrument of policy in any system and the introduction of

Islamic finance does not by itself affect its potency – which depends both on the credibility and professionalism of the central bank and the extent to which the system is oligopolistic – since in a unit banking system with a multiplicity of small banks it would be correspondingly difficult for a central bank to be effective. There is to date no evidence of how influential this instrument has been in systems like Iran, Malaysia, and Pakistan. In any event moral suasion is at best a supplementary instrument.

## 9.3 REGULATION AND SUPERVISION

It is also pertinent to inquire into the implications of Islamic finance for the prudential role of a central bank, particularly in view of the argument based on an analytic model, that an equity-based system is better suited to adjust to shocks that can lead to banking crisis than a conventional interest-based banking system, because shocks to the asset position are immediately absorbed by changes in the nominal value of shares (deposits) held by the public in banks (Khan, 1986). The real value of assets and liabilities would be equal at all points of time whereas in an interest-based banking system an adverse shock can create a divergence between the real and nominal values of assets and liabilities resulting possibly in negative worth for the bank, with no assurance as to how this divergence would be corrected and how long the process would take. While this reasoning is analytically valid, it does not necessarily hold in empirical terms judging by the high failure rate of equity-based financial institutions like investment trusts and mutual funds in existing systems. It is also difficult to agree with the proposition that in an Islamic system 'a further opportunity for enhancement of the control of the banking system is available to the central bank through its purchase of equity shares of banks and other financial institutions (Iqbal and Mirakhor, 1987, p. 7). Purchase of equity shares is more in the nature of a developmental instrument but does not in itself constitute a means of control unless it is part of the portfolio of the central bank for open market operations. This would also involve a conflict of interest between the supervisory and developmental roles of the central bank. On the other hand, a major function for a central bank would be the clear definition and enforcement of Islamic regulations relating to property rights and contracts in the financial and capital markets, since the prohibition of interest by itself generates a moral hazard problem in principal-agent contracts.

The experience of Iran and Pakistan is illustrative of the scope of supervision in an Islamic banking system. In Iran these regulations are far more detailed than are customary even in the most regulated of conventional banking systems. The Bank Markazi (central bank) (under the Law for Usury-Free Banking, 1983) is responsible for the supervision of the banking system and is required to determine: legal reserve requirements and the minimum ratio of liquid assets to short-term liabilities; bank-wise credit ceilings; minimum and maximum expected rates of return from various bank facilities; minimum and maximum profit shares for banks in their Mudarabah and Musharakha accounts; maximum rates of commission; maximum amount of credit facility granted by banks to each applicant; ratio of credit facilities to the bank's capital; acceptable ratio of credit facilities to that bank's capital and to various deposits; maximum commitment made by each bank under letters of credit, endorsement, guarantees as well as collateral for such commitments. The Bank Markazi oversees the indicative sectoral credit guidelines, but given the practical difficulties of supervision, it accepts deviations of plus or minus 2 per cent from the indicative guidelines. The Bank Markazi is also authorized to inspect and audit bank accounts and documents and to make additional regulations to strengthen its supervisory authority and to safeguard against threats of insolvency of banks.

The State Bank of Pakistan issued new prudential regulations in January 1992 to enhance the supervision and regulation of the banking system, which, however, have not been occasioned by the Islamization, *per se*, of the financial system. These include more stringent limits on credit concentration and on contingent liabilities, stiffer guidelines on the separation of bank ownership and management; tighter margin requirements on equity-based advances; and a strengthened system of classification and provisioning for nonperforming assets.

On the organizational side, there is, however, a real problem of finding suitable trained personnel with prior experience of Islamic banking, who would command the requisite capability to conduct both onsite inspection and offsite surveillance of Islamic banks. There is a tremendous variety of unfamiliar Islamic banking products which require considerable knowledge and experience for evaluation. For instance, in the Malaysian system there are twenty-one Islamic banking products, which, of course, also helps to widen the portfolio choice of depositors in a dual system and strengthens overall competition in the financial system (Bank Negara Malaysia, 1994, p. 186). The development of an appropriate framework of supervision for Islamic central banks is perhaps best undertaken by an international working group like the one organized by Egypt and the French Economic Community on the initiative of Senegal (Goedhuys, 1992, p. 43).

## 9.4 EVALUATION

In sum, the experience of Iran and Pakistan shows that the adoption of Islamic banking 'has not led to the collapse of the financial system as some had feared' (Khan and Mirakhor, 1990, p. 375). Islamic finance has been effective in mobilizing resources, as shown by the rapid growth of private sector Islamic deposits in Iran and Pakistan, but it is far more difficult to judge the efficiency of Islamic banking in allocating mobilized resources and to assess how the system would work in the absence of government and central bank intervention. This conclusion has to be qualified in so far as the study does not assess the extent to which the growth of deposits is due to Islamic finance, *per se*, rather than a cumulative result of numerous other factors, including the nationalization of banks in Iran and Pakistan, which, however, is not a corollary of Islamic banking but a reflection of 'perceived national priorities' (Khan and Mirakhor, 1990, p. 8). Nationalization may well have induced a greater inflow of funds from currency holdings consequent upon the enhanced confidence in commercial banks. In any event there is a heavy developmental agenda for Islamic central banks to address problems arising from: the inadequacies of the legal and accounting framework and the financial infrastructure; the shortage of trained and experienced personnel; the difficulty of devising appropriate noninterest-bearing instruments for financing government deficits; and higher transaction and information costs, which in a conventional system are largely reduced through government supervision and deposit insurance.

Although central banking in Islamic economies is still evolving, it could be said to be well past its formative stage considering that it has been operative over three decades in Saudi Arabia and over a decade in Iran and Pakistan. But to date there has been no in-depth analysis, based on empirical evidence, of the scope and limitations of central banking in Islamic financial systems. The experience of interest-free economies presents a unique continuing challenge to both analytic economics as well as to macroeconomic policy makers in Islamic countries, and 'students of banking theory and practice might find it informative to give close study to Islamic banking' (Goodhart, 1995a, p. 17). In sum, the policy issues posed by Islamic finance are by no means intractable and are no different from those posed by regimes of low and stable interest rates in conventional economies which also effectively precluded the use of interest rates as a policy instrument thereby obliging central banks to rely on other monetary policy instruments.

# 10 Transition Economies

> 'The issue that is important for us in the West to communicate to our colleagues in the East is that there is no single Western central bank model that is necessarily the one that we would recommend they follow.'
> —*Alan Greenspan*

The epigraph pinpoints the core of the unique challenges that face central banks in the formerly centrally planned economies (Russia, China, former Soviet Union and Eastern European countries, and Viet Nam) in their transition to market-orientated economies, a complex process that involves not merely the issue of new currencies and the creation of independent central banks but also comprehensive financial reforms and a radical reconstruction of the basic financial infrastructure. Most importantly, it involves a reformulation of their value systems from those of a command society to those appropriate for a market economy supported by a massive investment in the education and training of banking and financial personnel. Successful transition depends, among other things, on development of the institutional framework for monetary policy instruments and operations and the clearing and settlement systems for payments. Since these reforms are interdependent, they have to be pursued sometimes concurrently and sometimes in proper sequence, in a mutually reacting and reinforcing fashion (Baliño *et al.*, 1994). Consequently, the developmental and promotional role of central banks looms larger than the monetary and prudential roles. They have played a major role in the reform process – mainly shaping developments while also being shaped by them (Fleming and Cole, 1995, p. 54).

## 10.1 THE NEW NATIONAL CURRENCIES

A notable feature of economic reform in the former Soviet Union countries is the introduction of new currencies (Table 10.1), both as symbols of national and monetary independence and also because it gives them the necessary autonomy and authority to determine national monetary and exchange rate policies, which thereby also offer them a way to break away from the high inflation endemic in the ruble zone (Fleming and Cole, 1995, p. 57). Making the new currency legal tender involves a number of practical steps, notably enactment of the necessary legislation to give the central bank sole authority to issue it, the choice of an exchange rate regime, development of financial and foreign exchange markets, and procedures for intervention in the markets. It also requires concurrent actions at the micro-level – such as valuing the currency, deciding the quality of notes, using inventory models for estimating the demand for bank notes and the quantity of each denomination, limiting old currency inflows, disposal of old notes, mechanics of conversion, currency contracts and the necessary publicity to facilitate acceptance and circulation of the new currency. These measures also call for appropriate macro-level responses, insomuch

*Table* 10.1 New currencies in the former USSR states

| *Country* | (a) Legal tender as of September 1993 | *(b) New permanent currency* | *(c) Exchange regime as of 31 March 1994* |
|---|---|---|---|
| Armenia | Ruble | 1993 ruble | Independent float |
| Azerbaijan | Manat and 1993 ruble | Manat | Peg (Russian ruble) |
| Belarus | Ruble and ruble (coupon) | 1993 ruble | Managed float |
| Estonia | Kroon | Kroon[a] | Peg (Deutsche Mark) |
| Georgia | Coupon (82/92) | Lari | Independent float |
| Kazakstan | Ruble | 1993 ruble | Independent float |
| Kyrgyz Republic | Som | Som | Independent float |
| Latvia | Lats | Lats | Independent float |
| Lithuania | Litas | Litas[a] | Peg (US dollar) |
| Moldova | Coupon (7/27/93) | Leu (12/93) | Independent float |
| Russian Federation | 1993 ruble | 1993 ruble | Independent float |
| Tajikistan | Ruble | 1993 ruble | |
| Turkmenistan | Ruble | Manat (11/93) | Peg (US dollar) |
| Ukraine | Karbovanets | Grivna | Independent float |
| Uzbekistan | Ruble | 1993 ruble | |

*Note*: [a] Currency boards with 100 per cent foreign exchange backing for the domestic currency

*Source*: For (a) and (b) Hernàn Cortés-Douglas and Richard Abrams, 1993, p. 27; for (c) *Annual Report*, International Monetary Fund, 1994, p. 181.

as independent currencies alone are hardly sufficient for macro-economic stabilization unless supported by prudent monetary and fiscal policies, as in Estonia, Lithuania, and Latvia, where they were the crucial elements in reducing the average levels of inflation to a monthly rate of one per cent. On the other hand, in the Ukraine, the provisional currency (*Karbovanets*) depreciated even more rapidly than the Russian ruble, because of fiscal profligacy and lack of monetary discipline which accentuated inflation to levels even higher than in Russia. The persistence of inflationary pressures as a result of monetary indiscipline in the countries other than the Baltic republics has led to the adoption of a free float exchange rate regime in the expectation that a more actively managed rate might be feasible once domestic monetary conditions are under better control.

The successful operation of the Estonian Currency Board (since 20 June 1992) was based on a 100 per cent gold (using the pre-war gold reserves of Estonia restituted by the Bank of England and other countries) and foreign exchange backing for the new currency – the Krone – which was pegged to the Deutsche mark because of the transparency and credibility of a link with a single strong and reputed currency in preference to the Finnish mark or Swedish korona, even though the latter were the principal invoicing currencies in Estonia's trade. The currency board is operated by the Issue Department of the Bank of Estonia, and the Banking Department holds foreign exchange balances surplus to the Issue Department, including earned seigniorage as it accrues, and is responsible for any residual central banking functions, particularly the payments arrangements with the former Soviet Union. The Banking Department provides only emergency loans on a case-by-case basis for liquidity requirements to the banking system within the limits of its surplus foreign exchange resources. The central bank cannot act as lender of last resort to underwrite the banking system and the overall task of dealing with insolvency crises is a fiscal responsibility as was recognized in the rescue of a bank in early 1993. The distinctiveness of the Bank of Estonia as a unique hybrid of a currency board and a central bank derives from it two organizational features. The Issue Department balance sheet is not controlled by the authorities and is endogenous to the economy at large, 'while the Banking Department represents the exogenous, or policy side of the central bank' (Bennett, 1993, p. 456). The central bank cannot lend to the government, which is moreover committed to balance the budget, although a balanced budget is not a necessary corollary of a currency board. The successful macroeconomic performance of Estonia and Lithuania is largely attributable not only to the adoption of the currency board system but also the supportive monetary and fiscal policies. Even more instructive is the experience of Latvia, which is widely regarded as one of the success stories of new currencies and central banking in transition. This is best recounted in the words of Einars Repse, President of the Bank of Latvia, whose model recommendations for introducing a new currency to 'be loved and trusted' (1993, pp. 28–9) are:

- Liberalize your markets (foreign exchange and others);
- set up an independent central bank;
- introduce your currency;
- adjust your financial system to market principles;
- introduce floating exchange rates;
- follow a tight or extremely tight monetary policy;
- be ready to be blamed for everything.

It is noteworthy that this sequential strategy provided for an independent central bank as a precondition for introducing the new currency. The Central Bank of Latvia is autonomous in so far as no one can influence or overrule its decisions: the governing body of full-time members is appointed by parliament and cannot be dismissed; they are not permitted to engage in any other gainful activity, private or governmental. The success of the strategy is evidenced by the significant decline in the inflation rate and a stable exchange market. If the Estonian and Lithuanian programmes attest to the success of a rule-driven currency board regime, the Latvian programme attests equally to the efficacy of discretionary policies, thus demonstrating that there are no universal recipes in the central bankers' cookbook.

Alongside the introduction of new currencies, the transition economies have also witnessed the phenomenon of dollarization, or currency substitution – that is, the propensity of resident nationals to keep a large proportion of financial assets in the form of interest-bearing foreign currency deposits (normally US dollars) as a hedge against inflation. The dollarization of transition economies is largely a reactive phenomenon in contrast to the proactive dollarization of relatively steady state market economies such as Argentina, Chile, Egypt, India, Mexico, Pakistan, Peru, Sri Lanka,

Uruguay, and the Yemen Arab Republic, where it occurs because of the introduction of officially-sanctioned foreign currency deposits as a means of alleviating foreign exchange shortage, usually following widespread, often illegal currency substitution. While dollarization has become a significant phenomenon in transition economies the experiences of individual economies as measured by the behaviour of the dollarization ratio have varied in response to the respective inflationary pressures. Thus Russia and Ukraine have had among the highest inflation rates in transition economies and their dollarization ratios fluctuated between 30 per cent and 45 per cent in 1992–3. In the Baltic states the dollarization ratio, which peaked at around 60 per cent in Estonia (1992), 50 per cent in Lithuania (1993) and 35 per cent in Latvia (1993), was substantially reduced after the successful implementation of stabilization programmes during 1993. The lower decline in the case of Latvia was partly because of its liberal foreign exchange market, which 'provided a "safe haven" for flight of capital from other high-inflation states of the former USSR' (like Russia and Ukraine) (Sahay and Vegh, 1995, p. 37). The successful reversal of the dollarization process in several transition economies strongly contrasts with Latin America where dollarization has remained high even after inflationary pressures have abated. This shows how sound monetary and fiscal policies, which address the fundamental macroeconomic disequilibria, can induce a portfolio switch in favour of domestic currency-denominated assets with competitive real returns. On the other hand, some degree of dollarization could also reflect a natural outcome of portfolio diversification, particularly for institutional holders like social security funds, in a world of high capital mobility and globalized finance.

In the transition economies the predominance of cash payments in the household sector – reflected in the high average currency–deposit ratios – coupled with the large size and (unpredictable) variability of the payment float have proven to be major constraints on the efficacy of financial intermediation and monetary management particularly in the shift toward the use of indirect monetary policy instruments (see Table 10.2). There have also been periodic episodes of cash shortages, as for instance, the physical shortages of cash rubles in the former Soviet Union (FSU) during much of 1992 and 1993, which manifested itself in the suspension of full convertibility of sight deposits into currency at par. The cash shortage was a cumulative result of the special role of cash in making certain payments in FSU and the asymmetry 'of a monetary union under which every member had unlimited capacity to create deposit money but only one member, the Russian Federation was capable of providing cash rubles' (Hardy and Lahiri, 1994, p. 3).

*Table* 10.2 Currency–deposit ratio in selected transition economies (% of total deposits)

| | *1991* | *1992* | *1993* |
|---|---|---|---|
| Russian Federation | 20 | 31 | 50 |
| Ukraine | | 32 | 27 |
| Latvia | | 41 | 40 |
| Lithuania | | 25 | 8 |
| Kazakstan | | 30 | 67 |
| Poland | 28 | 24 | 26 |
| Romania | 22 | 38 | 49 |
| Czech Republic | 16 | 12 | 9 |
| Bulgaria | 22 | 18 | |
| Hungary | 29 | 28 | |

*Source*: Sundararajan and Sensenbrenner, 1994, pp. 646–7.

## 10.2 FINANCIAL INFRASTRUCTURE AND REFORM

A major problem is the outdated and inefficient payments systems in virtually all transition economies, with the exception of Czechoslovakia, which has had a high degree of automation at the start of reform. This problem accounts for the abnormally large size and unpredictable variability of the payments float in these economies. The float reflects differences in the timing between credits and debits of accounts caused by delays in transmission and in the subsequent registration of entries which are a cumulative result of several factors. The technical difficulties implicit in the changeover from a monobank to a two-tier banking system transformed the internal inter-branch float into a float involving multiple institutions, one of which became the central bank. The volume of payments too has increased substantially following privatization and the resultant creation of many private enterprises also means monitoring inter-enterprise arrears. This has been accentuated by the absence of penalties on payment delays, the inadequacy of computer facilities, inefficiency of communications, and the limited training of the operating personnel.

Although large floats can occur even in established and well-functioning payments systems due to errors in accounting, documentation or processing or because of communication, transportation or processing bottlenecks, they do not compare in size or volatility with those in the transition economies. The payment float in the Russian Federation fluctuated between 5 per cent and 35 per cent of reserve money during 1992–3 and between 12 and 30 per cent of reserve money in Bulgaria, whereas the corresponding range in the United States over the same period was 0.09–0.27 per cent (Sundararajan and Sensenbrenner, 1994, p. 651; Baliño *et al.*, 1994, p. 392). The float in the transition economies is unpredictable and large relatively to bank reserves which consequently weakens control over the supply of bank reserves, and prevents effective management of liquidity by both the central bank and the commercial banks as well as the use of indirect monetary policy instruments such as open market operations. Payment lags also sharply erode the real value of receipts under high inflation, like the negative effect of inflation and collection lags on tax revenues, and further aggravate the large inter-enterprise arrears, which, if monetized, impair the stance of monetary policy.

There have no doubt been some short-term efficiency gains through courier services, stepped-up use of cable and telegraphic networks for large-value payments, licensing of clearing houses, and consolidation of commercial bank accounts at the central bank. But large-scale systemic changes been generally limited, not only because of the time factor but also on the sheer complexity of the procedures involving many people and institutions. Above all, there is the risk that reform is being driven by technology instead of a policy strategy adapted to a market economy (Sundararajan and Sensenbrenner, 1994, p. 626). In recognition of these problems, several republics have established formal or informal committees under the aegis of their central banks, like the National Payments Councils in Kazakstan and Ukraine.

The progress of financial reform too has been noticeably limited in most of the transitional economies and there is still a tremendous amount of leeway to make up (Table 10.3). In sum, the inadequacies of the payments system and the slow pace of financial reform define the acute constraints on monetary policy in these economies. Financial reform and liberalization have generally been more successful, with the exception of Mongolia, in the transitional economies of Asia (TEAs) than in eastern Europe and the FSU countries (Rana, 1995). The difference in economic performance is explained by both initial conditions and policies in areas such as financial sector reform, price deregulation and enterprise reform as well as in sequencing. For instance, the TEAs (except Malaysia) placed microeconomic reforms ahead of macroeconomic ones. The same study, however, pointedly emphasizes that the 'TEAs need to supplement their reform programs with fiscal, monetary and external sector reforms on an urgent basis, without such actions the successes achieved so far could be at stake' (ibid., p. 1157). Its specific lessons for transitional economies are particularly noteworthy. First, in economies that rely on agriculture and light industry, fiscal and monetary policies are less important in the short term than standard doctrine would make them appear, but effective monetary and fiscal policies are indispensable in the medium term as macroeconomic instability develops. 'Dual pricing, exchange, fiscal and monetary systems may have to be maintained as long as enterprises with soft budget constraints and liberalized enterprises with hard budget constraints coexist' (ibid., p. 1167). The experience of TEAs suggests that evolutionary and pragmatic gradualism can work.

*Table* 10.3 Financial reform in transition economies

| *Little progress*[a] | *Some progress*[b] | *Substantial progress*[c] |
|---|---|---|
| Armenia | Albania | Croatia |
| Azerbaijan | Bulgaria | Czech Republic |
| Belarus | FYR Macedonia | Estonia |
| Georgia | Kyrgyzstan | Hungary |
| Kazakstan | Lithuania | Latvia |
| Tajikistan | Moldova | Poland |
| Turkmenistan | Romania | Slovakia |
| Ukraine | Russian Federation | |
| Uzbekistan | | |

*Notes*:
[a] Little progress beyond the division of the previous monobank into central and commercial banks
[b] Interest rate significantly influencing the allocation of credit
[c] Substantial progress on bank recapitalization, bank auditing and establishment of a functioning prudential supervisory system; significant presence of private banks; full interest rate liberalization with little preferential access to cheap refinancing

*Source*: Excerpted from *EBRD Transition Report*, October 1994, Table 2.1, pp. 10–11.

## 10.3 THE HUMAN FACTOR

Even more daunting than the challenge of building and modernizing the financial infrastructure in the transition economies is the acute shortage of qualified financial manpower.[1] Like the inherited problems of the pre-reform payment system, the staffing of financial institutions too is very much a legacy of the socialist regime when 'people went into banking if they could not perform any other reasonable job' and the 'lack of skill and interest of bank employees brought them little prestige which led in turn to a worsening of their standards' (Poenisch, 1991, p. 18). This is a particularly critical situation considering that 'the essence of banking lies in the assessment, monitoring and risk-handling of loans in circumstances where information is partial and asymmetric (p. 20) and 'it is the absence of expertise in such credit analysis that provides a major barrier to the development of proper Western banking in Eastern Europe and the former Soviet Union' (Goodhart, 1995, p.33). But even the expert credit analyst will have to school himself to think and act as a profit maker in societies where 'competition, profit, speculation, and entrepreneurship generally are still pejorative terms' (Greenspan, 1990, p. 182), a sentiment fully echoed by the Czech Minister of Finance, who remarked that 'there are many serious technical issues which must be solved, but the most pressing obstacle is the ideological prejudice against the market and its side effects' (Vaclav Klaus, 1990, p. 51). At the organizational and training levels also drastic changes in outlook and conduct are called for, in particular of the old managerial cadres who remain in the central bank and who have to learn to resist the temptation to twist the arms of their more dynamic subordinates and 'tell them what to do like providing loans to favored clients' (Poenisch, 1991, p. 17). Central banks too suffer from incompetence and lack of professionalism. The Central Bank of Russia has been evaluated as 'independent but incompetent.'[2]

The massive training programmes offered by international organizations and foreign central and commercial banks have run into serious problems, even allowing for the time and scale factors. These arise from the need to train personnel who have to work at the same time and who often lack the necessary knowledge of foreign languages, which usually the staff from the foreign and economic research and intelligence departments command, but they have no or limited contacts with operational bank staff. Consequently, 'the training carried out so far has thus often by-passed those most in need' and 'foreign travel for training is often considered a gift, which is handed out not to those who might benefit from it, but to 'those with the best contacts or greatest seniority' (Poenisch, 1991, pp. 18–19). Even the best training ceases to be of relevance when personnel find it difficult to apply its results for political or institutional reasons, like rigorous accounting standards in the face of persistent non-performing loans and the will to implement change and reform atrophies if the problem loans are not taken off the balance sheet. In sum, the formidable hurdles posed by culture lag and cognitive dissonance in transition economies have to be boldly faced if reforms are to bite.

## 10.4 MONETARY POLICY

Any evaluation of the monetary policy in the transition economies has to be duly qualified to take account of the difficulties of identifying, measuring and interpreting interest rate and money supply data, which therefore is 'an area in which there is not much scope for successful fine tuning as in developed economies' (Volcker, 1990, p. 8). For instance, analysts have noted the reluctance of the Central Bank of Russia to provide information, coupled with the frequent revisions of monetary statistics, which are often inconsistent (Aslund, 1995, p. 23).

With the progress of financial reforms, interest and exchange rates have become key elements in stabilization policies together with concerted moves to limit or eliminate central bank credit to the government, as, for instance, in Poland, where the independent National Bank is expressly debarred from financing the budget deficit or the state enterprises (National Bank of Poland Act and the Banking Act, 1991) and Hungary where the National Bank can finance the budget deficit on a sliding scale (from 5 per cent, later 4 per cent then 3 per cent) (Bod, 1994, p. 438). The thrust of monetary policy has been increasingly on the use of indirect instruments – primarily market-determined interest rates, open market operations, and refinance auctions, particularly in the central European countries, the Czech Republic, Hungary, and Poland, but in the region as a whole this movement has been hampered in varying degrees by the rudimentary character of financial markets (Table 10.4). The National Bank of Hungary (NBH) pioneered the

*Table* 10.4 Monetary policy instruments used by transition economies

| *Type of instrument* | *Definition* |
|---|---|
| *Direct* | |
| Credit ceilings and controls | Central bank imposes quantitative limits on, or influences the direction of, lending by commercial banks, either generally or selectively. |
| Administered interest rates | Interest rates are fixed directly by the authorities, not by market forces. |
| *Indirect* | |
| Reserve requirements | Every bank is required to hold obligatory reserves at central bank, calculated as percentage of the bank's loans or deposits. |
| Refinance auctions | Auctions at which domestic commercial banks bid for credit from the central bank; when introduced, credit is frequently unsecured, but collateralization is often subsequently introduced. |
| Secured lending | Short-term central bank credit facilities are offered against collateral, often at a penal interest rate. |
| Open market operations | |
| (a) Outright purchases or sales | Sales or purchases of securities by the central bank, as a means of influencing the liquidity of the banking system and short-term interest rates |
| (b) Repos (sale and repurchase agreements) | Sales of securities by the market to the central bank, with agreement to repurchase them on an agreed date at an agreed price; thus similar to a short-term secured loan with the central bank providing temporary liquidity to the market |
| (c) Reverse repos | Sales of securities by the central bank to the market, with an agreement to repurchase them on an agreed date at an agreed price, so temporarily withdrawing liquidity from market |
| (d) Foreign exchange transactions | Spot or swap transactions by central banks with intention of influencing liquidity of money market (may also have direct influence on exchange rate). |

*Source*: Fleming and Cole, 1995, p. 56.

issue of Treasury bills (1989) and their use in open market operations for monetary policy purposes, although indirect instruments were first used in 1987 when they replaced credit ceilings. In the same year reserve requirements also became available as a monetary policy instrument but little initial use was made of them. Currency swaps and repurchase agreements play an identical role in the NBH's refinancing operations, except that swaps are not available for a period of less than one month. The National Bank of Poland first issued treasury bills in 1990 followed by Czechoslovakia in 1992, where the central bank was also faced with the task of sterilizing the large capital inflows following the success of the reform programme, both by increasing reserve requirements and by sales of Czech National Bank bills and treasury bills. With the steady growth in the volume of open market operations maturity dates of securities have also been lengthened in these countries.

Elsewhere the effectiveness of monetary policies has been hampered by the shallowness of financial markets and by an increase in persistent high demand for credit despite rising interest rates due to the 'continuing monopoly power of many enterprises, incomplete price liberalization and slow progress with the pursuit of bankruptcy proceedings,' all of which has made demand for credit insensitive to its price (Fleming and Cole, 1995, p. 56). This conjuncture explains why, for instance, Romania relied on credit controls throughout 1991 and was able to employ more indirect tools like credit auctions to influence liquidity.

Interest rate deregulation has been a key element in the redesign of monetary policy, and has been crafted to address both the large monetary and debt overhang inherited from the socialist era and the price rises following decontrol. But it has not been too easy to determine the optimal level of interest rates which have to be positive in real terms in order to stimulate domestic currency savings, to prevent capital flight, to maintain the adopted exchange rate regime, and to contain inflation. Real rates have been positive in Poland (since February 1990), in Bulgaria (since 1991) and in Romania (since late 1993). Russia too has had a positive real interest regime from November 1993 with the abolition of all subsidized credits and raising of the refinance rate of the Central Bank of Russia (Aslund, 1995, p. 57). The activation of interest policies, however, has generated the inevitable conflicts between central banks with their interest rate stance as an anti-inflation weapon and the low interest bias of finance ministries to reduce costs of debt service.

A noteworthy feature of transition economies is the recourse to central bank credit auctions in Eastern Europe (Bulgaria, the Czech and Slovak Republics, Hungary, and Macedonia, Poland and Romania) and in the FSU countries (including Georgia, Lithuania, Kazakstan, the Kyrgyz Republic, Moldova, and Russia) both as a means to improve monetary control, in conjunction with other instrument, and to promote the development of money markets (Saal and Zamalloa, 1995). Credit auctions operate as a monetary control instrument through direct liquidity effects and through interest rate transmission mechanisms. In so far as banks are required to be in compliance with prudential and reserve regulations to participate in auctions. This also provides a linkage between monetary policy and supervisory roles. Although the amounts auctioned have been relatively small (generally below 20 per cent of the total flow of credit), there has been a gradual increase in the share of auctions in some countries, as, for instance, in Kazakstan (39 per cent in March 1994) and Moldova (80 per cent in January 1994). While the experiences of transition economies demonstrate their role in providing a suitable monetary control instrument and promoting the use of market-based indirect instruments it has also its limitations being a catalyst and a halfway house. It cannot be envisaged as a substitute for an interbank market, or as a lender of last resort for less creditworthy banks after the more creditworthy banks have moved on to interbank or deposit-based funds. On the whole, credit auctions in several East European countries 'appear to have successfully paved the way for the development of interbank markets and more refined open market operations, and do not appear to have resulted in excessive credit or monetary expansion' (Saal and Zamalloa, 1995, p. 204).

The more important lesson of the macroeconomic performance of the transition economies is that monetary policy alone cannot bear the burden of economic adjustment, which requires resolute fiscal policies and appropriate exchange rates supported by institutional legal and infrastructure reforms such as reducing the residual and still large power of the state, slimming down of enterprises, retraining of the work force, ensuring market access for exports and building sound financial institutions (*IMF Survey*, 14 August 1995, p. 255). The Czech Republic's performance, which stands out among transition economies in a number of important aspects stems from prudent and resolute macroeconomic policies, which despite fiscal strains arising from the transformation generated a budget surplus in 1993 and 1994. The Czech success story is well reflected in its unemployment rate (around 3 per cent in 1994), which is the lowest in the region and is considerably below the western European average, and its progressively upgraded credit rating which is higher than that of any other transition economy.

## 10.5 STATUS OF CENTRAL BANKS

The status of central banks in the transition economies is a study in contrast between the larger and the smaller economies which have more or less reached the steady state, with the possible exception of Poland, where a former President of the Bank has just issued a most plaintive appeal: 'Please, Respect the National Bank' (Baka, 1994/95, p. 65). The two major central banks (China and Russia) are still in a state of flux, the former despite the recent legislation. The People's Bank of China (PBC) since 1984, when it hived off its commercial banking activities in 1984, has confined itself mainly to central banking functions of currency issue, monetary policy, prudential supervision, and management of foreign reserves. Its position has now been formalized by the latest legislation (Law on the People's Bank of China adopted at the Third Session of the Eighth National People's Congress, 18 March 1995) which defines its functions as 'the formulation and implementation of monetary policy, establishing and perfecting macro control . . . and strengthening the supervision and control of the financial industry' (Article 1), which is subject to the leadership of the State Council (Article 2). The overall objective is defined as maintaining 'the stability of the value of currency and thereby promoting economic growth' (Article 3) which is in accord with the recent worldwide vogue of according price stability as the prime target of central banks. Likewise, the PBC is debarred from providing the state 'with overdraft facilities' or 'subscribing to and underwriting State and other government bonds' (Article 28) or from acting as guarantor for any organization or individual (Article 29). It is also debarred from providing loans to 'local governments or governmental departments at all levels' but 'may provide loans to banks, and to special financial institutions, as determined by the State Council'

(Article 29). Thus the obligations of the PBC as a lender of last resort are clearly defined. However, its effective independence is debatable in light of the leadership role of the State Council, which also prescribes (and reports to the Standing Committee of the National People's Congress for the record) the functions, organization and procedures of the monetary policy committee of the PBC (Article 11). The PBC is also 'subject to the budgetary control and supervision of the financial department of the State Council' (Article 37). The Law also provides for any losses sustained by the PBC to 'be offset by State allocations' (Article 38). In view of these provisions it is not correct to say that the Law provides 'for the skimpiest oversight by the National People's Congress' (*The Economist*, 15 April 1995, p. 70).

Given the shallowness of Chinese financial markets, which preclude effective money market operations, monetary policy will necessarily have to rely on variations of reserve ratios, the central bank's refinancing rate and its lending quotas, which because of the inflexibility 'in terms of quantity, regional demand, and maturity' are regarded as 'the day-to-day instrument of monetary policy' (Zhengying, 1991, p. 30).

Although the PBC has the most advanced regulatory and supervisory role among the central banks of the transition economies, it is still in the process of modernizing its systems with the help of a World Bank loan. It is fully responsible for regulating and supervising all the former groups of financial institutions (the specialized state-owned banks, the non bank financial institutions, including urban and rural co-operatives, commercial banks, foreign banks and Chinese banks overseas). Such a unitary approach provides, according to official sources, consistency of regulation and supervision, yet the 'lack of various institutions to check and balance one another', is said to be 'a major disadvantage' (Zengyin, 1991, p. 46). It is hard to fathom the rationale of such an ambivalent attitude to unitary supervision (reaffirmed by the Law of 18 March 1995), whose merits are being increasingly recognized all over the world as a corrective to regulatory overkill and regulatory arbitrage. It is interesting to note that the main objectives of bank supervision (onsite and offsite) include not only the protection of depositors and to ensure the implementation of monetary policy, but also to 'create an environment of fair competition' and 'to encourage economic development' (interview with Mr Wang Shugang, Deputy Director, Bank Supervision, in Pringle, 1993/94, p. 75). A high proportion (about 8000) of the PBC's total staff of 170 000 is involved in bank supervision at its peak.

The first annual report of the Russian Central Bank (1993) since 1936 sheds a revealing light on its status and problems since its emergence as a separate entity since 1992 (*Central Banking*, 1994/95, pp. 80–1). There have no doubt been some real reforms like the rudiments of a bank supervision and licensing system: foreign reserves management; a foreign exchange dealing desk; and central control of regional head departments. But its routine operation is still dominated by note issue which is administered through 1400 cash clearing centres operating across 12 time zones (ibid., 84). The bulk of centralized credits granted by the central bank are still routed through government lending committees and the central bank controls barely 4 per cent of its assets. It has just completed the preparatory work on a government short-term non-coupon bonds market, which makes it possible for the central bank to set up a primary and secondary market for government bonds. The amounts and terms of credit to government are set by legislative bodies of the Federation and as of January 1994 99 per cent of the budget deficit was funded by the central bank, which to date remains more of a fiscal agency than a central bank.

# 11 Central Bank Losses

> 'It is most desirable that the Bank of England should earn adequate profits; for the Bank ought to be free to pursue the right policy regardless of the effect on its profits . . . Why should not the Bank of England have both adequate profits and adequate reserves' — *J. M. Keynes*
>
> 'The college may totter but the Bursar's accounts still balance.' — *Sir Arthur Eddington*

## 11.1 THE PROBLEM

The experience of several central banks in recent years proves that, unlike Eddington's college, a central bank does not totter even if its accounts do not balance and generate losses. A central bank discharging traditional central banking functions in a steady and stable macroeconomic environment is normally expected to make profits because it is a monopoly supplying legal tender currency; an essential commodity, which, with an inelastic demand at least up to a minimum level, generates seigniorage. As privileged monopolistic enterprises central banks should not incur losses under normal circumstances. In fact the very notion of central bank losses sounds an economic oxymoron which perhaps accounts, among others, for the virtual absence of even a theoretical analysis of such possibilities in standard presentations of central banking doctrine (for example Sayers, 1967; and de Kock, 1974) as well as in historical reviews of central banking theory and experience (Collins, 1993). The only exceptions to this omission are the earlier treatment of the subject in Kisch and Elkin (1932) and Plumptre (1947).

Indeed, many central banking statutes do not contain adequate provisions regarding the treatment and financing of central bank losses. An IMF review of central banking laws in some sixty countries revealed that about one-third did not contain any specific provisions regarding the treatment of losses (Vaez-Zadeh, 1991, p. 70). Only a few central bank statutes provide for the contingency that the resources of the central bank would not be adequate to cover the losses, thus requiring a transfer from the government. Among these, the only two central bank laws which require transfers from the government are Jamaica and the Solomon Islands. This is the only procedure that would ensure a reduction in non-earning assets set off against a reduction in currency liabilities. Some other statutes (for example, Nepal, Oman, the United Arab Emirates) make the government responsible for compensating the central bank without specifying the procedures and mechanisms, or else require the losses to be imputed to a government advance account (for example, Belize). Some central banking laws (for example, Kenya, Republic of Yemen, Tanzania) by debarring the government from making further appropriations to finance the losses of the central bank, in effect, call for amalgamating central bank losses, which are basically quasi-fiscal deficits, in the government budget. Even where the legal provisions are adequate the tendency in countries where central bank losses had occurred has been to overlook them until they became sizeable enough to pose serious political and macroeconomic issues. Such insouciance in addressing central bank losses could be attributed to the notion that a central bank account cannot become insolvent because central banks, unlike commercial banks, can have persistent negative net worth so that their losses do not need to be funded (Robinson and Stella, 1988). This proposition implies that central bank losses are not of course grave because they can be financed through additional losses or through inflation, in which case the net worth would not remain persistently negative. This contingency can, however, arise when a central bank acquires liabilities of greater market value than the present value of its seignorage revenue (that is, social saving from the use of paper currency instead of gold), calculated for any steady state and service its liabilities only through accelerating inflation (Fry, 1992, pp. 85–6).

In recent years serious central bank losses have occurred in several developing countries, notably in Latin America (Table 11.1) but also in Africa (Gambia and Ghana). Asia (the Philippines), and Europe (Turkey). This problem has naturally engaged the concerns of the International Monetary Fund and the World Bank as part of their financial and technical assistance missions and their staff has also pioneered its analysis (Teijero, 1989; Vaez-Zadeh, 1991; Rodriguez, 1993; Leone, 1994). The data for Latin America show that central bank losses have attained significant proportions of GDP and in some of them they are the major contributors to the consolidated public sector deficit. But despite significant reduction of the nonfinancial public sector deficits, central bank losses 'have

*Table* 11.1 Central bank losses in selected Latin American countries[a] (in per cent of GDP)

| | *1987* | | | *1988* | | | 1989 | | | 1990 | | | 1991 | | | *1992[b]* | | |
|---|---|---|---|---|---|---|---|---|---|---|---|---|---|---|---|---|---|---|
| *Country* | *(1)* | *(2)* | *(3)* | *(1)* | *(2)* | *(3)* | *(1)* | *(2)* | *(3)* | *(1)* | *(2)* | *(3)* | *(1)* | *(2)* | *(3)* | *(1)* | *(2)* | *(3)* |
| Argentina | −0.7 | −4.1 | 4.0 | −0.5 | −4.3 | 2.5 | −4.5 | −12.1 | 2.4 | −0.7 | −1.7 | 2.7 | −0.4 | −0.9 | 3.1 | −0.1 | 0.6 | 4.2 |
| Chile | −3.1 | −0.4 | 4.5 | −3.2 | 2.5 | 4.0 | −1.8 | 5.3 | 4.1 | −2.2 | 3.8 | 4.0 | −1.1 | 2.3 | 4.4 | −1.2 | 3.2 | 4.4 |
| Costa Rica | | −3.5 | −0.3 | 10.0 | −3.3 | −0.3 | 11.0 | −2.8 | −2.9 | 10.0 | −2.0 | −3.0 | 1.9 | −0.2 | 9.5 | −2.0 | 0.5 | 11.0 |
| Guatemala | −2.2 | −1.4 | 9.1 | −1.6 | −1.9 | 8.6 | −1.3 | −3.5 | 9.0 | −2.1 | −2.7 | 7.8 | 8.9 | 0.4 | 7.5 | −1.2 | 0.2 | 7.7 |
| Jamaica | −5.7 | 0.1 | 14.2 | −5.4 | −0.1 | 15.6 | −5.4 | −7.3 | 15.2 | −5.0 | −1.3 | 1.3 | 13.4 | −4.3 | 12.8 | −5.6 | 5.1 | 15.0 |
| Peru | −5.4 | −7.9 | 8.8 | −3.2 | −9.2 | 3.4 | −0.4 | −7.9 | 4.3 | −1.1 | −5.4 | 4.2 | −0.4 | 2.6 | 4.3 | −0.2 | −2.7 | 4.1 |
| Uruguay | −2.8 | −1.5 | 4.4 | −3.1 | −1.9 | 4.5 | −3.4 | −3.5 | 4.2 | −3.6 | 0.5 | 4.3 | −2.2 | 1.3 | 4.3 | −1.6 | 2.1 | 4.1 |
| Venezuela | −1.4 | −5.4 | 13.0 | −2.9 | −9.4 | 6.2 | −1.8 | −1.4 | 5.2 | −2.0 | 1.0 | 5.7 | −1.7 | −3.4 | 8.0 | – | −6.2 | 8.3 |

*Notes*:
(1) Central bank losses
(2) Non-financial public sector balance
(3) Reserve money

[a] Central Bank losses are measured on an accrual basis. Data on reserve money were calculated as the ratio between the average of the stocks of currency issue plus banks' reserve deposits with the central bank at the end of the previous year and current years and the nominal GDP in the current year.

[b] Preliminary figures

*Source*: Excerpted from A.M. Leone, 1994, p. 739.

remained stubbornly high' (Leone, 1994, pp. 738–9). A complete financing of central bank losses would imply a substantial expansion of the monetary base.

## 11.2 CONCEPTS AND MEASUREMENT

Central bank accounting is unique because, among other things:

(1) it reflects the operating results of both its monetary activities and the fiscal activities assumed on behalf of the government, but the distinction between monetary and fiscal activities is not always clear-cut;
(2) its assets and liabilities are denominated in domestic as well as foreign currencies;
(3) it has several contingent liabilities, for example, credit guarantee and deposit insurance schemes; and
(4) its accounting conventions differ from those of the central government and also differ among central banks.

Central bank results (profit or loss) during a given accounting period may be defined and measured:

- on a cash basis relating to the net cash flow during that period;
- on an accrual basis taking account of accrued income and expenses instead of effective cash income and expenses, but excluding valuation changes and capital gains or losses which are captured in
- the changes in net worth concept.

These concepts are complementary and are equally relevant in the particular context for assessing the impact of central bank operations on the economy. Thus the net cash flow concept captures the immediate and consequent impact on monetary conditions, inflationary pressures, and the level of international reserves, and helps to 'assess the net impact that would take place should the losses be financed through reserve money expansion' (Leone, 1994, p. 740).

Likewise, the change in net worth concept is helpful in capturing the change, improvement or deterioration in the overall financial position of a central bank, its possible effects on the credit markets and the long-term effects on inflation and the balance of payments. A change in a central bank's net worth deficit may also have an immediate impact on current inflation even if not reflected in the bank's cash flow, if people perceive a future increase in the rate of money creation and reduce their money demand (Leone, 1994, pp. 740–1).

There are, however, major identification and measurement problems in regard to the financial statements of central banks, which, in general, are recorded on an accrual basis. But there is often a divergence between accounting and cash profits, which may reflect flaws and inadequacies in laws, accounting practices, information and management systems. Thus quite often fictional profit may be generated, given the practice of several central banks of underestimating accrued expenses, related to their most important liabilities, which are recorded in 'assets' accounts while accrued income is entered in 'profit' accounts. There are several factors which impair the transparency of the cash flow position (profits and losses) which is the most relevant magnitude for purposes of short-term monetary programming. It is usually difficult to identify and measure the effective flow of cash income and expense. The profits and losses resulting from daily transactions in foreign exchange are not identified correctly in the financial accounts because the accounting systems do not distinguish the profits or losses resulting from flow transactions from those arising from the revaluation of foreign assets and liabilities. These profits and losses depend on the volume of transactions as well as the spread between the buying and selling rates of foreign currencies. Unlike revaluation losses, losses on foreign exchange transactions, which can be substantial under regimes of multiple and subsidized exchange rates, have an immediate monetary impact. Often the estimation of possible losses on contingent liabilities (domestic and foreign) may not be realistic.

Similarly, the unrealistic valuation of domestic loan portfolio as well as foreign assets and liabilities can distort the true financial position and cash flow profits associated with foreign exchange transactions. A common failing is the widespread convention of many central banks of using a historical exchange rate, or a historical price for gold, for valuation of foreign assets and liabilities, which means that the profits or losses originating from exchange rate fluctuations are not being recognized. This practice can produce particularly serious distortions in accounts of central banks whose foreign liabilities exceed the value of their foreign assets. A related shortcoming is the practice of central banks of posting the counterpart of periodic revaluations of foreign assets and liabilities to a revaluation account that over time becomes a substantial non interest-bearing account. Admittedly, such revaluations, along with the often unrecorded arrears of interest, have no monetary significance but they do constitute capital gains or losses of a significant magnitude, which have to be taken into account to draw a true picture of the real net worth of a central bank and its overall financial position. In sum, the requirements of monetary programming and the need to safeguard the status and credibility of central banks underscore the case for revamping the opaque and outmoded accounting conventions of central banks and for creating realistic and transparent systems of financial statements and profit and loss accounts.

## 11.3 SOURCES: THE FISCALIZATION OF CENTRAL BANKS

Central bank losses, whether current or capital, can arise from the basic central bank activities of safeguarding the value of the currency or the so-called quasi-fiscal activities carried out by the central bank as an agent on behalf of the government as the principal. The quasi-fiscal activities generally refer to central bank activities that are not directly related to the objective of maintaining monetary and financial stability. Typically, they include such functions as management of domestic debt, exchange rates and reserves, prudential regulation and supervision, deposit insurance, economic and financial development, and the redressal of regional and income inequalities. The distinction between basic central banking and quasi-fiscal activities is not always clear-cut since they may straddle activities that affect price stability, even if indirectly. Some of them, like exchange rate and reserve management and prudential supervision, have a direct bearing on price and financial stability and often the central bank may be better fitted to discharge them than any other government agency.

Current losses originate in imbalances in receipts and expenses and occur when earnings from assets are lower than the cost of operations, whether domestic or foreign. The non earning assets of central bank, usually non interest-bearing government loans and securities and the quasi-fiscal activities, are a major contributory cause of current losses. Capital losses arise from differential variations in the value of assets and liabilities. Their accounting treatment also differs inasmuch as current losses (or gains) – whether realized or accrued – are always reflected in the financial results of the central bank. But some capital losses are not so recorded – such as a capital loss arising from an increase in net foreign liabilities due to a change in the exchange rate which is usually excluded from the computation of the annual profit and loss account. Such a loss may be transferred to a valuation account and shown as an item in the balance sheet. This convention allows the net worth and reserves of the central bank to remain intact as a consequence of such a loss until it is realized.

The most common source of capital losses relates to the role of central banks in foreign exchange management, in the course of which many central banks (for example, Argentina, Jamaica, and Turkey) incur substantial foreign liabilities, making them vulnerable to exchange rate fluctuations (Vaez-Zadeh, 1991, p. 75). The large devaluation of the Jamaican dollar (from 1.78 to 5.5 per US dollar during August 1983–February 1985) more than tripled the domestic currency value of the Bank of Jamaica's foreign liabilities and resulted in substantial losses for the Bank of Jamaica, whose non earning assets (that is, the counterpart of its losses) amounted to about three-quarters of its assets as at the end of March 1989. Turkey is an apt example of capital losses arising from the exchange rate guarantees or insurance schemes operated by the central bank, which fixed the debt service in terms of domestic currency. The Central Bank of Turkey on-lent external credits to domestic borrowers at interest rates that were substantially below the average rate of depreciation of the Turkish lira, which consequently amounted to substantial subsidies to them, and generated substantial losses during 1984–8 (Vaez-Zadeh, 1991, p. 76). The Bank Negara Malaysia recorded staggering losses in its foreign exchange operations amounting to RM $9 billion in 1992 and RM $5.7 billion in 1993, which by conventional accounting practices would have wiped out its paid-up capital (RM$100 billion) and its reserves of RM$3.6 billion built up over thirty-five years (Jayasankaran, 1994, pp. 29–31). The then Governor Tan Sri Jaffar Hussein admitted that the central bank had 'made mistakes and errors of judgement' (ibid., p. 29).

The experience of the Central Bank of Taiwan is a singular example of how the excessive appreciation of the domestic currency (NT dollar) against a foreign currency (US dollar) and the tremendous increase in the holdings of foreign assets from only 27 per cent of total assets (1980) to about 96 per cent in 1989 led to huge losses for the central bank as evidenced by the decrease in its net worth from approximately US$1.1 billion (1980) to a negative 1.3 billion in 1989 (Fan and Fan, 1990, pp. 94–5). The steep appreciation of the NT dollar against the US dollar meant a tremendous loss for the central bank, since its major liabilities were all in terms of NT dollars whereas its largest asset; foreign exchange reserves, was in US dollars. Technically, the bankruptcy of the central bank in terms of balance sheet losses did not really matter but the economic repercussions of foreign exchange accumulation were felt in terms of a sharp rise in money supply (from NT$669 billion in 1984 to NT$1905 billion in 1989). In response, the central bank raised the discount rate from 4.5 per cent to 6.5 per cent and the legal reserve requirement for chequing deposits from 25 per cent to 29 per cent, which only created an acute shortage in the required reserves of commercial banks, exacerbated by the central bank's refusal to extend temporary credit. It could not use open market operations because it did not possess a significant amount of government or other securities to sell, since 96 per cent of its total assets were in foreign exchange, which if sold to tighten the money supply would, concomitantly, have led to a further appreciation of the Taiwan dollar. This singular conjuncture of modern mercantilism, central bank bankruptcy, and the limitations of monetary policy posed a policy dilemma which could not be resolved by the central bank alone 'unless a stimulative fiscal policy is adopted' (Fan and Fan, 1990, p. 99). This unusual experience of the Central Bank of Taiwan is instructive in showing that excessive foreign assets and excessive appreciation of the domestic currency can be as much a source of central bank losses as excessive foreign liabilities and depreciation of the domestic currency, except that a negative net worth (the balance sheet position) is less of a problem than losses on the profit and loss account. It also substantiates the point that a central bank can incur losses even when it does not carry quasi-fiscal activities. More importantly, it shows up that monetary policy whether in depression, stagflation, or in a huge current account surplus, cannot be effective unless buttressed by appropriate fiscal policies. The moral: central bank independence as an instrument of monetary policy is not a sufficient condition for an effective macroeconomic management.

The loss experience of the Central Bank of the Philippines (CBP) is an instructive case study of how both internal and external factors can combine to produce a chronic deficit situation (World

Bank, 1992, pp. 28–30). A major source of losses was the debt-service commitments of the CBP on the foreign exchange liabilities of certain public and private enterprises amounting to P 100 billion (*c.* 1986). The CBP also advanced the payment of moratorium interest on maturing obligations of certain public corporations guaranteed by the National Government of the Philippines (NG) the peso equivalent of which had not yet been paid to the CBP. These liabilities led to substantial realized and unrealized losses, as a result of which the CBP had been *de facto* financing the fiscal deficit of the NG. The CBP also did not have adequate foreign reserves to provide forward cover to oil companies to enable them to maintain oil price supports and, consequently, had to enter into swap arrangements to maintain two-tier exchange rates. The mechanics of losses through forward and swap transactions were broadly as follows. Under a forward cover, the CBP agreed to provide foreign exchange at a guaranteed peso price at a future date, but if in the interim the peso depreciated, as it actually did to a level below the stipulated price, the difference was met by the CBP. But a much larger source of losses was the swap arrangement of the CBP with commercial banks in the mid-1980s, whereby the CBP would exchange a swap in peso loan for a foreign currency loan with a major bank. These swap commitments, being contingent liabilities, were treated as off-balance sheet items. The depreciation of the peso in excess of the forward rate meant losses for the CBP. The nature of its foreign liabilities and the related transactions also led to substantial losses for the CBP which accounted on average for about 55 per cent of the consolidated public sector deficit. The fiscal deficit of the NG averaged a modest 3 per cent during 1987–90 only because these losses were *de facto* transferred to the CBP. The domestic transactions of the CBP, like open market operations and loans to financial institutions, were another source of losses although of not of the same magnitude as the foreign transactions. The CBP's large-scale open market operations through sales of its own securities – CB bills – until end 1986 generated losses because of the negative spread on these operations. The CBP's emergency loans to sick financial institutions during the crisis years (1980 and 1987) became non performing assets, in addition to which the CBP accumulated large arrears on its credits to rural banks.

Although quasi-fiscal deficits are common in both Latin American and South Asia, there are significant differences in their magnitudes and generating factors (Rodriguez, 1993, p. 27). Latin American experience suggests that the most common sources of quasi-fiscal deficits are:

- quasi-fiscal expenses such as deposit guarantees
- loan collateralization
- coverage of losses of nationalized banks, often due to interest rate controls and credit rationing systems;
- service of the central bank's debt
- foreign exchange losses
- commercial banking financing of fiscal deficits.

In South Asia (India, Bangladesh, Pakistan) it is noteworthy that the central banks have not been the primary source of public sector financing. Rather their quasi-fiscal deficits result mainly from servicing of domestic public debt that financed primary deficits and losses from directed credit and interest rate controls, which for the most part occurred in the state-owned commercial banks.

Given the diversity of loss experience, it is difficult to generalize about the causes of central bank losses in the developing countries, much less to disaggregate and quantify their relative magnitudes, which cannot be read off from the usually opaque and bland published financial statements and reports. It is only rarely that one finds quantitative orders of magnitude as in the annual report of the Banco de Portugal (1987) which showed in its profit and loss accounts that interest rate subsidies represented 50 per cent of the reported profits for that year (Fry, 1992, p. 89). It is, however, possible to present a taxonomy of the various contributory causes of central bank losses and quasi-fiscal deficits (Table 11.2) as a programme for a feasible corrective agenda to address the problem of identifying, preventing and correcting such losses.

Losses can recur in the performance of even basic central banking functions such as open market operations but the bulk of them are attributable to the performance of fiscal activities, such as

(1) collection of seigniorage;
(2) administration of selective and directed credit policies targeted to channel credit to priority sectors, groups, or regions at subsidized rates of interest through differential rediscount rates or ratios or by portfolio restrictions on commercial banks;

*Table* 11.2 Sources of central banks' losses: a taxonomy

| | *Current losses* |
|---|---|
| 1. | Non-earning assets, such as revaluation accounts, non-interest-bearing government securities and loans, non performing loans |
| 2. | Excessive administrative expenses: for example, establishment outlays, provision of free services such as bank supervision, clearing and payment mechanism; interest on financial institutions' deposits at central bank; cost of issuing high-powered money (minting of coins and printing notes) |
| 3. | Trading losses in domestic open market operations and foreign exchange operations |
| | *Quasi-fiscal activities (subsidies)* |
| 1. | Interest-free or below market rates of interest loans to the government and non financial public sector |
| 2. | Subsidized credit to, and recapitalization of, distressed and sick financial institutions facing liquidity and solvency problems: for example, covering losses of nationalized state banks. |
| 3. | Subsidized credit and rediscounts to priority sectors (such as housing, food procurement, civil supplies, agriculture, strategic industries, nontraditional exports); direct subsidies for export finance |
| 4. | Subsidized implicit or explicit deposit insurance |
| 5. | Onlending with the central bank assuming the foreign exchange risk of foreign finance to the government, financial institutions, and private sector |
| 6. | Net interest costs of government and private sector foreign debt transferred to the central bank |
| 7. | Foreign exchange purchases (sales) at a more depreciated (appreciated) rate than the market rate of exchange in multiple exchange rates, forward operation, swaps, and so on |
| | *Capital and valuation losses* |
| 1. | Use of historic rates of exchange or historic prices for assets (for example, gold). |
| 2. | Adverse fluctuations in the exchange rate of foreign currencies and in prices of foreign securities in the central bank's portfolio |
| 3. | Adverse fluctuations in the prices of domestic securities held by the central bank |
| 4. | Devaluation of the domestic currency when external liabilities exceed external assets |
| 5. | Unrealistic pricing of contingent assets and liabilities (including foreign exchange guarantees) |
| 6. | Non performing and uncollectible loans in the central bank' portfolio (typically related to financing of subsidized sectors and activities) |
| 7. | Purchase of assets of distressed financial institutions at above market prices |
| 8. | Assumption of government and private sector debt at a more appreciated exchange rate than the market rate |
| 9. | Exchange rate guarantees or insurance schemes offered by the central bank that fix the debt service in terms of domestic currency |

*Source*: This table is a modified and enlarged version of Table 2 in A.M. Leone, 1994, p. 745.

(3) foreign exchange operations at non-market clearing prices and foreign exchange guarantees;
(4) subsidizing implicit or explicit deposit insurance and recapitalizing insolvent banks; and
(5) miscellaneous fiscal activities such as tax collection and operation of civil supplies (for example, food and the essential commodities) procurement and trading programmes.

The significant features of central bank profit and loss accounts in developing countries are that: 'as a general rule central bank profits are well below the amount implied by calculations of seignorage revenue' and 'the difference is far larger than any conceivable expenditure on normal central banking activities' such as maintaining the quality of the note issue and 'outlays on staff salaries and benefits' (Fry, 1992, p. 85). The discrepancy between central bank profits and estimates of seigniorage is therefore accounted for by the acquisition of substandard and non performing assets and liabilities, domestic and foreign, not matched by assets of equal value.

## 11.4 MACROECONOMIC IMPLICATIONS

The losses of a central bank have adverse macroeconomic consequences, both directly through their impact on monetary expansion and on the efficiency of monetary policy and management. The public perception that a central bank is not financially sound would understandably undermine its authority and credibility to regulate and supervise the banking and financial system. Likewise, its autonomy in internal management would be most certainly diminished by pressures to make its administrative budget, or even prudential and monetary policies, subject to approval by the government or the legislature, as a means to limit its losses. It has been argued that, 'from a macroeconomic point of view, losses of the central bank are a problem only if they endanger attainment of monetary targets' (Vaez-Zadeh, 1991, p. 77), and that 'central bank losses have created problems in the effective design and implementation of International Monetary Fund programs because of large and unexpected or unexplained movements in "other items net" in the balance sheet of central banks' (Leone, 1994, p. 38). This approach, however, offers a somewhat narrow and limited perspective from the angle of monetary programming and management. It can be readily conceded that central bank losses do create problems for IMF adjustment programmes but it is certainly not the case that they are a problem only if they jeopardize attainment of monetary targets. The operations of the central bank in both domestic and foreign currency affect total liquidity in so far as the central bank's expenditures inject liquidity into the economy, and its receipts constitute a withdrawal of liquidity. The net impact of foreign currency operations on domestic liquidity may occur with a greater time lag. But sooner or later central bank losses lead to money creation (and inflation) and the drain of foreign reserves. Central banks can, of course, postpone the expansionary monetary effect by issuing interest-bearing debt, which, however, only adds to interest liabilities at a future date. This creates a vicious circle of mounting losses and rising remunerated liabilities accompanied by increases in interest rates in each round, which can be avoided as long as the central bank's losses are offset by surpluses in other parts of the public sector. However, surpluses may not be able to match the growing losses, with the result that interest rates would also have to rise, eventually reducing investment and growth, since the public will hold a growing volume of public debt only at increasingly higher rates of interest, with adverse effects on investment, via the crowding-out effect among others, and economic growth. If a central bank can service its debt only through accelerating inflation and decelerating growth, it should be considered insolvent (Vaez-Zadeh, 1991, p. 77).

Central bank losses, especially if they are persistent and large relative to the monetary base, can lead, among other things, to inconsistent use of monetary policy instruments, as in Jamaica, and generally hamper efficient monetary management, whether the central bank relies on indirect market-orientated instruments like open market operations or direct instruments such as regulated interest rates and credit ceilings. Under the indirect method of open market operations, central bank losses lead to progressively higher and more volatile interest rates and complicate both interest rate management and financial programming, besides hampering the development of the money market. Such a scenario may well compel recourse to direct techniques of monetary policy and the resultant distortion of interest rates may impede efficient allocation of resources.

The implications of central bank losses for monetary policy become evident when monetary sterilization is required to offset the impact of fiscal deficits or substantial capital inflows and the resultant appreciation of the local currency. In both cases greater central bank losses will result with negative effects on the overall public sector deficit and monetary control. The pressures for an expansionary monetary policy in order to increase the proportion of non remunerated liabilities in its portfolio, and thereby reduce losses, conflicts with the objective of reducing liquidity to maintain monetary stability.

The experience of Jamaica is particularly instructive in illustrating the macroeconomic implications of central bank losses. The Bank of Jamaica was faced with the task of continuous sterilizing of the monetary impact of its losses (1985–92) by absorbing liquidity from the financial institutions through open market operations, which, however, had to be reinforced by raising the penalty rate for liquidity support to as high as 60 per cent a year in 1989. These measures complicated the management of daily fluctuations in liquidity and further impeded the development of the money market, while they were not adequate to reduce liquidity to the desired level, with the result that the Bank of Jamaica was obliged to continue issuance of its securities (certificates of deposit). The Bank of Jamaica had also incurred substantial net foreign liabilities in order to support the exchange rate and the massive devaluation of the Jamaican dollar (from 1.78 to 5.5 per US dollar during August 1983–February 1985) more than tripled the domestic currency value of its foreign liabilities, resulting in substantial losses for the bank. This scenario explains why central bank losses 'embody inherent bias toward generating inflationary surprises' (Vaez-Zadeh, 1991, p. 78).

## 11.5 SOLUTIONS: ACCOUNTING REFORMS AND DEFISCALIZATION

An essential prerequisite for any effective programme for addressing the problem of central bank losses is a visible improvement in the transparency and purposiveness of central bank accounts, covering flow variables (profit and loss statements) and stock variables that affect the net worth (balance sheet statements), using both accrual-based and cash-based accounts, coupled with techniques of early recognition of liabilities, hidden and contingent, and their regular monitoring. There has been to date a woeful lack of appreciation of the uniqueness and importance of central bank accounting as a tool of monetary and fiscal management whose key element is liability management. There is no central banking counterpart to the concept of effective government accounting (Premchand, 1995). Perhaps this is only one more manifestation of the inexplicable neglect of central bank accounting in mainstream monetary and financial economics even though one of its central concepts – liquidity – is based on application of the balance sheet concept approach. Even the high priest of economic theory, Sir John Hicks, proudly styled himself as an 'accountant among economists' (A. Klamer, 1989, p. 180) but the Levites are still strangely coy in recognizing the contributions that accounting concepts can make toward economic rationality. Hicks pointedly observed: 'I have actually seen business decisions being made on the basis of projected balance sheets. I think that is the rational way to make a business decision.' This stance is equally relevant to central bank decision making and management.

There are several conceptual and practical problems involved in the rationalization of central bank accounts. To begin with, the distinction between monetary and fiscal activities of the central bank is not always clear-cut and a central bank's fiscal activities are not only substantial but quite often hidden and are not easy to quantify, as for instance, contingent liabilities for deposit insurance – credit guarantee programmes. There are also major discrepancies between central bank and non financial public sector accounting, which arise both from use of different accounting criteria and the routing and recording of financial relations between the central bank and the central government and the non financial public sector in multiple accounts which results in improper consolidation or asymmetrical treatment of transactions between the central bank and the non financial public sector (Teijero, 1989, p. 5, 9).

There are also several sources of inconsistencies between central bank and non financial public sector accounting such as adjusting operating results for the effect of inflation, use of multiple exchange rates, differences in the timing, valuation, and recording of transactions, accounting of loans, and treatment of nominal capital gains or losses on foreign exchange transactions. In the final analysis,

> an item by item connection of accounting income and loss statement is preferable, since it allows for an item by item consolidation with nonfinancial public sector deposits which is required for a meaningful

> analysis of the overall deposit composition, and any suggested short cut is therefore appropriate as a consistency check of above the line estimates or as a final global estimate of the central bank's results when the line correctors are not feasible. (Teijero, 1989, p. 17)

However, it is only realistic to recognize that 'in many cases data problems may force the short cut of calculating the central bank result from the changes in its assets and liabilities' (ibid., p. 17). Whatever the data problems, which may be difficult but are certainly not insuparable, the rationalization of central bank accounts merits high priority on the agenda of central banks as well as in the technical assistance programmes of international agencies, particularly the IMF, which is well placed to initiate a programme of internationally accepted accounting standards for central banks. The adequacy and transparency of central bank accounts, both in terms of flows and stocks, is a vital precondition for the efficiency and accountability of its decisions and policies as well as for establishing its effective autonomy or independence.

Concomitantly, appropriate norms have to be specified for accounting and auditing, including norms for distribution of realized central bank profits, the timing of their transfer to the government; and modalities of covering any possible losses. A major institutional reform would be to upgrade the status and powers of the internal auditor in a central bank, who is usually treated as one among several departmental heads, so that the incumbent reports directly to the governor and the board of directors. The format and information content of central bank accounts should in principle accord with the best standard commercial accounting practices. It is a rare central bank that publishes unaudited estimated balance sheets and no profit and loss account (for example, the Saudi Arabian Monetary Agency, *Annual Report*, 1992, pp. 220–1).

Given an adequate and transparent accounting framework, a central bank should aim at both adequate profits and adequate reserves while pursuing the right policy regardless of the effect on its profits. This implies that a central bank does not necessarily behave as a profit maximizer, but more like an efficient market-orientated institution that aims at maintaining its income position and adds adequately to its reserves to cover any possible risks and resultant losses.

A strong income position presupposes a sound balance sheet because of the concept of capital adequacy which, although generally neglected in the literature, is valid for central banks if they are required to behave as market-orientated profit-maximizers. Arguably, a central bank can also become technically insolvent. The uncritical application of capital adequacy ratios formulated for commercial banks, such as those of the Basle Committee, would be misleading given the vastly different intrinsic character of central banks, and 'rough calculations of the capital ratios of central banks based on their published accounts produces widely different results' (O'Grady Walsh, 1991, p. 110). Each central bank should review periodically its capital and reserve position 'because a weak position might oblige it to seek some form of support – financial or legislative – from its government, thereby undermining its independence' (Ibid., p. 110), a dimension so often ignored by advocates of central bank independence. There are also some central banks which do not have any capital – like the Saudi Arabian Monetary Agency (under Article 3 of its charter) (Abdeen and Shook, 1984, p. 149).

An appropriate two-step programme to address the problem of central bank losses would, first, aim at eliminating accumulated past losses and existing non earning assets (through recapitalization) and replace them with market-related interest-bearing assets. As regards improperly priced off-balance sheet items, the option of realistic pricing should be explored if elimination is not deemed feasible. This could take the form of an actuarially adequate premium or fee to cover contingent liabilities. The second and more basic step is the defiscalization of central banks through divestiture of their quasi-fiscal activities and their transfer, along with all foreign liabilities, to the government budget, leaving the central bank to concentrate exclusively on its basic monetary, regulatory and prudential activities, using cost-effective techniques such as charging fees for bank inspection and supervision and for maintenance and improvement of clearing and payment systems, and reliance on government rather than central bank securities, for open market operations. Even after shedding its quasi-fiscal activities, a central bank would still require a strong capital and reserves position. This could be easily eroded, for instance, by appreciation of the domestic currency, which would necessitate writing down the value of its gold and foreign currency assets, or by the trading losses on domestic open market operations. The financial reorganization of central banks would require appropriate and well-defined arrangements governing the relationships between the central bank and the government, including the critical issue of defining the limits of central bank credit to government (discussed in Chapter 13). However, the transformation from a 'loss producing' to a 'profitable bank' is very much in the nature of a 'zero-sum' game since the 'mirror image' of a viable financial position of a central bank 'may be a deterioration in the fiscal stance of the nonfinancial public sector' (A. M. Leone, 1994, p. 748), which may be alleviated by total elimination of some of the quasi-fiscal activities or their transfer to the private or external sectors. Pending transfer of quasi-fiscal activities to the government their costs should be made transparent in central bank accounts. The government may also consider making a provision, as in Brazil, for any subsidies provided indirectly through the central bank. It should, however, be stressed that credit and financial subsidies, whether carried on the books of central bank or government, cannot be treated as open-ended commitments and as such should be subject to rigorous periodic cost-benefit reviews with a view to abolition.

# 12 Organizational Reform

> '... it is not powers or policies that determine competence or effectiveness in the main. It is the quality of personnel and the system of incentives and disincentives that prevails that makes a central bank command the respect it deserves.' — *I. G. Patel*

One of the more glaring ironies and oddities of the prolific debate on central banking reform alike in the industrial and developing countries is the virtual absence of any discussion of the most crucial determinant of the effectiveness of a central bank – the quality and motivation of its personnel at all levels, the chief executive, management and staff. In the ultimate analysis it is the adequacy and efficiency of the central bank's human capital more than its financial structure and range of instruments and statutory powers that will underwrite its credibility as an independent and respected policy-making entity. It is also the most difficult, challenging and time-consuming task that faces any central bank. As a former governor of the Central Bank of Barbados aptly observed, 'the literature on central banking has been concerned primarily with policy issues and with the relationship between the central bank and government rather than with the problems of institutional [and personnel] management' (Blackman, 1993, p. 90). Although central banks are the single most important public enterprise in the developing countries, the overwhelming bulk of research studies relates to the managerial problems of state-owned commercial, industrial and financial enterprises, as for instance, most notably in the World Bank's *Development Report*, 1983 (chapter on 'Management in Development'). The *World Development Report*, 1989, which was devoted to financial systems and policies, recognized the importance of timely and accurate accounts and financial information and of 'good compensation and career prospects', but it did not analyse the staffing problems of financial institutions, particularly the central banks. Hence its somewhat plaintive self-serving confession that it 'has treated in a perfunctory way the human and political dimension of the subject, both in discussing the origins of the financial problems and in offering prescriptions for change' (ibid., p. 132). This institutional stance of the unbenign neglect of personnel and managerial problems is faithfully reflected in the total dearth of published literature on central bank management following the pioneering article by Rudolph Kroc (1972), who advised on the establishment of the Central Bank of Barbados and served as its first General Manager. Kroc observed perceptively:

> Most managers of central banks, especially in developing countries, think of their institutions as being well-managed. In arriving at this judgement, they apply the simple criterion that so far, it has been able to carry out the functions for which it was created. From this narrow point of view, it is difficult to fault their judgement. However, if the performance of these managers is viewed from the vantage point of optimal efficiency in attaining the aims of the central bank in the long run, and in accomplishing its various functions continuously and effectively, the judgement may be quite different.[1] (ibid., p. 43)

His observations, although still relevant, merit reappraisal in the context of the new information age as well as the changing perspective of the functions and objectives of central banks as independent entities in macroeconomic and microeconomic management. This issue can be approached from two angles: first, from a new model of central bank management formulated by Courtney N. Blackman, former Governor of the Central Bank of Barbados, and second, from the general standpoint of bureau and public choice theory.

## 12.1 THE BLACKMAN MANAGERIAL MODEL

Blackman models the central bank as 'an information system utilizing knowledge workers to process inputs of data into outputs of decisions, advice, and education' and explores its managerial implications before leading up to the question: 'How do we measure the performance of a central bank?' (1993, p. 91). The basic elements of the central bank as an information system operating in the domestic and international economy are input, process, output, feedback from output to process to allow for monitoring and correction of performance, and feedback of results back to input. The central bank's information from its principal roles as banker to government and banks, supervisor, fiscal agent of government and foreign exchange manager is collected, classified, retrieved and analysed by the central bank staff of economists, statisticians, computer analysts, accountants, lawyers, and managers subsumed under the category of knowledge workers who constitute an increasing proportion of the staff of a central bank and make it a knowledge institution *par excellence*, using professional, technical and intellectual skills. He believes that to realize the potential of knowledge workers requires a radical reorientation of the management approach in the central banks of the [the Caribbean] region which continue to employ mechanistic–industrial models of management with hierarchical structures and bureaucratic procedures rewarding seniority rather than performance. The productivity of the knowledge worker derives not from the hours worked but from the quality of his or her intellectual contribution, which requires leadership more than direction and supervision. But a knowledge organization is not only a thinking but a perpetually learning organization which requires training, retraining and new learning. Blackman emphasizes four main elements in the organizational design for an effective knowledge-based central bank, which is equally relevant for other developing countries too (ibid., p. 96).

(1) The organizational structure must accommodate lateral communication between knowledge workers because central bank tasks require a mix of different skills and knowledge workers have to be in continuing communication across departments which makes the 'task force' the classic organizational technique of knowledge institutions.
(2) Organizational structures will be increasingly flatter inasmuch as electronic data processing provides for the instantaneous flow of operating results from the frontline to top management thus eliminating several layers of middle management. Also, self-directed knowledge workers do not need detailed and continuous supervision.
(3) Knowledge workers, freed by computerization from repetitive tasks, can be orientated toward multiple rather than specific tasks, and to routinely communicate across departmental and functional barriers.
(4) With the task of top management shifting from command to leadership the organizational structure of the central bank will become less formal and relationships among managers will reflect shared values rather than hierarchical status.

## 12.2 THE ORGANIZATION CHART

Blackman's provocative essay, however, fails to address the intriguing question: why despite advances in managerial science, do the organization charts of central banks the world over, including the radically reformed Reserve Bank of New Zealand, remain stubbornly conventional in retaining the pyramidal structure with variations only in the hierarchical gradations – see Figures 12.1 (Malaysia), 12.2 (Israel), 12.3 (Bulgaria), 12.4 (New Zealand)? The universal persistence of the pyramid would suggest that it is not without enduring merits provided it allows scope for more lateral communication. It is significant that the extensive internal reorganization of the Bank of England (July 1994), while retaining the pyramidal management structure, was

> designed to focus the Bank's management structure as close as possible on the achievement of the Bank's core purposes – monetary stability, financial stability, and the promotion of efficient and competitive financial markets' and to bring the operational and analytical sides of the Bank's work more closely together. (Bank of England 1994, p. 1)

This approach would seem to be relevant even in the developing countries whose central banks have the same goals. In fact as long as the central bank allows the concentric and lateral principle to operate in the management and policy process, the pyramidal structure, far from being a hindrance will be seen as very much of an organizational necessity. This is, however, not to deny the scope for substantial organizational reforms in the central banks of developing countries, many of whom suffer typically from excessive layers of authority and insufficient lateral communication. For instance, the Reserve Bank of India (3) and the Central Bank of Sri Lanka (2), the National Bank of Bulgaria (3) have more than one deputy governor and an intermediate layer of executive directors between the deputy governor and the departmental heads, an arrangement which needlessly clogs the chain of command. The highly efficient Bank of Israel has a noticeably lean and muscular chain of command with the senior department heads and the internal auditor reporting directly to the governor (Figure 12.2). The Central Bank of Cyprus too has a slim chain of command but the head of internal audit reports to the governor through his divisional audit. A universal lacuna in almost all central bank

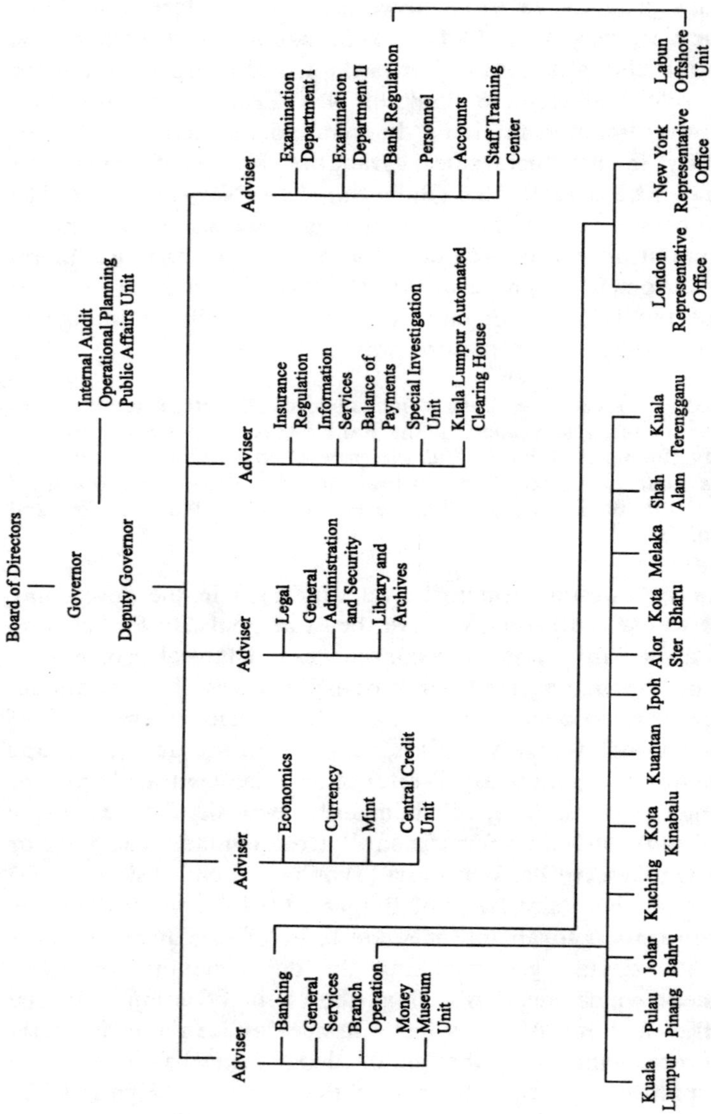


*Source*: Annual Report, 1993, Bank Negara Malaysia, p. 328.

*Figure* 12.1 Bank Negara Malaysia organization chart, 1993

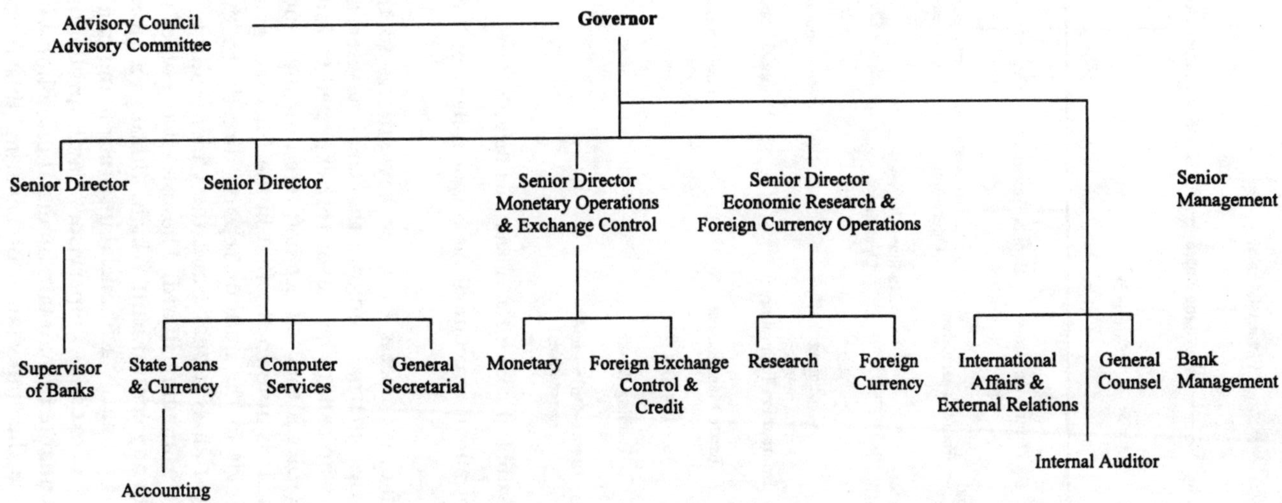


*Source*: Office of Executive Director for Netherlands and Israel, IMF.

*Figure* 12.2 Bank of Israel organization chart

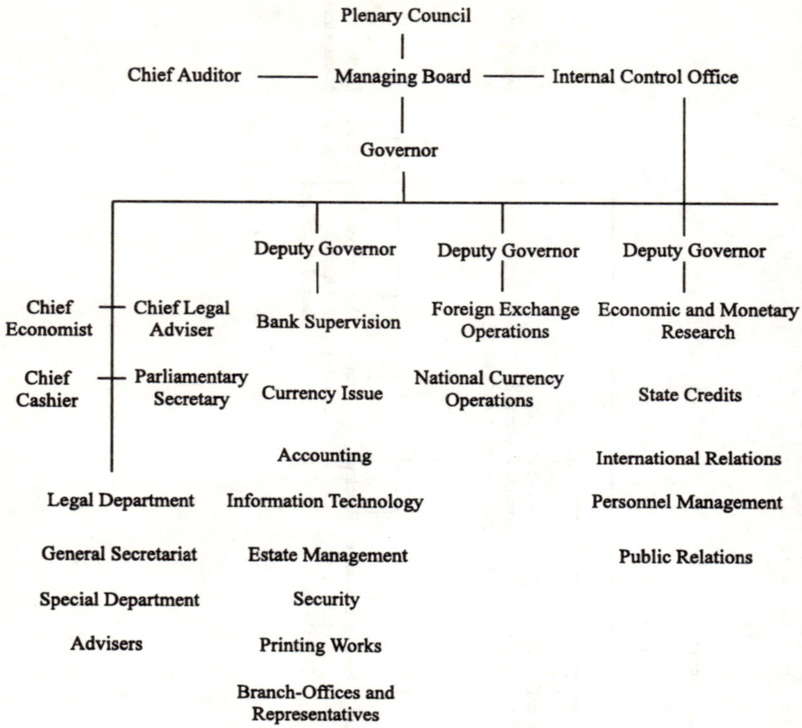


*Source*: Office of Executive Director for Netherlands and Bulgaria, IMF.

*Figure* 12.3 Organizational structure of the National Bank of Bulgaria

statutes is lack of direct access by three key officers to the governor – namely, the internal auditor, the legal adviser and the economic adviser, who cannot be reasonably expected to fulfil their highly responsible roles if their advice is filtered through successive layers of authority. It is noteworthy that in the 1994 reorganization of the Bank of England the auditor reports directly to the Governor. In the Bulgarian National Bank the Chief Auditor reports even higher, to the Managing Board. The role of the chief internal auditor is critical in any central bank which, although a knowledge-based institution, is primarily a financial institution and can scarcely be expected to exercise supervisory and prudential responsibilities if it is unable to maintain financial discipline within the organization. Hence the importance of ensuring this functionary

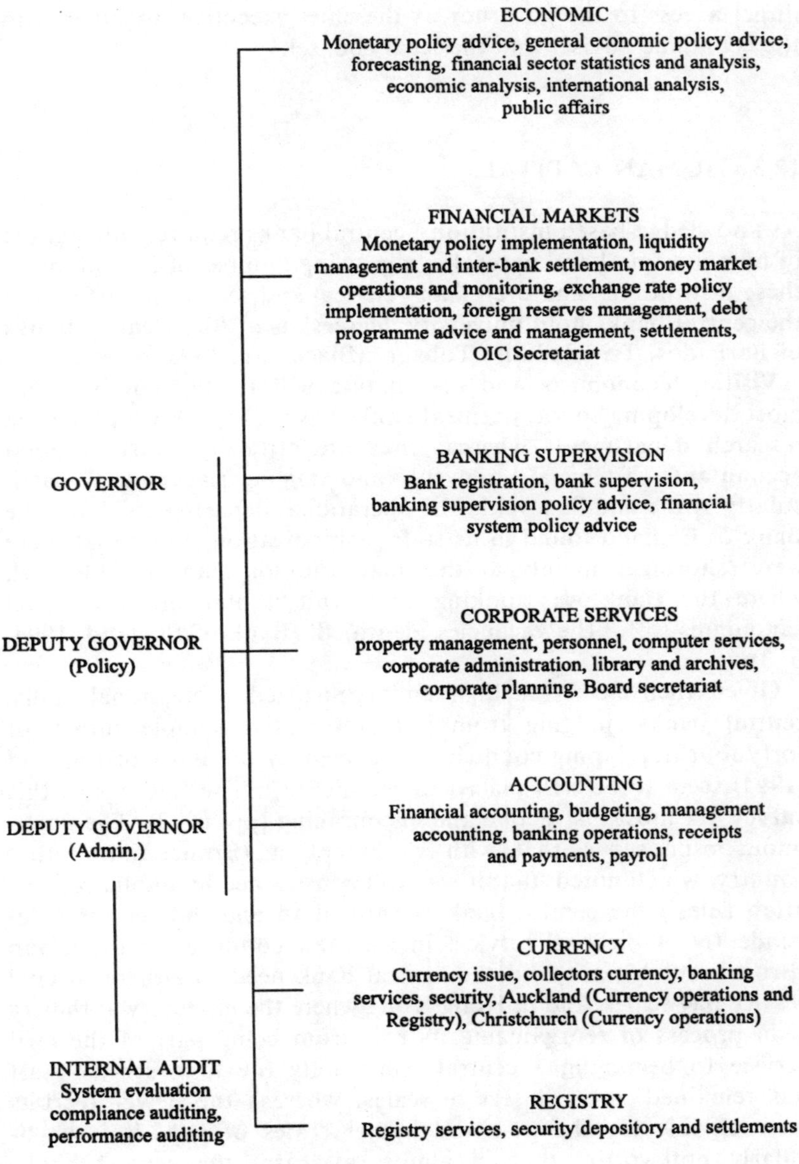


*Source*: Reserve Bank of New Zealand.

*Figure* 12.4 Reserve Bank of New Zealand organization chart.

direct access to the governor as the chief executive, together with the economic adviser and the legal counsel.

## 12.3 HUMAN CAPITAL

As knowledge-based institutions, central banks require a high grade of human capital and naturally 'a growing number of PhDs inhabit these institutions' and even many clerical and secretarial officers at the central banks hold university degrees' as at 'the Central Banks of Barbados, Trinidad and Tobago' (Blackman, 1993, p. 95).

Visiting economists and consultants will readily confirm that most developing country central banks have reasonably well-staffed research departments whereas they are critically short of good accountants, financial analysts, and managerial cadres particularly at the middle level in the operational departments. Even the Bank of England found in its staff reorganization (1994) that there were 'shortages mainly at the analyst/junior management level, where the Bank was looking to recruit a number of external candidates to fill the vacancies identified' (Bank of England, 1994, p. 3).

Given their need for high and specialized professional skills, central banks, judging from a representative sample survey of forty-four developing countries conducted by the Bank of England (1994) seem to be well placed to recruit staff. The findings of this survey are most instructive and encouraging (pp. 60–2). The unanimous response was that, with two exceptions (Brunei and another country, which noted 'that it was still constrained by public corporation rules') the central bank is entitled to and did recruit independently of the civil service. In very few countries of the group (Brunei and Mexico) did the central bank need to adhere to civil service pay scales, and in Hong Kong where the monetary authority is in process of reorganizing its role from being part of the civil service to becoming a central bank, only the long service staff has remained on civil service scales, whereas the newer recruits were eligible for the new and higher scales of pay. It is particularly noteworthy that in almost all cases the central banks with separate pay scales 'reported that these were higher than those of the civil service, in several cases being based both on market forces and on comparable civil service pay scales.' Some reported that their scales were 'close' or 'similar to those in the civil service' (Bangladesh, Botswana, Chile, Saudi Arabia, Swaziland) and 'two central banks just stated that their pay scales were 'different' (Kuwait and Namibia). On the whole, the pay scales were uniformly reported as higher except for Pakistan, 'which stated that its central bank pay scales 'were lower'. The survey concluded that 'given the higher pay scales (than the civil service) and the relatively high esteem, status and public service role of the central bank (combined with the low market risk)' central banks are relatively well placed to recruit job seekers. It is not known whether the survey also included the various fringe benefits such as subsidized housing and transport, concessional loans for housing and cars, medical facilities, and so on, which central banks are also known to offer on a better scale than the civil service, and which further increase the differential of total remuneration and net advantages in favor of the central banks. The autonomy of central banks in recruitment and scales of pay is also a contributory factor to their independence. A good example of this process is the new Act (1986) of the Central Bank of the Netherlands Antilles which confers on the Bank 'the authority to determine its own salary structure, which became independent from the Government's salary structure and rather competitive with that of the commercial banking sector,' a measure which has improved the average quality of the Bank's staff members' (Benard, 1993, p. 104).

The incentive structure of central bank's staff comprises not only the aggregate compensation package and the psychic income from working for a centre of excellence but also from the security of tenure, as in the civil service, which is traditionally associated with central bank service. The self-esteem engendered by the sense of belonging to an elite corps rather like the Brigade of Guards in the army is a material factor in attracting quality staff and sustaining the staff morale and efficiency. Equally, as dynamic knowledge-based institutions perennially on the leaning curve, central banks have to strike a nice balance between maintaining a strong permanent cadre and the need for what Pareto called the 'circulation of elites', and the turnover of decision-makers. As Kenneth Arrow remarks, 'if we think of education as the primary source of information [knowledge] then it is introduced into an organization by its youngest and newest members' but 'the prime need in organizational design is increasing capacity to handle a large agenda' (1974, p. 59). Keeping these desiderata in mind central banks have to maintain a delicate balance between staff and line positions, between tenure and contract jobs, and between seniority and merit in promotions, if they have to stave off intellectual inbreeding and ossification. The human capital of central banks has to face the concurrent tasks of renovation and maintenance through a combination of on-the-job training and working sabbaticals in other central banks, universities, as well as in the private sector. Some central banks (for example, India, Philippines, Sri Lanka) have their own staff training institutes and most of them also seem to provide for training in universities (for example, The Gambia, Jamaica, Malta and Singapore) as well as deputation to international and inter-regional central banking courses. While central banks are generally conscious of the ongoing need for staff training they still seem to suffer from the pervasive malaise of failing to bridge the internal divide between the analytic and the operational staff which often generates a pernicious two cultures ambiance. Transfers to basic departments like currency issue and accounts and to branch offices are traditionally regarded as punitive, rather than as standard personnel procedures. Too often central bank economists readily lapse into a *corps élite* attitude for which the sovereign remedy might be free transferability of professional staff between the analytic, operational and policy departments. Nothing would concentrate young minds so wonderfully as the certainty of periodic transfers.

An important but neglected element in staff morale is an assurance of legal immunity for their official actions and decisions in good faith, which is not always clearly spelt out in central bank statutes. The consequences of such an omission can be serious judging by the experience of the Central Bank of the Philippines whose supervisory staff at one time had to contend with a virtual epidemic of civil suits from bank customers who felt that their legitimate civil rights of access to credit were being denied.

## 12.4 THE GOVERNOR'S ROLE

It is evident that the central bank's unavoidably pyramidal structure has to have strong and effective leadership at the chief executive's level, whether or not one agrees with Blackman that 'the days of the super-star Governor with a large supporting cast are certainly numbered' (1993, p. 129). The governorship of a central bank is one of the most critically important and demanding jobs in any country which consequently requires appropriate dignity, independence of status and reasonable tenure rather like the Chief Justice or the Auditor-General. The office terms of governors, judging from the available data (Table 12.1 and Appendix Table A.2), show a wide range extending from one year to indefinite terms, with the five-year term as the single largest group.

*Table* 12.1 Terms of office of governors/presidents (summary)

| *Term in years* | No. of banks |
|---|---|
| Indefinite | 19 |
| 8 | 2 |
| 7 | 6 |
| 6 | 22 |
| 5 | 58 |
| 4 | 15 |
| 3 | 10 |
| 2 | 1 |
| 1 | 1 |
| Data not available | 36 |

*Source*: *Reprinted from the Morgan Stanley Central Bank Directory*, 1994, published by Central Banking Publications Ltd, with permission of the Editor.

There are no priori criteria for the ideal term of office but it is possible to lay down a few guidelines. First, very short terms of one or two years are much too short to allow the new incumbent to settle down and to master the basics of an increasingly complex bailiwick, regardless of the size of the bank or its economy, and his or her previous experience or knowledge even as an internal candidate. In fact there are examples of very senior and experienced incoming governors who even volunteered to understudy the serving governor before formal assumption of office, as in the case of Benegal Rama Rau, the second governor of the Reserve Bank of India, who understudied the first Indian Governor, C. D. Deshmukh, for a few months. It is said that even Gordon Richardson, one-time Governor of the Bank of England, despite his background in merchant banking, took 'two years to settle into the saddle' as 'he didn't have any idea of economic policy' (Fay, 1988, p. 70). This episode carries a stern moral. Central banks in developing countries might do worse than making it obligatory for the governor-designate to understudy the serving governor for a minimum period which, while adequate for the necessary learning experience, should be flexible. This means that the search process for a successor should commence well ahead of the expiry of the incumbent's term of office. Second, the concept of indefinite terms seems hardly to commend itself despite its adoption by sophisticated central banks such as those of Italy and Finland, since an exceptional governor can always be reappointed. Third, the tendency in some central banks (for example, the Reserve Bank of India) to make very frequent short-term appointments, sometimes even for a few days, amounts to a grotesque caricature of the office which undermines the credibility of not only the incumbent but even more of the bank.[1] It is invidious to nominate to such high office some appointees for a statutory term and others for a derisory short-term when presumably they are deemed eligible to hold the office.

Given the requisite status and adequate length of tenure, what then are the necessary and desirable qualifications and characteristics of a governor, since statutes specify them in understandably general terms of knowledge and experience, and the negative grounds of ineligibility, which are of course applicable to all public office? A statute is rarely as concrete and specific in listing the desirable qualifications for a governor as is the Report on the Central Bank of Chile, which set out 'judgement, tact, broad economic knowledge, initiative, energy, and executive ability' as the desirable virtues of a prospective President of the Bank (Kisch and Elkin, 1932, p. 60). Unquestionably, the office of governor demands a rare combination of the talents of a technocrat, a skilled generalist, and above all that of 'masters of public business' a quality which Alexander Hamilton and James Madison (in *The Federalist Papers*) sought in their politicians and legislators. The notable central bank governors in the developing countries like Blackman (Barbados), Deshmukh, Patel, Manmohan Singh (India), Rachmet Saleh, Arifin Siregar (Indonesia), Arthur Brown (Jamaica), Tun Ismail (Malaysia), Mancera (Mexico), Cuaderno (Philippines), Poey Ungphakorn (Thailand), have all had a strong background, both academic and practical, in economics, banking and finance (Appendix, Table A.1). A more delicate and sensitive issue for a governor is to ensure that, regardless of his or her personal knowledge and experience as an economist, the status and influence of bank's economic adviser is not undermined – in a way an occupational hazard which can occur alike in central banks and international organizations.[2] The central issue of making the right choice of central bank governors raises a number of questions which are well addressed by a former governor of the Reserve Bank of India in an unusually candid appraisal which is pertinent for other central banks too.

> Some conventions should also be followed in regard to making the appointment of RBI Governors as non-political or non-personal as possible. There is no reason why this important post should be the preserve of senior finance ministry officials as it has tended to be for so many years now. Much of what I have said about bank chairmen applies here also, e.g., long tenure and a more explicit role for an independent Board of Directors in the filling up of all vacancies on the Board including that of the Governor. Age bars and short tenures of two or three years are totally misplaced when one wants continuity in this very important job. All that should matter is that there is a good fit between the man and the job and that he has sufficient stature to command respect across party lines. (Patel, 1994, p. 50)

While every central bank statute defines the duties and responsibilities of the governor, the individual status, capability and influence of a governor does impart an extra dimension to the credibility and effectiveness of a central bank, as attested by the role of charismatic governors like Deshmukh (India), Arthur Brown (Jamaica), Horowitz (Israel), Cuaderno (Philippines), Tun Ismail (Malaysia) and Mancera (Mexico). Even in authoritarian regimes central bank governors have shown a rare spirit and courage in resisting the excesses of the executive – for example, Hjalmar Schacht's opposition to Hitler's rearmament drive and Pei Tsu-Yi of the Bank of China who did 'an extraordinary job keeping inflation in China within reason during World War II' but was thrown out by the generalissimo, 'because he was a T. V. Soong man' (Alsop, 1992, p. 230). But the role of individual charisma can be overblown because, as Keynes wisely reminded, there is a distinction between 'the fleeting policies of governors' and 'the policies of the Bank' a nuance which by inference underscores the enduring contribution of a soundly managed professional central bank which does not depend on the accidents of office.

## 12.5 IMPROVING MANAGEMENT: LEARNING FROM NEW ZEALAND

The far-reaching reforms in the structure and policy-making role of the Reserve Bank of New Zealand (RBNZ) (founded in 1934) in the Act of 1988 have also been accompanied by a radical and successful reorganization of its management, which has instructive lessons for central banks in developing countries as it is based on replicable business management concepts (Mendzela, 1994).[3]

Central bank governors traditionally tend to focus on policy issues and external relations rather than internal management even when they have formal responsibility for managing the central bank which in practice devolves on career staff, usually a deputy governor. In the case of the Reserve Bank of New Zealand (RBNZ) the governor took personal responsibility for the restructuring over the period 1988–92 and its results are well reflected in the organization chart after reorganization (1992). The RBNZ as part of New Zealand's economic and political reform, moved from vague multiple objectives, rigid and overstaffed bureaucracy subservient to the ruling government and limited external scrutiny to a single explicit objective of achieving and maintaining stability in the general level of prices, with a leaner staff, operating autonomy, and tight accountability.

Any strategy for improvement involves the twin concepts of 'effectiveness' which 'refers to how well an organization meets its operational responsibilities', and 'efficiency' which 'refers to the quantum of resources applied to operations': that is, 'to be effective means to produce planned outputs; to be efficient means performing activities with minimum inputs' (ibid., p. 1). Admittedly, the effectiveness of a central bank in terms of macroeconomic results is not always easy to measure but the available evidence does substantiate the effectiveness of the RBNZ, judging by the abatement of inflationary expectations consequent upon the achievement of price stability defined as a measured inflation rate of 0.2 per cent in terms of the Policy Targets Agreement. The effectiveness is also borne out by other economic indicators like increasingly accurate liquidity forecasting, smooth functioning of financial markets and interbank settlements, reduced volatility in money and foreign exchange markets. The new accountability mechanisms have worked smoothly. The Policy Targets Agreement set out in formal public agreements with the RBNZ as well as the goals and activities of the bank are monitored in detail through a comprehensive annual report presented to the minister of finance, which is subsequently tabled in Parliament and the RBNZ also appears before a committee of Parliament. A separate five-year funding agreement between the RBNZ and the minister of finance ensures the cost-effectiveness and operating efficiency of the RBNZ. This agreement, which is renegotiable if the bank's functions change substantially, specifies a level of operating expenditure (excluding interest and other costs of servicing financial liabilities), which the bank can deduct in calculating the net profit available to the government. Expenditure in excess of this amount is deducted from the bank's reserves; underspending is added to reserves which are large in relation to annual expenditure. The bank's expenditure is in practice constrained mainly by vigilant public scrutiny.

The operating results of the bank showed startling efficiency gains as reflected in the fall of staff numbers by 43 per cent in five years and a fall in operating expenses of 34 per cent in nominal terms and 43 per cent in real terms. The unification of the note and coin issue by transfer of coinage from the treasury and appropriate changes in currency denominations and formats helped to reduce the cost of new notes by one-third, coupled with increased efficiency in the processing of used notes. To promote efficient property management of the substantial spare office space, the bank charged market rentals to departments, rationalised its own use of space, and increased rental income. It is noteworthy that the key elements in this dramatic turnaround in the managerial efficiency of the RBNZ were neither new nor unusual. Rather the novelty consisted mainly in the resolute application of business concepts to a central bank in contrast to the accepted tradition whereby central banks draw their role models and comparators from the central banking community rather than from business enterprises. But a central bank is a market-orientated organization whose main resource and the main cost in terms of staff time are its personnel. Accordingly, the RBNZ calculated charge-out rates to emphasize the value of staff time and these were used in pricing and resource allocation decisions. The most radical change was the abolition of tenured lifetime careers. All new job contracts for over one-third of the staff, including all senior staff, are for fixed but renewable terms, subject to organizational needs and performance in keeping with the new employment legislation in New Zealand which requires all employers and employees to negotiate and codify individual contracts in supersession of the regulated system based on centralized bargaining and collective industrial awards. The meritocratic principle of appointing the most suitable person, from inside or outside, for the job is now established, and senior vacancies are often advertised externally. The remuneration systems identified the full cost of each employee to the organization based on a 'cash package' remuneration, dispensing with complex fringe benefits. Remuneration, based on cash packages in place of 'cumbersome fringe benefits' is now linked lightly to market norms and individual performance, not length of service, with all staff required to achieve 'effective' rather than 'satisfactory' performance rating in order to be offered renewed contracts or increased remuneration (ibid., p. 21).

The second innovation was to orientate planning, budgeting, and information away from departments to outputs which crossed departmental lines and were defined from the standpoint of the users (customers), linking the expense to its product. The 1992 output lists about 120 outputs classified into eleven functions or 'product groups': monetary policy formulation, market operations; financial system oversight; currency operations; foreign reserves management; banking services; registry services; overseas investment; commission, secretariat; other outputs; property management; service codes; and overheads.

Planning and budgeting (zero-based and participative) were integrated and supported by performance audit and an internal audit with its focus on monitoring internal control measures of managers. Many non core functions have been contracted out but the RBNZ maintains quality control through specifications, tenders and performance standards. The RBNZ publishes detailed information about its objectives, operations, financial results, budgets, and plans and its external reporting has been favourably received by government and parliament and awards from the New Zealand Society of Accountants. The transparency of its activities and reports facilitates public scrutiny but the bank itself has consciously aimed at a high public profile and its efficiency gains have greatly contributed to its credibility and worldwide acclaim.

Concomitantly, there has been a dramatic shift, not without transitional problems, in the organizational culture of the bank with a greater reliance on initiative and judgement and less on rules and precedents. The bank has tried hard to mitigate redundancy issues through mutual consent, early negotiated retirement, and generous cash settlements. The emphasis of staff training has shifted toward ongoing skill development for all staff rather than graduate and post-graduate study for a few. It is noteworthy that the radical managerial transformation of the Reserve Bank of New Zealand has been accomplished without changing the pyramidal structure of the organization, which shows: that hierarchy *per se* is a neutral feature; that it is possible to graft the desirable feature of a concentric structure by developing lateral communication through the concept of an output which embodies interdepartmental inputs.

To conclude, 'the RBNZ achieved major efficiency gains without a loss of effectiveness by applying business management concepts' which can 'with minor limitations, be successfully applied in [other] central banks to increase efficiency' (Mendzela, 1994, p. 23). While this finding would not be controverted it has to be borne in mind that this managerial transformation was accomplished in a small homogeneous, well-governed democratic welfare state, based on a broad socio-political consensus, in support of the price stability objective in the 'best governed country in the world and the most easily governed' (Popper, 1977, p. 112). Would this prescription work, for instance, in central banks like the Reserve Bank of India (RBI) with a strong Luddite trade union that has managed successfully to obstruct even the introduction of rudimentary first generation word processors, and where the governor's time is more likely to be taken up with industrial relations than with monetary policy? Although redundancy in central banks in countries with virtually no social safety nets is likely to pose its own problems, it should not militate against improving management in central banks. An inefficient bank will simply lack the capacity to discharge its basic functions and serve only to undermine its autonomy and its credibility.

## 12.6 BOARD OF DIRECTORS

The role of the board of directors in a central bank is still very much a grey area which has not evoked much systematic discussion, beyond defining the statutory requirements of qualification, size, quorum, composition and term of office – which perhaps conceals an unconscious assumption that a board tends in practice to be more of a rubber stamp than a constructive sounding board with a purposive role in a collegiate decision and policy-making process. Such a role assumes that a board should be regarded as a body of knowledgeable experts, who bring varied qualifications and backgrounds to bear on decision-making, rather than as representatives of special interests which would in effect transform them into paid lobbyists. But an otherwise eligible person should not be disqualified from membership of the board on grounds of being a shareholder in a banking and financial institution, provided there is full disclosure and the shares are put in a blind trust for the duration of office. Any overly restrictive provision would debar many deserving nominees from public service.

It is, however, difficult to determine the optimum size of a board, which varies from three for the Monetary Board in Sri Lanka to nineteen in India and forty in Switzerland (see Table 12.2). A more important consideration is the need for a quorum, which should include government representatives, and the specification of voting majorities, particularly to cover difficult situations involving, for instance, the lender of last resort responsibilities of the bank, even though the normal business is best conducted on a consensual basis. The quorum is better specified in the statute rather than the by-laws and regulations. As regards the term of office, as important as the appropriateness of the length of tenure – preferably not less than three years – is the need to ensure some overlap between incoming and outgoing members in order to provide for the necessary element of continuity. But a board can only be as active as the governor intends, which is an important responsibility of the chief executive. Board passivity is a common phenomenon in developing countries and this is more often than not a subconscious anxiety not to offend the powers-that-be for fear of undermining their professional and business interests.

## 12.7 PUBLIC RELATIONS

Transparency is a prime requisite for an independent and accountable central bank and explaining the rationale of decisions and policies, through the annual reports, press communiqués, press

*Table* 12.2 Composition of the board of directors of central banks – selected countries

| *Country* | *Term of office* | *No. of board members (including the governor)* | *Government representatives on the board* |
|---|---|---|---|
| Germany | 8 | 21[a] | Minister of Finance and Minister of Economy, on invitation without vote (may deter decisions for 2 weeks) |
| India | 4 | 16–19 | Government official |
| Indonesia | 5 | 5–7 | None |
| Japan | 4 | 7 | Representative of Ministry of Finance and a person representing Economic Planning (without vote) |
| Korea | 3 | 9 | Minister of Finance (with vote; may request reconsideration of decisions by the board) |
| Malaysia | 3 | 7–10[b] | Secretary General to the Treasury (with vote) |
| Netherlands | 7 | 5–7[c] | None |
| New Zealand | 5 | 7–10[c] | None |
| Pakistan | 3 | 10[d] | Government official (including one deputy governor with a maximum of 6 deputy governors) |
| Philippines | 6 | 7 | Secretary of Finance, Director General of National Economic Development Authority, and Chairman of the Board of Investment |
| Singapore | 3 | 7 | Minister of Finance who is Chairman and Permanent Secretary of Finance |
| Switzerland | 4 | 40[e] | None. |
| Taiwan | 5 | 11–15 | Minister of Finance and Minister of Eco nomic Affairs (also 2 deputy governors) |
| Thailand | unspecified | 7 | None |
| UK | 4 | 18 | None |
| USA | 14 | 7[f] | None |

*Notes*:

[a] Ten appointed by the government.

[b] None appointed by the government; Parliament elects all the board members.

[c] Depending on the number of deputy governors and non-executive directors appointed

[d] At least ten depending on the number of deputy governors appointed

[e] Twenty-five appointed by the government

[f] All appointed by the government; monetary policy actions are taken by the Federal Open Market Committee composed of the seven governors and six of the twelve Presidents of the Regional Federal Reserve Banks. All of the Presidents of the Federal Reserve Banks are appointed by the Federal Reserve Board.

*Source*: respective statutes.

conferences, speeches, and so on is an important responsibility. This, however, does not necessarily warrant the creation of a special functionary designated as 'public relations officer' except in the larger central banks, like the Reserve Bank of India, which has a full-time officer in charge of public relations. The smaller central banks could well utilize the services of the secretary to the bank and the board of directors. A more delicate issue is the role of the governor/deputy governors in public relations, which is best limited to explaining major changes in policy in appropriate forums. It is only too tempting to strive for higher visibility supported by a compulsive logorrhea. There is always a golden mean between the extremes of a Trappist monastery and the Tower of Babel.

## 12.8 BRANCHES AND OFFICES

A central bank should have an adequate network of branches in the main centres, not only to provide a minimum infrastructure for supply of currency notes, acceptance of tax payments, servicing of public debt, foreign exchange transactions but also serve as purveyors of regional economic intelligence. For instance, the Presidential Commission on Finance and Banking in Sri Lanka pointed out the obvious need for opening regional offices in other centres (besides the three in operation) such as Kandy and Galle but also added that 'the Central Bank should examine how effectively these regional offices have achieved their objectives' (para. (2) xi – 25 of Report, 1992, p. 125). Significantly, the commission also noted: 'If staffing has been a constraint to their effective functioning, it should be ensured that postings of staff to regional offices are made sufficiently attractive in terms of remuneration and perquisites and that there is a systematic rotation of staff as part of the career development process' (ibid., p. 125). The larger central banks such as Indonesia, Malaysia, Philippines, also have representative offices in the main overseas financial centres such as London, New York, Frankfurt, and Tokyo to serve as their eyes and ears and also for operational purposes like loan floatations and similar activities. The banks which do not have such offices like the Reserve Bank of India may well consider opening of such representative offices as part of organizational reform. This should not preclude consideration of having a structure akin to the US Federal Reserve Board which classifies its jurisdiction into districts, which might be particularly suitable for central banks in large federations like India, Brazil, and Nigeria.

## 12.9 ASSESSING A CENTRAL BANK'S PERFORMANCE

Assessing the performance of a central bank is not an easy exercise because of its unique composite and complex character as a knowledge-based apex financial institution which has to function as a public interest bureau while observing the norms of a cost-effective business firm. This suggests some fruitful applications of public choice and bureaucratic theory to developing countries, which to date has been applied extensively to central banks in the industrial countries using maximands such as prestige and self-preservation (Chant and Acheson 1972), reward structure (Goodfriend, 1988), and expense-preference (Boyes *et al.*, 1988). There are several variables that can enter a bureau's utility function such as salary, perquisites, public reputation, power, patronage, on-the-job leisure, output of the bureau, ease of management and fiscal residuum – that is, the surplus over and above the emoluments payable to administrative staff. But a central bank is a *sui generis* public interest bureau whose behaviour has to be explained in terms of a maximand that can capture output variables such as efficacy of monetary, exchange rate and prudential policies. The input variables, however interesting, are subsidiary to public interest. But to date bureau theory has not been applied to analysis of central bank behaviour in developing countries.

Although it is not feasible, and even not very meaningful, to employ quantitative measures of performance, it is possible to specify the broad performance criteria, which also subsume the obligatory in-house performance audit, and relate them to the objectives of the central bank and the quality of the services rendered to each group of its clients, namely, the government, the banking and financial community and the public. The measurement of performance is complicated by 'the fact that whereas the inputs of a central bank are purchased on the market place – labor, supplies, equipment – its outputs are generally not saleable' and also by the variety of its clients and services (Blackman, 1993, p. 98). There are real but not insuperable problems which can be resolved through the type of output accounting adopted by the

Reserve Bank of New Zealand, which compares the cost of an output with the benefits obtained using an output chart with a list of about 120 outputs which fall into eleven functions or product groups, including monetary policy formulation, currency and market operations, financial system oversight, banking and registry services, and foreign reserves management (Mendzela, 1994, pp. 30–7). Illustratively, one can list a few typical measures of cost-effectiveness and operating efficiency as follows:

(1) Processing time for disposal of application for release of foreign exchange, tax payments, replacement of soiled or damaged currency notes, clearance of cheque, payment transfers, minimization of the float, and so on;
(2) Completion of bank inspections as per scheduled cycles;
(3) Rate of return on foreign exchange reserves, using, for instance, pace-maker portfolios farmed out to established international portfolio managers, operating under identical criteria of performance, so as to serve as a standard of performance for the central bank's in-house portfolio manager;
(4) timely publication of statistics, reports and annual accounts.

The indicators of macroeconomic performance such as price targets, if any, are easily identifiable, but it is overly cavalier to say that 'central bank profit is virtually useless as a measure of performance' (Blackman, 1993, p. 98). Although a central bank is not a profit centre, it has to generate an adequate operating surplus to maintain adequate reserves and most certainly to avoid losses, which undermine its credibility and effectiveness. Equally important are the qualitative indicators of performance like the professionalism, integrity and objectivity of the bank.

## 12.10 INTER-CENTRAL BANK CO-OPERATION

Central banks in developing countries can learn and profit not only from their counterparts in the developed countries and the international organizations but also from among their own fraternity, an aspect whose full potential has yet to be tapped. To date the limited inter-central bank co-operation among developing countries has been confined to the subregional level through:

(1) clearing unions such as the Asian Clearing Union (1974), the Asian Clearing House (1971), West African Clearing Union (1976), the Multilateral Clearing Facility of the Caribbean Community (1977);
(2) multilateral balance of payments support entities like the Arab Monetary Fund (1976), the ASEAN Swap Agreement (Association of South-East Asian Nations, 1977), the Andean Reserve Fund (1978); and
(3) research, training and consultative arrangements like the Center for Latin American Studies (CEMLA) in Mexico (1952), the Southeast Asian Central Banks Research and Training Center (SEACEN) in Kuala Lumpur, Malaysia (1977), and the SEANZA (Southeast Asia, Australia and New Zealand) Central Banking Course (1957).

A good example of fruitful inter-central bank co-operation is the Southeast Asian Central Bankers' Group (Fiji, Indonesia, Malaysia, Nepal, Singapore, Sri Lanka and the Indochina countries, with Burma and Korea as observers), which was set up in 1965 to exchange views on current issues such as the amendment to the IMF Articles of Agreement, and commodity problems. Since then it has 'evolved into a policy group for representation in Bank and Fund meetings, with executive directors from our region able to carry on views into the implementation stage' (Vijit Supinit, Governor, Bank of Thailand, 1991, p. 21). Many other countries have expressed interest in the group which meets twice a year, usually in January and during the Fund-Bank Annual Meeting. The SEACEN Center is a concrete result of collaboration by this group. This policy group is an integral part of the Annual Conference of Governors of South East Asian Central Banks, which has been in operation for the last twenty-eight years. Similarly, clearing arrangements have been understandably more productive than payments unions, although some clearing arrangements have not been able to enlarge their membership (for example, the Asian Clearing Union, founded with six members in 1975, has added only one more member (Burma in 1977). On the other hand, there has been hardly any attempt at inter-regional co-operation of central banks in developing countries, which is a reflection alike of the lack of political will as well as of a central organization to evolve and implement a consensus agenda. There is still a widespread notion that developing country central banks can only learn from their counterparts in the industrial countries. Hence the well-merited stricture that

> the carefully cultivated ignorance of people in any country about the experience of people in other countries and the belief . . . that somehow One's Own Country is a unique specimen is perhaps even more applicable to the less developed nations who are often more conversant with ideas and techniques of the developed countries than of similarly placed countries whose experience in particular fields or even generally is likely to be of far greater economic relevance to them. (Johnson, 1976, p. 6)

This reflects 'a habit based on the fallacy that the value of training increases with the distance traveled to get it,' which is followed 'by a natural unwillingness to admit that a neighbor has better facilities than one's own' (Mills, 1961, p. 109).

The belief that technical assistance can only be a one-way street from the industrialized country to the developing country is a particular manifestation of not only ethnocentrism but also misplaced aggregation – in this instance envisaging technical assistance as a vast undifferentiated mass. But in specific areas a less developed country may well have a stock of relevant exportable technical knowledge, depending upon its stage of development, even if the country as a whole is not regarded as technically advanced. This applies equally to central banking and financial technology. There are several areas of financial know-how and technology with a proven track record in many LDCs which are capable of transfer and emulation (such as the Grameen Bank for landless poor in Bangladesh, deposit insurance (India and Pakistan); credit risks insurance (India, Malaysia); pigmy deposits (India); postal giro systems, computerization of financial services (Singapore); rural banking (Ghana); transformation of passive savings banks into active savings and credit institutions (Sri Lanka, Malaysia); mobilization of local savings for local investment (Thailand); inspection and supervision of banks (Singapore, Sri Lanka); constructive monitoring of nonbank financial intermediaries and informal finance (Thailand and Korea); open market operations (Indonesia, Philippines); credit auctions (Bolivia); financial liberalization (Indonesia, Malaysia, Chile, Korea). This points to the formulation of an integrated programme of technical co-operation rather like the TCDC (Technical Co-operation among Developing Countries) of the UNDP, among central banks (TCCB) to promote mutual technical assistance by filling gaps in financial structure and manpower, through advisory services, secondment and exchange of personnel at middle and senior management levels;[4] to create a think-tank and clearing house of know-how and ideas for transfer of appropriate financial technology.

# 13 Independence: Rhetoric and Reality

> '. . . the limitations imposed on new or reorganized banks . . . arise more from the fear and mistrust of political interference than from the needs of Central Banking.' —*Montague Norman* (1927)

> 'One of the primary tenets of accepted central banking thought has been the importance of keeping central banks politically independent.' — *A.F. W. Plumptre* (1939, 1947)

No other aspect of central banking has evoked more attention and discussion in every conceivable forum, academic, financial, and political, than the advocacy of central bank independence of political authority primarily as a countervailing power against the alleged inflationary bias of the executive and the legislature. But this high-powered debate has been conducted largely in the context of the industrial democracies, albeit without much historical perspective, and the terms of the Maastricht Treaty with its absolute prohibition of automatic access for the member countries of the European Community (EC) to credit from the proposed European Central Bank (ECB).[1]

The inflationary bias of governments is explained by three motives: the seigniorage revenue motive; the employment motive; and the balance of payments motive (Cukierman, 1992). The relative importance of these motives varies with the institutional and structural features of countries. Thus the importance of the seigniorage revenue motive (that is, the amount of real resources acquired by the government through new base money increases as a percentage of total government revenues inclusive of the increase in base money) is greater relative to the employment motive in countries with shallow capital markets whose governments cannot issue substantial amounts of public debt. Recourse to seigniorage revenues can also occur due to circumvention of legal limits on government borrowing at the central bank (CB). The evidence suggests that the quantitative impact of political instability on seigniorage is large by comparison with the other explanatory variables. For instance, for the period 1971–82, the following standardized estimates of the coefficients were obtained: political instability, 0.593; agriculture, 0.415; foreign trade, –0.206; GDP per capital, –0.287; urbanization, 0.466; industrialization dummy, 0.571 (Cukierman, 1992, p. 76). Significantly, the same estimates confirmed that political instability, measured by frequency of government change, is a semipermanent feature of the observed countries. Unstable countries collect a large share of their revenues in seigniorage and political polarization induces and accentuates greater reliance on seigniorage (Ibid., p. 76).

In practice, both the revenue and employment motive affect monetary policy. During high inflation, both the employment and the revenue motive are operative but the revenue motive for monetary expansion rises relative to that of the employment motive. In fact, the revenue motive is the dominant inflationary force in developing countries, which also tends to be self-accentuating when lags in tax collection erode the real value of tax revenues (the Olivera–Tanzi effect). This further stimulates the propensity to inflate in order to recoup the lost revenues and raises the rate of monetary expansion. But from this sequence to argue that 'high inflation tends to erode the independence of the central bank', (Cukierman, 1992, p. 77) almost suggests that central bank independence is an intrinsic good, whereas its rationale has to be argued on more substantial grounds of independence as an instrumental good to contain inflation. The perils of such circular reasoning warrant a careful analysis of the real meaning and rationale of central bank independence in developing countries.

## 13.1 INDEPENDENCE: RATIONALE AND CONSTITUENTS

How can independence of the central bank contribute to the effectiveness of monetary policy in achieving internal and external stability in the developing countries? This is a highly complex issue whose several pertinent nuances are only too apt to be overlooked in the somewhat monotheistic advocacy of central bank independence as the panacea for the fiscal aberrations of the executive and the legislature, which has been so characteristic of much of the literature on the subject. A useful starting point for the rationale of central bank independence is:

> The ancient doctrine of the Separation of Powers . . . the issue . . . is political – even institutional – as well as economic. There is the technical economic problem of the Instrument; but it is tied up with the political problem of how to secure that it is used decisively . . . monetary regulation is a major function of government . . . if it is to be exercised decisively, it needs to be separated, in . . . the constitutional sense, from other functions . . . The judicial function, in well-ordered states, is recognized to be a function of government, but a function that is better separated. So it is with the monetary function. (Hicks, 1977, p. 132)

The concept of an independent central bank separates the power to create money from the power to spend money (vested in the executive). The doctrines of separation of powers, and its corollary of checks and balances, are universal in democracies and in pluralist societies, and are particularly relevant in federations where the constitutions provide for curbs on the federal government's financial powers. This explains the strong statutory independence of central banks in federations like the USA, Germany and Switzerland, but not in federations among developing countries like India, Brazil, Malaysia and Nigeria. The doctrine of separation of powers is predicated on an orderly democracy and the rule of law, whereas most developing countries are authoritarian states, where all the other organs of the state, including the central bank, are agents of the executive. But even a constitutional separation of powers offers no safeguard against subsequent encroachment through, for instance, judicial activism which can undermine central bank autonomy, as in Venezuela where the supreme court forced the central bank to set limits on interest rate barely a month after it had freed interest rates in February 1989 (Galbis, 1993, p. 5). On the other hand, democracy by itself offers no assurance of the independence of central banks, as borne out by the experience of the Reserve Bank of India (RBI), the largest and oldest central bank in a functioning democracy under a federal constitution (discussed later, in Section 13.4).

Even abstracting from the political climate, the monetary function, strictly speaking, despite its many sui generis characteristics, is a shared function of the executive and the central bank. For instance, even if monetary policy is the prerogative of a central bank, exchange rate policy is often shared or wholly vested with the government. As the Radcliffe Committee (UK) rightly observed every monetary action has a fiscal content. Conversely, every fiscal action has monetary consequences. Therefore, 'the so-called "separation of powers" is properly speaking a distinction of authorities' (Oakeshott, 1985, p. 145), with the central bank classified as the monetary authority, alongside the executive, an independent judiciary and a democratically elected legislature.

The case for independence of central banks derives essentially from the technocratic argument for insulating monetary policy by entrusting it to organizations that 'will not be tempted by the sirens of partisan politics' (Nordhaus, 1975, p. 188; Lindbeck, 1976, p. 18). From this standpoint 'the central bank can be seen as the repository of reason against the short-term claim of passion' with 'the exchange rate and the price level as 'crucial parameters that under no circumstances should be transformed into political control variables' but then 'the removal of monetary policy [from] the political sphere is itself a political act' (Elster, 1988, pp. 90–1). In contemporary discussions the most decisive argument is that 'central bank independence can be viewed as one way of committing monetary policy to focus mainly on the objective of price stability' (Cukierman, 1992, p. 8). But the arguments for independent central banks are not basically different from those used in support of an objective nonpolitical civil service (Plumptre, 1947, pp. 13–29)

There is arguably an even stronger case for independent central banks in the developing countries given the greater frequency and arbitrariness of political changes coupled with the politicization of finance and the ever present pressures of strident economic populism. But would politicians in such countries respect the autonomy of central banks, even though it might not compromise their ultimate accountability to governments? Equally, would the newly independent central banks command the requisite professional capacity and political will to resist fiscal importunities of governments? 'Is it therefore realistic to postulate a politically independent central bank as an oasis of stability in the midst of political turbulence? If anything, as recent research demonstrates, political instability causes instability at the central bank too, although the spillover varies across country groups and types of political traditions' (Cukierman, 1995). These are hard questions which have not been addressed in the prolific debate on central bank independence which was really initiated in the late 1960s by the International Monetary Fund in a very forceful supportive pronouncement.

> I am in favor of a high degree of central bank independence. This does not mean that I suppose that the central bank can live outside of the

> institutional framework of government (in the broader sense), is divorced from sharing the role of over-all policy making, and can go its blind way ignoring the needs of the country and the broad objectives of government . . . What is meant by independence is that the central bank must be allowed to be a full-fledged partner at the stage when major economic policy decisions are made affecting the price level, the balance of payments, and monetary and credit conditions; and must be enabled to help to carry out such policies with vigor and courage. This means . . . that the government should avoid creating situations of *fait accompli*, where its commitments can be honored only through endorsements of public deficits by the central bank . . . the central banker must, with equal resolution, withstand the demands from the private sector for too easy credit. It is encouraging that in many countries strong and properly independent central banks have emerged. It is also illuminating that these tend to be economically successful countries. (Frank Southard, Jr, Deputy Managing Director, IMF, 1968, p. 19)

Surprisingly, the injunction of central bank independence seems to have lapsed gently into institutional oblivion. It does not seem to have figured either in the Fund's technical assistance or as an element of conditionality in its adjustment programmes. Is this an implicit recognition that central bank independence *per se* is less important than might appear at first blush in the policy menu of successful adjustment programmes which seem unrelated to the degree of independence, judging by the Fund's own review of such programmes (Chapter 3)?

## 13.2 THE CONCEPT

Central bank independence is far from being an unambiguous monistic concept. It can connote several nuances, almost approximating to William Empson's classic 'Seven Types of Ambiguity', which run in dichotomies: political and economic; de jure and de facto; constitutional and statutory; macroeconomic and microeconomic; independence within or from government; strategic (to formulate policy) and tactical (day-to-day operations); independence of choice in instruments or targets; and independence of the executive, judiciary and the legislature. Besides the kinds of independence, there is also the added dimension of the 'relative degrees of independence now possessed by central banks' (Norman, 1932, p. vi). Given the ambiguities, the concept, measurement and legislative formulation of independence becomes problematic and it is therefore particularly instructive to note the major changes in central bank legislation in Latin America, where 'the focus on central bank independence and rooting out old destructive practices have been stronger . . . than anywhere else in the world' (Lindgren and Dueñas, 1994, p. 312). Chile (1989) pioneered the movement for new central bank legislation followed by El Salvador (1991), Argentina, Colombia, Ecuador, Nicaragua, Peru, Venezuela (1992), Bolivia and Mexico (1993). In Mexico the concept of central bank independence has been embodied as a constitutional amendment which is unique among central banks since even the status of the three most independent central banks in the industrial countries, Germany, Switzerland and the USA is statutory and not constitutional. In sum, virtually all countries in Latin America, except Brazil and the Caribbean, have amended or are in the process of revision of central bank legislation which aims at achieving three types of independence, namely, political, macroeconomic, and financial independence. Political independence implies a clear, preferably, a single objective like price stability, separate from others; independent board of directors, appointed for relatively long, staggered terms, but not representing specific interest groups; accountability of the central bank's actions to the public and legislature, and mechanisms for conflict resolution and coordination (Ibid., p. 312). Macroeconomic independence represents the freedom to formulate monetary and exchange rate policy, to choose appropriate policy instruments, and limits on credit to government and banks. Typically, market-based policy instruments strengthen central bank independence. Financial independence requires transparency of accounts, prudential norms such as prohibition of quasi-fiscal subsidies – for example, preferential interest rates, exchange rate guarantees, prohibitions on distribution of non-cash profits, and linkages of losses and net worth to the government budget. But it is important to understand that 'legal independence is not absolute and no state's formal constitution proclaims the independence of a central bank,' which, in a democratic state, needs to be independent subject to diversified accountability (Lastra, 1992, p. 481).

The cross-country tests of correlation using regressions of legal and actual independence of central banks on inflation are, of course, also subject to the usual problems of simultaneity, reverse causality, unobserved variables and measurement errors. The results suggest that formal independence is insignificant in explaining inflation for a wide group of developing countries using the components of formal independence (Tables 13.1 and 13.2), whereas actual independence, measured in terms of governor turnover rates better explains differences in inflation rates. However, the uncritical use of turnover rates, as an index of independence can be positively misleading since a compliant governor may last much longer than the one willing to resist a profligate government.

*Table* 13.1 Central bank independence and inflation 1950–89

| | *Industrial countries* | *Developing countries* |
|---|---|---|
| Legal independence[a] | –1.54 | 0.01 |
| significance level | 5% | Not significant |
| T-statistic | –0.06 | 0.11 |
| Informal authority[b] | –0.08 | 0.28 |
| significance level | 10% | 1% |
| T-statistic | –1.81 | 4.80 |

*Note*:
[a] Legal independence is an aggregated index of differentially weighted aspects of independence stipulated in central bank charters.
[b] Informal authority is governor turnover. Inflation is transformed (geometric decade average of annual inflation divided by one plus annual inflation) to reduce the weight of outliers.

*Source*: Excerpted from Cukierman *et al*., 1992, (fn. 1), 372.

*Table* 13.2 Components of legal independence

| | *High independence* | *Low independence* |
|---|---|---|
| Rules stipulated in central bank charter | | |
| Terms of governor's appointment | long-term litle executive branch role | short-term large executive branch role |
| Policy process | bank has final word in conflict with executive | executive has final word in case of conflict |
| | bank alone formulates monetary policy and has active role in budget process | bank has no role in budget process |
| Central bank objectives | price stability preeminent | conflicting goals stipulated |
| Central bank lending to government | low, stipulated in absolute cash terms | high, specified as percentage of government spending |

*Source*: Maxfield (1994, p. 559).

To date the most comprehensive econometric study of inflation and central bank independence, which also includes the role of the exchange rate regime (Table 13.3) shows that 'for countries with pegged exchange rates, the connection between central bank independence and the country's inflation performance was much weaker than in countries where no such rule was in place', whereas 'for countries whose exchange rate regime has changed over the decade, the relation between central bank independence and inflation was entirely perverse' (Anyadike-Danes, 1995, pp. 339–40).

There are, of course, may influential variables which are difficult to quantify like the professionalism of the staff, the personality and leadership of the governor, and, above all, the traditions governing government–central bank relations. In fact, the disjuncture between formal independence and effectiveness in curbing inflation is well substantiated by the records of the central banks of Thailand, Mexico, Brazil and South Korea (Maxfield, 1994, pp. 560–1). For instance, 'the Bank of Thailand charter does not mention central bank autonomy; the executive board has unconditional authority to dismiss the governor; the Bank has no legal authority in formulation of monetary policy; government borrowing from the central bank is relatively unrestricted. Yet in terms of its ability to influence economic policy broadly, the Bank of Thailand is one of the strongest central banks in the world' (ibid., p. 560), whereas in contrast, while 'the legal independence of the South Korean central bank is the same as that of the Bank of Thailand, yet the Bank of Korea has very little actual authority' (ibid., p. 561). Subsequent research studies based on the comparative performance of the Bank of Japan, one of the more formally dependant central banks, and the US Federal Reserve also contradict the statistical association between formal independence and inflation performance which weakens or disappears with changes in model specification, time periods, and the countries included in the regression (Cargill, 1995, p. 161). The same study also underscores the pitfalls of the transfer function from central bank laws to a numerical index which obscures the important historical, institutional and structural changes occurring in a given country. It rightly concludes that 'the claimed statistical association between low inflation and formal central bank independence should not be given the importance it has been afforded in discussions of how to structure a price stabilizing central bank' (ibid., p. 169). Analysts should also look 'at the incentives financial structures give government politicians,

*Table* 13.3 Inflation and Central bank independence, 1980–9

| *Exchange rate category and country* | *Average annual rate of inflation (%)* | *Turnover rate of central bank governor* | *Index of legal central bank independence* | *Transformed rate of inflation (%)* |
|---|---|---|---|---|
| *Pegged* | | | | |
| Malta | 3 | 0.20 | 0.44 | 0.02 |
| Panama | 3 | 0.20 | 0.22 | 0.02 |
| Ethiopia | 4 | 0.10 | 0.40 | 0.03 |
| Malaysia | 4 | 0.20 | 0.36 | 0.03 |
| Qatar | 4 | 0.00 | 0.20 | 0.03 |
| Romania | 4 | 0.20 | 0.30 | 0.03 |
| Bahamas, The | 6 | 0.20 | 0.41 | 0.05 |
| Barbados | 7 | 0.10 | 0.38 | 0.05 |
| Honduras | 7 | 0.10 | 0.43 | 0.05 |
| Botswana | 10 | 0.40 | 0.33 | 0.09 |
| Kenya | 10 | 0.20 | 0.44 | 0.09 |
| Nepal | 10 | 0.10 | 0.18 | 0.08 |
| Zimbabwe | 12 | 0.10 | 0.20 | 0.11 |
| Venezuela | 19 | 0.50 | 0.43 | 0.16 |
| Tanzania | 27 | 0.10 | 0.44 | 0.21 |
| Nicaragua | 128 | 0.40 | 0.45 | 0.71 |
| *Flexible* | | | | |
| Morocco | 7 | 0.20 | 0.14 | 0.06 |
| Korea, Rep. of | 8 | 0.50 | 0.27 | 0.07 |
| India | 9 | 0.30 | 0.34 | 0.07 |
| Indonesia | 9 | 0.20 | 0.27 | 0.07 |
| Philippines | 13 | 0.20 | 0.43 | 0.11 |
| South Africa | 14 | 0.20 | 0.25 | 0.12 |
| Nigeria | 18 | 0.10 | 0.37 | 0.16 |
| Colombia | 21 | 0.20 | 0.27 | 0.17 |
| Costa Rica | 23 | 0.40 | 0.47 | 0.19 |
| Turkey | 41 | 0.40 | 0.46 | 0.28 |
| Uruguay | 45 | 0.30 | 0.24 | 0.34 |
| Mexico | 50 | 0.30 | 0.34 | 0.38 |
| Yugoslavia | 73 | 0.20 | 0.17 | 0.51 |
| Brazil | 119 | 0.80 | 0.21 | 0.68 |
| Argentina | 143 | 1.00 | 0.40 | 0.74 |
| *Combined* | | | | |
| Singapore | 3 | 0.60 | 0.29 | 0.20 |
| Thailand | 6 | 0.10 | 0.27 | 0.04 |
| Pakistan | 7 | 0.30 | 0.21 | 0.06 |
| China | 8 | 0.30 | 0.29 | 0.07 |
| Western Samoa | 12 | 0.56 | 0.30 | 0.11 |
| Egypt | 16 | 0.30 | 0.49 | 0.13 |
| Chile | 19 | 0.80 | 0.46 | 0.16 |
| Zambia | 25 | 0.50 | 0.33 | 0.20 |
| Ghana | 37 | 0.20 | 0.31 | 0.28 |
| Zaire | 45 | 0.20 | 0.43 | 0.34 |
| Israel | 72 | 0.20 | 0.39 | 0.47 |
| Uganda | 72 | 0.20 | 0.38 | 0.47 |
| Peru | 108 | 0.30 | 0.43 | 0.64 |

*Source*: Anyadike-Danes (1995, p. 337).

private financiers and industrialists, rather than at central bank laws' (Maxfield, 1994, p. 588). The imbalance of research on central bank behaviour in relation to inflation has been well redressed by two important studies which use a political economy approach to suggest how an accommodation of political forces and interests in developing societies 'might be reached to support a more autonomous but not fully independent central bank' (Bowles and White, 1994, p. 234). Similarly, another provocative study 'argues for a view of monetary policy that is driven by political interests in the society because central banks will take strong anti-inflationary action only where there is a coalition of interests politically capable of protecting it' which in industrial countries is represented by the financial sector (Posen, 1994, p. 2). It substantiates why central bank independence does not cause low inflation and that there is no institutional fix for politics.

## 13.3 LIMITS ON CREDIT TO GOVERNMENT

There is, however, one institutional contrivance whose scope and efficacy merits consideration, namely, the limits on central bank credit to government (Tables 13.4 and 13.5), which are, arguably, the most relevant of institutional guarantees of central bank independence (Cukierman *et al.*, 1992), even though there is the example of a wholly independent central bank (New Zealand) which does not rely on explicit constraints on central bank credit to the government. The relevance and efficacy of constraints on central bank credit is essentially an empirical issue, influenced by several country-specific factors, but it is important to recognize that institutional constraints can be circumvented, or if necessary, abrogated, as in the USA, where the President is authorized to grant direct credit to the Treasury when foreign commerce is adversely affected (Cottarelli, 1993, p. 31). Moreover, monetary policy, regardless of the institutional framework, is affected by fiscal policy, as shown by the 'unpleasant monetarist arithmetic' of Sargent and Wallace (1981). Therefore, the issue is not the necessity or sufficiency of institutional constraints on central bank credit as the extent to which they can tilt the balance in favor of the central bank, forcing fiscal policy to adjust to monetary policy. Equally there are occasions when monetary policy has to adjust to fiscal policy, which only serves to underscore the importance of efficient

*Table* 13.4 Regulation of central bank credit to the government (% composition)

| | *Industrial countries* | Developing countries | *Total* |
|---|---|---|---|
| Overdraft facility | | | |
| Prohibited | 43.8 | 56.1 | 52.6 |
| Constrained | 41.8 | 36.6 | 38.6 |
| Unconstrained | 12.4 | 7.3 | 8.8 |
| Total | 100.0 | 100.0 | 100.0 |
| Fixed-term loans and advances | | | |
| Prohibited | 43.8 | 22.0 | 28.0 |
| Constrained (d) | 25.0 | 70.7 | 57.9 |
| Constrained (m) | — | 2.4 | 1.8 |
| Unconstrained (d) | 18.8 | 4.9 | 8.8 |
| Unconstrained (m) | 12.4 | — | 3.4 |
| Total | 100.0 | 100.0 | 100.0 |
| Purchase of government paper (primary market) | | | |
| Prohibited | 25.0 | 19.5 | 21.1 |
| Constrained (d) | 6.2 | 58.6 | 43.9 |
| Constrained (m) | 6.2 | 2.4 | 3.5 |
| Unconstrained (d) | 56.4 | 19.5 | 29.8 |
| Unconstrained (m) | 6.2 | — | 1.7 |
| Total | 100.0 | 100.0 | 100.0 |
| Purchase of government paper (secondary market) | | | |
| Prohibited | — | 19.5 | 14.0 |
| Constrained (d) | — | 26.8 | 19.3 |
| Unconstrained (d) | 100.0 | 53.7 | 66.7 |
| Total | 100.0 | 100.0 | 100.0 |

*Note*: d = discretionary; m = mandatory.
*Source*: Cottarelli, 1993, p. 33.

*Table* 13.5 Alternative ways of expressing constraint on central bank credit to the government

| | *Industrial countries* | Developing countries | *Total* |
|---|---|---|---|
| Fixed in nominal terms | | | |
| In % of | | | |
| (a) current revenue | 8.2 | 20.3 | 24.6 |
| (b) past revenue | 16.7 | 41.4 | 35.8 |
| (c) current expenditure | 16.7 | 7.3 | 9.4 |
| Fixed growth rate | — | 4.9 | 3.8 |
| Other | — | 17.1 | 13.2 |
| Total | 100.0 | 100.0 | 100.0 |

*Source*: Cottarelli, 1993, p. 34.

co-ordination of monetary and fiscal policy rather than a single-minded pursuit of the primacy of monetary policy.

Subject to these caveats, it is possible to specify the criteria of such constraints, which should ensure that the ceiling be set in terms of flows rather than stocks; that all central bank credit to the government be discretionary, securitized, and at market rates, which are features of credit through open market operations through the secondary market (Cottarelli, 1993, p. 26). There is however, the critical condition that, ideally, the most effective and meaningful constraint would be not on central bank credit to government but on total domestic central bank credit (ibid., p. 26). But to extend this logic, even this constraint would not be adequate unless there is also a ceiling on the total public debt of government, as in the USA. The fact that the US national debt ceiling, first imposed in 1941, has had to be periodically revised upward carries its own moral. It has had embarrassing consequences for the US Government from time to time resulting 'in the curious paradox of Congress refusing to permit the Government to obtain the funds needed to carry out the programs that Congress itself has approved' (M.A. Robinson, 1959, p. 5), culminating in the shutdown of the US Government (*c.* November 1995) following the refusal of Congress to raise the debt ceiling above $4.7 trillion. In fact, the national debt ceiling in the US is shown as having: fostered budgetary subterfuge; hampered proper debt management; interfered with compensatory measures during recession; jeopardized long-run defence policy; and increased the cost of financing the government (M.A. Robinson, 1959, p. 102). An expert witness before a Committee of the Ninety-Ninth US Congress concluded that 'the debt limit itself is an anachronism' and 'the balanced budget amendment is upside-down economics . . . the real issue is the level of Federal outlays' (Snyder, 1986, pp. 34–5). In sum, central bank credit and public debt ceilings are better viewed as speed-breakers, a means of exercising constitutional control over public borrowing, rather than absolute barriers.

## 3.4 THE RESERVE BANK OF INDIA: CENTRAL BANK OR FISCAL AGENCY?

The history of the Reserve Bank of India (RBI) is an instructive case study in institutional attrition in a functioning democracy. Since its establishment (1935) the RBI has functioned under an inherent constraint because 'there is no constitutional provision indicating the lines of demarcation between the Government and the Reserve Bank in the field of monetary authority', as stated by a former governor.[2] An official publication of the RBI noted candidly 'that in practice the regulation of money supply is not wholly or even largely under the Bank's control. It is considerably affected by the budgetary operations of the Government, over which the Bank has no control' (Reserve Bank of India, 1957, p. 11). There was only one period (1951–6) during which there was perfect co-ordination between the Finance Minister (Deshmukh) and a former governor, and the RBI under Bengal Rama Rau, an admiring friend 'an all-time demonstration of the importance of equal partnership of a kind which was not much in evidence in the years to come' (de Costa, the official historian, 1985, p. 59). In the event the RBI under Iengar, Rama Rau's successor, 'readily agreed . . . to increase the net bank credit to the government' which 'reached a peak in the Second Plan' (ibid., p. 83).[3] Thus, India presents the curious contradiction of a political separation of powers without a corresponding separation of economic powers between the government and the central bank. As a former deputy governor notes perceptively, 'there is no clear understanding as to where, and in what measure, its [RBI] authority should generally be respected by the government' and 'it is this deliberate fudging of jurisdiction that has adversely affected the capability and moral authority of the RBI and hence its effectiveness' (Krishnaswamy, 1985, p. 37). According to him, 'the Emergency settled once for all the issue in favor of the Government by force majeure' and the long process of requiring the Reserve Bank to seek formally or informally the 'approval' of the Government of India on matters of banking administration and policy, including internal administration, was complete' (ibid., p. 35).[4] This assessment is fully corroborated by a former economic consultant to the Government of India who remarks that for decades the RBI 'has acted as a faithful implementer of the wishes of the Finance Ministry' and 'almost all its practices [credit regulation] can be traced to the orders of the Finance Ministry at one time or another' (Desai, 1994, p. 133).

The attrition of the RBI has been further accentuated by the creation of the ill-conceived Banking Department in the Government of India, which a former governor justifies as being necessary to 'mastermind and implement a financial as well as a physical plan of rationalization and restructuring of the nationalized banks' since it is doubtful whether 'the RBI . . . can or should do the job on its own' (Patel, 1994, p. 45). The underlying rationale, although not explicated, is questionable considering that nationalization 'only accelerated the politicization and emasculation of the RBI (Krishnaswamy, 1985, p. 35). Meanwhile, this set-up has only served to foster bureaucratic in-fighting on the relative roles of the Government of India's Departments of Economic Affairs and of Banking *vis-à-vis* the RBI and between the latter and the RBI's Department of Banking Operations (ibid., p. 35).

In light of all this it strains credibility when a former Governor can confidently assert 'that government respects the autonomy of the Reserve Bank' (Venkitaramanan, 1992, p. 20). The crowning irony, seldom noticed even by Indian commentators, is that the RBI, which was envisaged even in the colonial regime, as 'an independent authority which can act with continuity' (Sir George Schuster, Finance Member, c. 1933, cited in Reserve Bank of India, 1970, p. 39), enjoyed more autonomy before independence under both British and Indian governors on varied issues like gold and silver sales, bank rate changes, sterling balances (Deshmukh, 1948). It is no secret that Deshmukh overcame the strong internal and external opposition to the creation of a Research Department in the RBI. It remains to be seen whether the recent agreement between the Government of India and the RBI (9 September 1994), whereby the automatic monetization of the budget deficit through the issue of ad hoc treasury bills is to be phased out over a period of three years and abolished altogether from 1997–8, would impart genuine flexibility in its monetary policy and, concomitantly, initiate the process of greater autonomy. Meanwhile, RBI experience serves as an instructive lesson on how easily a highly professional central bank can slide down the Gadarene slope to virtual ineffectiveness. Its post-independence record is one of exponential enlargement of quasi-fiscal activities such as industrial and agricultural finance concurrently with an abdication of monetary control and some egregious regulatory failures as in respect of the great securities scam of c. 1992–3.

## 13.5 THE PRIVATIZATION OPTION: COMPLETE OR PARTIAL?

A transparent institutional mechanism for 'keeping central banks politically independent' is 'the election of directors by private shareholders or by the commercial banks, in short by some group other than the Government of the day' (Plumptre, 1947, p. 23). But Plumptre thought such an attempt 'is doubly doomed to failure' because, first, 'there is no such thing as an "unbiased" or "scientific" monetary policy' and, second 'shareholder election is practically certain to result in a board with strong biases in certain directions because it will be composed of a group of men with very similar outlooks' (ibid., p. 25). The second reason sounds like a non sequitur and today monetary policy is much more scientific. Therefore, the relevant issue, which has hardly figured in public discussion,[5] is whether privatization of central banks, in full or in part, can be viewed as a feasible option to ensure independence through market discipline.

Admittedly, there is no unique correlation between the ownership of a central bank and its responsibilities and performance. Thus the privately owned Bank of England functioned as a responsible central bank even before its nationalization (1946) and any criticism of its policies was unrelated to its ownership. Today the overwhelming majority of central banks are wholly state-owned. The South African Reserve Bank is the only central bank which has been fully owned by private shareholders since its inception in 1920, a fact which has in no way constrained its monetary and exchange rate policies or its prudential responsibilities. Its shareholders are entitled to only a fixed rate of return which is an added safeguard. There are only six central banks (Austria, Belgium, Italy, Japan, Switzerland, and Turkey) which have mixed state and private ownerships whose record compares favourably with those of the wholly state-owned central banks.

Most central banks in developing countries were established as fully state-owned institutions and even those which were initially privately owned were subsequently transformed into state-owned entities (for example, Afghanistan, Bolivia, Costa Rica, India, Indoneisa, Iraq, and Nicaragua). Although the rationale for full state-ownership of central banks has never been fully spelt out, it is implicitly based on the assumption that given the macroeconomic responsibilities of the central bank as the controller and regulator of the cost, availability and supply of money and its prudential functions and powers, its ownership cannot be wholly vested in a privately owned profit-making corporation. Nevertheless, it is surprising that in the burgeoning debate on financial liberalization and privatization hardly any voices have been raised to plead for full or partial privatization of central banks when so many established public institutions, including even the post office, are touted as prime candidates for privatization. Ownership, *per se*, does not necessarily make any material difference to the policy independence of a central bank – as evidenced, for instance, by the German Bundesbank which is perhaps the most independent of central banks despite being fully owned by the state. Furthermore, it may not be practical politics or even sound economics for central banks in developing countries to be fully privatized. Nevertheless, the case for at least partial privatization of central banks in developing countries could be argued on grounds of its merits as an effective supplementary means of strengthening the independence of central banks by enabling the representation of influential and knowledgeable directors from the private sector, who would thereby be able to offer constructive inputs in monetary decision and policy-making while reflecting the legitimate concerns of the private sector in an open forum subject to public scrutiny through the periodic meetings of the board and its annual reports. Such an arrangement would function as a part of the process of checks and balances as well as enhancing the transparency of the policy-making process. Directors elected by private shareholders may be relied upon to be more vocal and articulate than directors nominated by the government. For instance, the annals of the pre-independence Reserve Bank of India typify the role of private members of the board of directors – for example, the late Sir Purshotamdas Thakurdas, a notably constructive public gadfly, whose efforts were supported by several inglorious but seldom mute Miltons among private shareholders of the *pro buono* species whose heckling was duly followed up by letters to the press. Old-timers recall that the annual meetings of the pre-independence Reserve Bank of India had all the vivacity and ambiance of a New England town meeting or a New Hampshire political forum. The lacklustre post-nationalization boards of the Reserve Bank of India, although not lacking in talent, have been sadly deficient in public spirit.

The debate preceding the post-independence nationalization of the Reserve Bank of India is in fact especially instructive and relevant on the economic as distinct from the political merits of private and mixed ownership of a central bank. The principal justification for establishing the Reserve Bank of India as a shareholders' bank in the pre-independence days was well put by Sir George Schuster, the British Finance Member of the Government of India, that 'Government, as the chief user of money, shall not themselves be the authority controlling the creation of money, but that when they needed money, they should have to go to an independent authority and make out their case just as any private individual had to do' (Reserve Bank of India, 1970, pp. 510–11). The then Finance Member of the Government of India, Sir Archibald Rowlands stated (1946) that 'the real reason why it [the Reserve Bank of India] was not nationalized in the first instance was that the Legislature was not prepared to commit to the sole charge of an irresponsible executive an institution which plays such an important part in the economic life of India' (ibid., p. 507). This point of view is eminently in consonance with the doctrine of checks and balances and separation of powers as important props of the requisite independence of the central bank. This stance was further endorsed by the categorical statement of the first Indian governor of the RBI after independence (c. 1948) that 'as things stood, nationalization of the Bank was neither called for nor was it likely to be beneficial' and 'the Board of the Bank was "a body of very responsible business or public men who may be trusted to take a dispassionate view of the matter from the point of view of the country's economy (ibid., p. 515). The Reserve Bank also felt that nationalization would not lead to any increased efficiency in the running of the bank, but rather that its processes would be slowed down and its efficiency impaired owing to the intrusion of extraneous factors (communication of Deputy Governor Charles Trevor to the Government of India: ibid., p. 508). Thus on grounds of independence and efficiency alike the Reserve Bank of India resisted nationalization, which in the event was consummated more for political and ideological reasons as a concomitant of the country's fully-fledged independence.

The case for mixed ownership through partial privatization as a mechanism for enhanced professionalism and autonomy, and greater market-orientation merits serious consideration. The proportion of state and private ownership could vary within a range of 60:40 per cent with provision for external private audit and a variable dividend, subject to the distribution of surplus profits, after the necessary transfers to reserves, to the government, and listing on the stock exchange (as in Switzerland and South Africa). It would be desirable to provide simultaneously for limiting the number of votes any one shareholder can exercise as in the original Reserve Bank of India Act 1935 to prevent concentration of voting rights and to permit a variable dividend, unlike the ceiling of 5 per cent for the RBI shares or the fixed rate of dividend in the case of the South African Reserve Bank. A variable dividend would be more appropriate for a market-orientated institution. The central bank's stock price might well emerge as a reliable bell-weather. Such an arrangement would provide the central bank with an excellent sounding board and also subject it to some degree of market discipline and access to market intelligence. The retention of the government as the majority shareholder would recognize official responsibilities of the central bank for monetary policy and prudential functions.

# 14 Conclusion: Toward Effective Central Banking

'... it is of the utmost importance that the policy of the Bank and the policy of the Government should at all times be in as complete harmony as possible.' —*Montague Norman* (*c.* 1926)

'... the economic problem in the developing countries ... can be tackled only through simultaneous adoption – and adaptation – of the monetary-fiscal policies and other instruments of economic policy.' —*C.D. Deshmukh* (1969)

'It is important for monetary and fiscal policy to stay on the same page.' —*R.M. Solow* (1994)

It is not mere happenstance that the pronouncements of two luminaries among central bank governors, from the industrial and developing world respectively, and separated by over four decades, should emphasize the simultaneity and harmonization of different elements of national economic policies – a stance uncannily echoed by an economics Nobel laureate three decades later. This is a recognition and a much-needed reminder that macroeconomic management is a seamless web whose intertwined threads comprise not only monetary, fiscal and exchange rate policies but also incomes, prices and supply-side policies. It also serves to highlight the real challenge facing central banks: how effectively can they contribute to the implementation and harmonization of macroeconomic objectives and policies through monetary and exchange rate policies aimed at protecting the internal and external value of the currency and help generate the maximum policy synergies?

The statutory primacy of price stability as a central bank objective confers no assurance of its feasibility, which in fact depends on a close concordat between the central bank and the government as so well exemplified in the agreement between the Reserve Bank of New Zealand and the Government of New Zealand (The Fiscal Responsibility Act, 1994). But such social contracts presuppose a strong anti-inflationary social and political consensus as in Germany where it serves to bolster the commitment of the Bundesbank. The 'control of inflation is ultimately a political problem' which 'can be kept down if you have the political will to do so, as the Germans do because of their bitter experience of hyperinflation' (Thatcher, 1993, p. 707). Central bankers too would concur with this diagnosis. Thus, 'a large fiscal deficit . . . often reflects a country's inability to resolve social conflicts over income and wealth distribution' (Bruno, 1991, p. 252). The control of inflation has therefore to arbitrate between the conflicting claims of different income and occupational groups on the national dividend, which implies an incomes policy, whether implicit or explicit, acting as a necessary adjunct to monetary and fiscal policies. Therefore, the real challenge before the developing countries is to evolve and implement a 'therapy by consensus' (ibid., 1991) against inflation rather than establishing the mere statutory primacy of price stability. Too often developing countries are habitual victims of misplaced concreteness in this as in other spheres of economic organization and policy.

This in turn poses the question: given a favourable socio-political conjuncture, does a central bank have the requisite number and range of instruments to aim at monetary, exchange rate and price targets? This includes not only the usual monetary policy instruments but also the exchange rate, a dimension often overlooked by advocates of central bank independence who seem only too willing to concede the optional nature of exchange rate policy for the central bank, and let the government retain responsibility for the exchange rate regime. Central banks are supposed to be primarily managers of foreign reserves and intervention policies but often have little or no part in the choice of the exchange rate regime. This is a strategic instrument and objective in which the central bank should have an equal input with the government.

The efficacy of indirect monetary policies operating through open market operations and interest rate management is contingent upon liberalized interest rates and financial systems with wide and active dealer-based securities markets, primary and secondary. This presupposes that reserve ratios (remunerated) are best kept at a prudential minimum and that statutory liquid asset ratios, which only serve as a captive market for government borrowing and hamper monetary policy are abolished. Equally important is the divestiture of all quasi-fiscal developmental activities of the central bank which conflict with its monetary policy and prudential roles. Divestiture need not preclude a positive stance toward development of the financial infrastructure, particularly an efficient clearing and payments system. Concomitantly the prudential role of a central bank in maintaining systemic stability becomes even more important in liberalized financial systems.

How relevant is the so-called independence of central banks to their efficiency considering that this legitimate term of art has become a monotheistic mantra with all the overtones of a strident monetary evangelism redolent of the litany of single and simple panaceas like currency boards, balanced budgets, debt ceilings, single taxes (Henry George) flat taxes and social credit (Major Douglas). But independence *per se*, no matter how defined, offers no assurance of the technical and institutional capability of a central bank, which, as a knowledge-based public interest bureau, derives its credibility from the professionalism and integrity of its staff at all levels. Above all, it requires the resolute leadership of governors who answer to the Federalist Papers description of 'masters of public business' and who come to their office with the requisite apprenticeship in banking and finance, including a necessary stint as understudy to the outgoing incumbent. The adequacy and efficiency of the human capital of central banks has been all but overlooked in the contemporary bemusement with the formal status of central banks. The radical personnel and organizational reforms of the Reserve Bank of New Zealand give point and substance to its formal independence, a feature which has hardly evoked any attention in the midst of the universal acclamation of its independence. Even more instructive are the inspiring examples of highly effective central banks like those of Thailand and Mexico, based on their superb professionalism and unblemished rectitude. The Bank of Thailand does not enjoy formal independence and yet has played a decisive role in monetary, prudential and fiscal policies, and acquired a moral and political stature far transcending its legal authority. The Bank of Mexico's widely acclaimed effectiveness and reputation vastly antedate its recent acquisition of statutory independence. The Bank of Israel's authority and influence are unrelated to its formal status. As a counterpoint there is the stern object lesson of how even a professional central bank like the Reserve Bank of India, which, ironically, enjoyed genuine independence in the colonial days, can be swiftly transformed after independence into a fiscal agency and a dysfunctional monetary and regulatory authority, with governors subject to kaleidoscopic tenures.

A crucial but little discussed element in the professionalism of central banks in developing countries is the weakness of hands-on market contacts and the tendency to equate expertise too uncritically with academic credentials and analytic skills to the neglect of market-based judgmental skills, insights, and on-the-job experience. The market orientation and market discipline of central banks in developing countries would only be enhanced if they were to be partially privatized and listed on the stock exchange, an overlooked option which merits serious consideration.

Central bank–government relations are known to carry the potential for conflicts, whether arising from endogenous factors, such as choice of instruments and objectives, responses to liquidity and solvency problems, or exogenous factors like constitutional and institutional rigidities, jurisdictional disputes, and personality conflicts. The prevailing obsession with a hypothetical inoperable concept of independence carries the real risk of generating an adversarial in place of a collegial economic culture based on avoidance of conflicts through coherent mechanisms and procedures for coordination of monetary, exchange rate, and fiscal policies in consonance with 'the common funnel theorem' (Tobin, 1982, p. 18). This theorem posits that it is 'the total size of a demand management package, whatever its fiscal-monetary mix, that helps determine the combination of output and employment results . . . and nominal wage and price movements' which implies that 'relative to those objectives, monetary and fiscal instruments are not independent but collinear' (ibid., p. 18). Even in the nineteenth century Walter Bagehot perceived that 'all monetary policy originates with the Treasury'. Yet among the many gaps of contemporary discussion is the virtual absence of research on co-ordination and policy synergies considering that the most critical errors in policy-making originate in co-ordination failures and trade-off problems. Neither central banks nor monetary policies can function as stand-alone entities and instruments. This reasoning points to a separation of authorities rather than powers, but with powers shared at the strategic levels which is wholly consistent with the desirable goal of maximum operational (tactical) autonomy for the central bank, headed by a chief executive with a status and tenure guaranteed by the constitution and on par with that of the Chief Justice and the Auditor General.

It is, however, only realistic to recognize that independence is not synonymous with the infallibility of central banks. Central bank failures too have the same degree of probability as the better known and more discussed market and government failures. Even a central bank whose books balance, like those of Eddington's college bursar, can fail. Yet the prolific advocates of central bank independence are too coy to refer even obliquely to the unprecedented phenomena of central bank losses and even wholesale restructuring of central banks in recent years.

What then is the key message? Central banking, more than any other branch of economics, is a uniquely complex amalgam of ideas, traditions, institutions, techniques, and operations which does not yield a corpus of settled unambiguous conclusions. Nevertheless, it points to a decisive shift in the paradigm from independent to effective central banking, based on the highest professionalism and integrity, lest central banks fail in their appointed role of Platonic bastions of the economy and become the Potemkin villages of the financial system. Central bankers are an epistemic community charged with the responsible and historic bailiwick of 'discretionary control of the monetary system' (Sayers, 1957, p. 1). Even the gold standard in its heyday was in fact 'A Model of Discretion' (Flanders, 1993). In the final analysis, the only genuine safeguard against fiscal profligacy and economic populism is the technocracy, rectitude, and political courage of central banks coupled with the Ulysses constraint of the fiscal authorities, and not legal nostrums. Perhaps it might assuage the bruised hubris of central bankers to recall that 'long before the invention of money as a means of exchange, the historical empires . . . already had their fiscal agents' and 'though the tax collector is a well-known figure in the Bible, the central banker is barely mentioned' (Patinkin, 1965, pp. 392–3).

# Appendix I

*Table* A.1 Establishment of central banks and monetary authorities (in chronological order)

| *Year* | *Central bank* |
|---|---|
| 1668 | Sveriges Riksbank (Sweden) |
| 1694 | Bank of England |
| *Nineteenth century* | |
| 1800 | Bank of France |
| 1811 | Bank of Finland |
| 1814 | The Netherlands Bank |
| 1816 | National Bank of Austria |
| | Central Bank of Norway |
| 1818 | National Bank of Denmark |
| 1828 | Bank of the Netherlands Antilles |
| | Bank of Java (nationalized in 1951 as central bank under the name Bank Indonesia) |
| 1829 | Bank of Spain (initially established as Bank of San Fernando) |
| 1846 | Bank of Portugal |
| 1850 | National Bank of Belgium |
| 1879 | Bulgarian National Bank |
| 1880 | National Bank of Romania (renamed in 1965 as National Bank of the Socialist Republic of Romania) |
| 1882 | The Bank of Japan |
| 1883 | National Bank of Serbia |
| 1893 | Bank of Italy |
| *Twentieth century* | |
| 1904 | National Bank of Panama |
| 1907 | Swiss National Bank |
| 1911 | National Bank of Bolivia (Central Bank of Bolivia in 1928) |

*Table* A.1(*continued*) Establishment of central banks and monetary authorities (in chronological order)

| *Year* | *Central bank* |
|---|---|
| | National Bank of Haiti (Bank of Haiti in 1979) |
| 1914 | Federal Reserve System, USA |
| 1919 | Bank of Estonia (re-established in 1990) |
| | Bank of Lithuania (re-established in 1990) |
| 1921 | South African Reserve Bank |
| 1922 | Reserve Bank of Peru (reconstituted as Central Reserve Bank of Peru in 1931) |
| | Bank of Latvia (re-established in 1990) |
| | Bank of Lithuania (re-established in 1990) |
| 1923 | Bank of the Republic of Colombia |
| 1924 | National Bank of Hungary |
| | Commonwealth Bank of Australia and Bank of the Republic of Uruguay converted into central banks |
| 1925 | National Bank of Albania |
| | Bank of Mexico |
| 1926 | National Bank of Czechoslovakia (State Bank in 1950) |
| | Central Bank of Chile |
| | Central Bank of Guatemala (reconstituted as Bank of Guatemala in 1946) |
| 1927 | Central Bank of Ecuador |
| 1928 | Central Bank of China (State Bank of People's Republic of China in 1948) |
| | National Bank of Iran (Central Bank of Iran in 1960) |
| | Bank of Greece (in place of National Bank of Greece) |
| | National Bank of Iceland converted into a central bank (Central Bank of Iceland in 1961) |
| 1929 | National Bank of Yugoslavia (in place of former National Bank of Serbia) |
| 1931 | Central Bank of the Republic of Turkey |
| 1932 | Bank of Mexico converted into a central bank |

| | |
|---|---|
| 1934 | Reserve Bank of New Zealand |
| | Central Bank of El Salvador |
| 1935 | Bank of Canada |
| | Reserve Bank of India |
| | Central Bank of the Argentine Republic |
| 1936 | Bank of the Republic of Paraguay (reconstituted as Bank of Paraguay in 1944) |
| 1937 | National Bank of Costa Rica (Central Bank of Costa Rica in 1950) |
| 1939 | Bank of Afghanistan (reconstituted in 1945 as Da Afghanistan Bank) |
| 1940 | Central Bank of Venezuela |
| 1941 | National Bank of Nicaragua converted into a central bank |
| 1942 | Central Bank of Ireland |
| | Bank of Thailand |
| | State Bank of Ethiopia |
| 1945 | Da Afghanistan Bank |
| | National Bank of Poland (in place of Bank of Poland) |
| 1947 | Central Bank of the Dominican Republic |
| 1948 | State Bank of Pakistan |
| | Bank of the German States – Bank Deutscher Lander (in place of Reichsbank in West Germany) |
| | Central Bank of the Philippines (reconstituted as Bangko Sentral ng Pilipinas in 1993) |
| 1949 | National Bank of Iraq (Central Bank of Iraq in 1956) |
| 1950 | Central Bank of Ceylon |
| | National Bank of Cuba |
| | Bank of Korea |
| | Central Bank of Honduras |
| 1952 | Central Bank of Belgian Congo (replaced by Monetary Council in 1960 and by National Bank of Congo in 1964) |
| | Union Bank of Burma converted into central bank |

*Table* A.1(*continued*) Establishment of central banks and monetary authorities (in chronological order)

| *Year* | *Central bank* |
|---|---|
| | Central Bank of Paraguay (in place of Bank of Paraguay) |
| | Bank of Issue of Associated States of Indo-China (split into the National Banks of Cambodia, Laos and Vietnam in 1955) |
| | Saudi Arabian Monetary Agency |
| 1954 | Bank of Israel |
| 1955 | National Bank of Libya (renamed Bank of Libya in 1963) |
| 1956 | Central Bank of Syria |
| | Central Bank of Iraq (in place of National Bank of Iraq) |
| | Bank of Rhodesia and Nyasaland (split into Reserve Bank of Rhodesia, Bank of Zambia and Reserve Bank of Malawi in 1964) |
| | Nepal Rastra Bank |
| 1957 | German Federal Bank – Deutsche Bundesbank (in place of Bank Deutscher Lander) |
| | Bank of Ghana |
| | Central Bank of Surinam |
| 1958 | Central Bank of Nigeria |
| | Central Bank of Malaya (renamed Bank Negara Malaysia in 1963) |
| | Central Bank of Tunisia |
| 1959 | Bank of Morocco |
| | Reserve Bank of Australia (Commonwealth Bank split into Reserve Bank and Commonwealth Banking Corporation) |
| | Central Bank of West African States |
| | Central Bank of Equatorial Africa and Cameroon |
| 1960 | Bank of Republic of Guinea |
| | Bank of Sudan |
| | Bank of Jamaica |

| | |
|---|---|
| | National Bank of Somalia converted into a central bank |
| 1961 | Central Bank of Egypt (in place of National Bank of Egypt) |
| | Central Bank of Nicaragua (in place of National Bank of Nicaragua) |
| | Central Bank of Iran (in place of National Bank of Iran) |
| | Central Bank of Iceland (in place of National Bank of Iceland) |
| 1962 | Central Bank of Algeria (in place of Bank of Algeria) |
| | Bank of Republic of Mali |
| | Bank of the Netherlands Antilles |
| 1963 | Central Bank of Cyprus |
| | National Bank of Ethiopia (in place of State Bank of Ethiopia) |
| | Central Bank of Jordan |
| | Bank of Sierra Leone |
| 1964 | Banque Nationale du Congo (Bank of Zaire 1970) |
| | Central Bank of Lebanon |
| | Central Bank of Trinidad and Tobago |
| | Bank of Burundi |
| | National Bank of Rhodesia (Reserve Bank of Zimbabwe, 1980) |
| | National Bank of Rwanda |
| 1965 | National Bank of Zambia |
| | National People's Bank of Kampuchea |
| | Central Bank of Brazil |
| | Bank of Guyana |
| 1966 | Central Bank of Kenya |
| | Bank of Tanzania |
| | Bank of Uganda |
| 1967 | Brunei Currency Board |
| | Bank of Mauritius |
| | Central Bank of Uruguay (in place of Bank of Republic of Uruguay) |
| 1968 | Central Bank of Malta |

*Table* A.1(*continued*) Establishment of central banks and monetary authorities (in chronological order)

| *Year* | *Central bank* |
|---|---|
| | Central Bank of Mali (in place of Bank of Republic of Mali) |
| | People's Bank of Union of Burma (Central Bank in 1976 and now Union of Myanmar Bank) |
| | Central Bank of Kuwait |
| 1969 | Central Bank of Republic of Equatorial Guinea |
| | Monetary Authority of Bermuda |
| 1971 | Central Bank of The Gambia |
| | The Bangladesh Bank |
| | Cayman Islands Currency Board |
| | The Monetary Authority of Singapore |
| | Central Bank of Yemen (merged with the Bank of Yemen [People's Democratic Republic] after the unification of the two countries in 1990/1) |
| 1972 | Central Bank of Barbados |
| 1973 | Bahrain Monetary Agency |
| | Bank of Central African States |
| | Reserve Bank of Fiji |
| | Central Bank of Mauritania |
| | Bank of Papua New Guinea |
| | Central Bank of Madagascar |
| 1974 | The Central Bank of the Bahamas |
| | National Bank of Liberia |
| | Central Bank of Oman |
| | Monetary Authority of Swaziland (Central Bank of Swaziland in 1979) |
| 1975 | Bank of Botswana |
| | National Bank of Guinea Bissau |
| | Bank of Mozambique |
| 1976 | National Bank of Angola |
| | Bank of Cape Verde |
| | Bank of Nauru (took over activities of Bank of New South Wales) |

| | |
|---|---|
| | Monetary Authority of Belize (Central Bank of Belize in 1982) |
| 1977 | Central Bank of Comoros |
| | National Bank of Djibouti |
| 1979 | Central Bank of Seychelles |
| | Central Bank of Lesotho |
| 1980 | Central Bank of the United Arab Emirates |
| | Reserve Bank of Vanuatu |
| 1981 | Maldives Monetary Authority |
| 1982 | Royal Monetary Authority of Bhutan |
| 1983 | Eastern Caribbean Central Bank |
| | Luxembourg Monetary Institute |
| | Central Bank of Solomon Islands |
| 1984 | Central Bank of Samoa |
| 1986 | Central Bank of Aruba |
| 1989 | National Reserve Bank of Tonga |
| 1990 | Armenian Republican Bank |
| | Azerbaijan Republican Bank |
| | National Bank of Belarus |
| | Bank of Estonia |
| | Georgian Republican Bank |
| | National State Bank of Kazakstan |
| | Bank of Latvia |
| | Bank of Lithuania |
| | National Bank of Moldova |
| | Bank of Namibia |
| | Central Bank of the Russian Federation |
| | State Bank of Uzbekistan |
| 1991 | Central Bank of Croatia |
| | National Bank of Tadjikistan |
| | National Bank of Ukraine |
| 1992 | National Bank of Slovenia |
| | National Bank of Turkmenistan |
| | National Bank of the Republic of Macedonia |
| 1993 | Czech National Bank |
| | National Bank of Eritrea |
| | Hong Kong Monetary Authority |

*Table* A.1(*continued*) Establishment of central banks and monetary authorities (in chronological order)

| *Year* | *Central bank* |
|---|---|
| | Slovak National Bank |

Note: The year refers to the date of commencement of operations and may not be the same as the year of enactment of law.

*Source*: *Morgan Stanley Central Bank Directory*, 1994.

# Appendix II: Some Notable Central Bankers

**Blackman, Courtney N.** (1933– ): educated Harrison College, Barbados; University College of West Indies; Inter-American University, Puerto Rico; Columbia University; Personnel Officer, Alcan Jamaica Ltd. (1956–8); teacher, Kingston College, Jamaica (1958); Professor, Hofstra University, 1971–2; first Governor, Central Bank of Barbados, 1972–6; Visiting Professor, Pace University, New York City, 1977.

**Brown, George A.** (1920–93): educated London School of Economics, 1947–50; Jamaican Civil Service, 1950–6; Chief, Central Planning Unit, 1957–61; Inspector, Financial Secretary, Government of Jamaica, 1962–6; Governor, Bank of Jamaica, 1967–72; Member, Economic Council of Cabinet, Jamaica, 1973–8; Associate Administrator, United Nations Development Programme, 1979–89; Governor, Bank of Jamaica, 1989–92; Special Adviser to Prime Minister, Jamaica, 1992–3.

**Burns, Arthur F.** (1904–88): educated Columbia University; Chairman, US President's Council of Economic Advisors; J. B. Clark Professor of Economics, Columbia University and President, National Bureau of Economic Research; Counsellor to the President of the United States, 1969–70; Chairman, Board of Governors of the Federal Reserve System, 1970–8.

**Coombs, Herbert Cole** (1906– ): Educated University of Western Australia, London School of Economics; Education Department, Western Australia, 1929; Assistant Economist, Commonwealth Bank of Australia, 1935; Economist to Commonwealth Treasury, 1939; Member, Commonwealth Bank Board 1942; Director of Rationing, 1942; Director-General of Post-War Reconstruction, 1943; Governor, Commonwealth Bank, 1951–60; Governor and Chairman, Reserve Bank of Australia, 1960–8; Chancellor, Australian National University, 1968–76; Chairman, Australian Elizabethan Theatre Trust, 1954–68; Australian Council of Arts, 1968–74; Australian Council for Aboriginal Affairs, 1968–70; Royal Commission on Australian Government Administration, 1974–6.

**Corea, Gamani** (1925– ): educated Universities of Ceylon, Cambridge, Oxford; Director, Economic Research, Central Bank of Ceylon, 1960–4; Secretary, Cabinet Planning Committee and Permanent Secretary, Ministry of Planning and Economic Affairs, 1965–70; Deputy Governor, Central Bank of Ceylon, 1970–3; Ambassador of Sri Lanka to European Economic Community, Brussels, 1973; Secretary General, UNCTAD, 1974.

**Cuaderno, Sr, Miguel** (1890–1975): educated Philippine Law School and London School of Economics; President, Philippine Bank of Commerce, 1941; Chairman, Central Bank Council, 1946; Chairman, Philippine Financial Mission to USA, 1948; Professor of Banking and Finance, Far Eastern University, Manila, 1949–51; Chairman, Foreign Investment Committee, 1954; Governor, Central Bank of the Philippines, 1949–60.

**Currie, Lauchlin Bernard** (1902–93): educated London School of Economics, Harvard University; Instructor, Harvard University, 1927–31, Professor, Fletcher School 1931–4; Deputy Director, Department of Investigation, Federal Reserve Board, 1934–9; Economic Assistant to President Roosevelt, 1939–45; Administered the lend-lease programme for China, 1941–2; Deputy Chief, Foreign Economic Administration, 1943–4; Chief, World Bank Mission to Colombia, 1949; Economic Consultant, Government of Colombia, 1959–66; Dean, Faculty of Economics, National University Bogota, 1967; Professor of Economics, Simon Fraser University, Vancouver, 1967–71, Visiting Professor, Universities of Glasgow and Oxford, 1968–9; Advisor, National Planning Department, Colombia, 1971–80; Professor of Economics, University of Los Andes, Bogota, 1981.

**Deshmukh, Chintaman D.** (1896–1983): educated Elphinstone College, Bombay, and Jesus College, Cambridge; joined Indian Civil Service, 1918–39 (Revenue and Finance Secretary, Central Provinces and Berar, Secretary, Second Round Table Conference); Liaison Officer, Reserve Bank of India, Jul.–Sept. 1939; Secretary, Reserve Bank of India, Oct. 1939–Nov. 1941; Deputy Governor, Reserve Bank of India, Dec. 1941–10 Aug. 1943; Governor, 11 Aug. 1943–30 Jun. 1949; Indian Delegate, Bretton Woods Conference, July 1944; Member, Board of Governors, IMF and IBRD, 1946–56; Special Financial Ambassador of India, 1949; Chairman, Joint Annual Meeting of IMF and IBRD, Paris 1950; Finance Minister, Government of India, 1950–6; Chairman, University Grants Commission, India, 1956–60; Vice-Chancellor, University of Delhi, 1962–7; Chairman, Indian Institute of Public Administration, 1963–4; President, Indian Statistical Institute, 1945–64 and Institute of Economic Growth, 1965–74.

**Einaudi, Luigi** (1874–1961): Professor, University of Turin; Governor, Bank of Italy, 1945; Deputy, Italian Constituent Assembly, 1945; Minister of Budget, 1947, Italy; Senator, 1948; President, Italian Republic, 1948–55.

**Horowitz, David** (1899–1979): educated Lwow and Vienna; Director, Economic Department, Jewish Agency, 1935–48; Liaison Officer to UNSCOP, 1946; Member, Jewish Delegation to Lake Success (UN Partition Resolution), 1947; Governor, Bank of Israel, 1950–71; also served as Director General, Ministry of Finance, Economic Advisor to Government of Israel, Lecturer, School of Law and Economics, Tel Aviv.

**Ismail, tun Mohamed Ali** (1918– ): educated University of Cambridge and Middle Temple, London; joined Malayan Civil Service, 1946 and served in

Selangor State, 1948–50, Federal Treasury, 1950–3, Penang 1954–5; Minister, Malaysian Embassy, Washington, DC 1957–60; Executive Director, IBRD, 1958–60; Deputy Governor, 1960–2; Governor, 1962–80, Central Bank of Malaysia.

**Mancera Aguayo, Miguel** (1932– ): educated Technological Institute of Mexico and Yale University, employee, Bank of Commerce, 1953–6; Professor of Political Economy, Free Law School, 1957; Professor of International Trade, ITAM, 1958–64, and CEMLA, 1962–4; economist, Bank of Mexico, 1958–62; Administrator, Fund for the Export of Manufactured goods (FOMEX), 1962–7; Manager, Department of International Affairs, Bank of Mexico, 1967–71; Subdirector, International Affairs, Bank of Mexico, 1971–3, Subdirector General of Finances, Bank of Mexico, 1973–82; Director General, Bank of Mexico, 1982–.

**Norman, Montague Collett (Lord Norman)** (1871–1950): educated Eton and King's College, Cambridge; Deputy Governor, 1918–20, Bank of England; Governor, 1920–44.

**Patel, Indraprasad G.** (1924– ): educated University of Bombay and King's College, Cambridge; Professor of Economics and Principal, Baroda College, M.S. University of Baroda, 1949; Economist, later Assistant Chief, International Monetary Fund, 1950–4; Deputy Economic Adviser, Ministry of Finance, India, 1954–8; Alternate Executive Director for India, IMF, 1958–61; Chief Economic Adviser, Ministry of Finance and Planning Commission, 1962–4, 1965–7; Visiting Professor, Delhi University, 1964; Special Secretary and Secretary, Department of Economic Affairs, 1967–72; Deputy Administrator, UN Development Programme, 1972–7; Governor, Reserve Bank of India, 1977–82; Director, Indian Institute of Management, Ahmedabad, 1982–4; Director, London School of Economics, 1984–90; Chairman, Aga Khan Rural Support Project, India, 1990.

**Pohl, Karl Otto** (1929– ): educated Gottingen University; Division Chief for Economic Research, IFO-Institut, Munich, 1955–60; Economic Journalist, Bonn, 1961–7; Member Executive, Federal Association of German Banks, Cologne, 1968–9; Division Chief, Federal Ministry of Economics, Bonn, 1970–1; Departmental Chief in Federal Chancellery (Head, Department for Economic and Fiscal Policy), Bonn, 1971–2; Secretary of State, Federal Ministry of Finance, 1972–7; Deputy Governor, Deutsche Bundesbank, 1977–9; Governor, Deutsche Bundesbank, 1980–91.

**Prebisch, Raul** (1901–86): educated University of Buenos Aires, Deputy Director, Department of Statistics, Argentina, 1925–7; Director, Economic Research, National Bank of Argentina, 1927–30; Under Secretary of Finance, Argentina, 1930–2; Adviser, Ministries of Finance and Agriculture, Buenos Aires, 1933–5; Director General, Central Bank of Argentina, 1935–43; Professor, Political Economy, University of Buenos Aires, 1925–48; Executive Secretary, Economic Commission for Latin America, 1950–

63; Director General, Latin American Institute for Economic and Social Planning, Santiago, Chile, 1950–63; Secretary General, UNCTAD, 1963–9; Special Adviser to UN Secretary General on Development, 1973; Under Secretary General, 1974.

**Rasminsky, Louis** (1908– ): educated University of Toronto and London School of Economics; Economic Section, League of Nations, 1930–40; joined Bank of Canada, 1940; Foreign Exchange Control Board, Canada, 1940–3; Executive Assistant to the Governor of the Bank of Canada, 1943–54; Deputy Governor, Bank of Canada, 1955–61; Governor, 1961–73.

**Saleh, Rachmat** (1930– ): educated University of Indonesia, Jakarta; staff, Bank Indonesia, Jakarta, 1956; Representative, Bank Indonesia, New York, 1958; Secretary, Board of Directors, Bank Indonesia, Main Branch Office, Amsterdam, Netherlands, 1958; Head of Research, later Vice Director, Bank Indonesia, 1961; Director, Bank Indonesia, 1964; Chairman, Director of Foreign Exchange, Jakarta, 1968; Governor, Bank Indonesia, 1973–83; Member, Monetary Council.

**Schacht, Hjalmar** (1877–1970): educated Universities of Kiel, Berlin, Munich, Leipzig and Paris; doctoral research in economics in London; Currency Commissioner and President, Reichsbank (1923–30) and (1933–9); Adviser, Governments of Egypt, Syria, and Indonesia (*c.* 1952–3).

**Singh, Manmohan** (1932– ): educated Punjab, Cambridge, and Oxford Universities; Lecturer 1957–9; Reader, 1959–63, Professor of Economics, 1963–5, Punjab University; Consultant, UNCTAD, 1966–9; Professor, Delhi School of Economics, 1969–71; Economic Adviser, Ministry of Finance, Government of India, 1972–6; Secretary, Ministry of Finance, Government of India, 1976–80; Member-Secretary, Planning Commission, Government of India, 1980–2; Governor, Reserve Bank of India, 1982–4; Deputy Chairman, Planning Commission, Government of India; Secretary-General, the South Commission, Geneva, 1987–90; Chairman, Economic Advisory Council, 1990–1; Minister for Finance, Government of India, 1991–6.

**Siregar, Arifin M.** (1934– ): educated Netherlands School of Economics, Rotterdam and University of Munster, Germany; United Nations, New York, 1961–3, Beirut, 1963–5; International Monetary Fund, 1965–71; Managing Director, Bank Indonesia, 1971, Governor, 1983–7; Minister of Trade, 1988–92; Ambassador to the United States, 1993–.

**Strong, Benjamin** (1872–1928): High School of Montclair, New Jersey; entered private banking firm of Jesuf Paton and Co. (later Cuyler, Morgan and Co.); Assistant Secretary, Atlantic Trust Co. 1901; Secretary, Bankers' Trust Company, 1903; President, Bankers' Trust Company, 1914; Governor, Federal Reserve Bank of New York, 1914.

**Towers, Graham Ford** (1897–1975): Assistant General Manager, Royal Bank of Canada, Montreal, 1933–4; Governor, Bank of Canada, 1935–54.

**Volcker, Paul A.** (1927– ): educated Princeton, Harvard, London School of Economics; Special Assistant, Securities Department, Federal Reserve Bank of New York, 1953–57; Financial Economist, Chase Manhattan Bank, New York, 1957–62; Vice-President and Director of Forward Planning; 1965–9; Director, Office of Financial Analysis, US Treasury Department, 1962–3; Deputy Under-Secretary for Monetary Affairs, 1963–5; Senior Fellow, Woodrow Wilson School of Public and International Affairs, Princeton University, 1974–5; President, Federal Reserve Bank of New York, 1975–9; Chairman, US Federal Reserve Board, 1979–87; Commission on the Public Service, 1987–90; Chairman, James D. Wolfensohn since 1988; Frederick H. Schultz, Professor International Economic Policy, Princeton University since 1988.

**Ungphakorn, Puey** (1916– ): educated Thammasat University, Bangkok and London School of Economics; Economic Counsellor, Royal Thai Embassy, London; Budget Director; Member, Executive Committees, National Economic Development Board and National Education Council; Chairman, Council of Economic Advisers to the Prime Minister of Thailand; Member, Legislative Assembly, Thailand; Professor and Dean, Faculty of Economics, Thammasat University; Visiting Professor, Woodrow Wilson School, Princeton University; Governor, Bank of Thailand; Visiting Fellow, Wolfson College, Cambridge.

**Zijlstra, Jelle** (1918– ): educated Netherlands School of Economics; Assistant (1945) and Professor, Netherlands School of Theoretical Economics, 1948–52; Professor, Public Finance, 1963–6); Free University of Amsterdam, 1963–6; Minister of Economic Affairs, 1952–8; Minister of Finance, 1959–63; Prime Minister, 1966–7; President, Netherlands Bank, 1967–81; President, BIS, 1967–82.

**Zolotas, Xenophon** (1904– ): educated Universities of Athens, Leipzig and Paris. Professor of Economics, University of Thessaloniki, 1928, University of Athens 1931–68; Member, Supreme Council of Greece, 1932; Chairman, Board of Directors, Agricultural Bank of Greece, 1936–40; Joint Governor, Bank of Greece (after Liberation), 1944–5; Member, Currency Committee, 1950, 1974–81; Governor, Bank of Greece, 1955–67; 1974–81; Minister of Economic Co-ordination, Jul.–Nov. 1974; Prime Minister of Greece, 1989–90.

# Notes

## 1. Nature, Objectives and Functions

1. The President of the American Federation of Labor noted critically: 'neither the committee [Open Market Committee of the Federal Reserve – FOMC] nor the reporters covering them are likely to mention the Fed's legal obligation, under the 1978 Humphrey–Hawkins Act (*sic*) to take steps to reduce unemployment whenever it is above 4 per cent as it is today . . . the Fed [should] take seriously its legal obligation to promote full employment as vigorously as it preserves price stability. If it continues to ignore this clear mandate, the Fed must be held accountable' (Lane Kirkland, 'Not in Our Best Interest,' *The Washington Post*, 14 November 1994, p. A21).
2. The Governor of a South Asian central bank once remarked to the author that he never felt inhibited by the central bank law in undertaking any new activities which he thought were in the best interests of the bank and the country. A good example in point is the one time venture of the Central Bank of Sri Lanka in opening a gold sale boutique at the international airport at Colombo, which although profitable, was in clear violation of the injunction in its statute against the Bank having a direct interest in any commercial undertaking. These outlets were subsequently hived off to commercial banks.

## 2. Central Banks: Origins and Variants

1. '– the simple expedient of providing for a 100 per cent cover for the colonial currency' meant that 'any increase in the currency circulation in the dependent area resulted in a de facto loan by it to the metropolis. . . . It did actually impose limitations to the extension of "Keynesian" policies in the short period after the War before independence was won' (T. Balogh, 1974, p. 83).
2. See Osband and Villanueva (1993); Bennett (1994); and Williamson (1995) for an analytical discussion of currency boards; Clauson (1944), Hanke and Schuler (1993) for a historical perspective on currency board operations and episodes.
3. 'It would be wrong to infer that the Bank was prejudiced against the transition to central banking in general; quite the contrary; in fact the Bank [was] in the forefront to see these currency boards of colonies grow into the central banks of the politically transformed countries of the new Commonwealth' (Sayers, 1976, p. 521). This is borne out by the general tenor of recommendations of successive Bank of England advisory missions to the dependencies (for example, Mynors, Southern Rhodesia, 1949; Fisher, Nigeria, 1952; Watson-Caine, Malaysia, 1956;

Loynes, Nigeria, 1957; Hall, Barbados, 1969). These missions, while not disputing the case for eventual establishment of central banks, were rightly concerned more with the timing for such actions. This stance is typified by the recommendations for Nigeria which stated '– it would be inadvisable to contemplate the establishment of a Central Bank at the moment . . . Given further development of the indigenous banking system and growth in the financial mechanism, the establishment of a Central Bank would be a logical and useful step in due course' (J.L. Fisher, Adviser, Bank of England, 1953, p. 18).

4. This is based on the author's experience as Economic Advisor to the Bank of Libya (1959–60 and 1965–6). The Bank was in fact critical of the government's complacency in controlling inflation and even published a report to support its findings and views.
5. Professor Edwin Walter Kemmerer of Princeton University served as economic advisor or headed financial missions to Latin America, Philippines, South Africa (1924–5), Poland (1926), China (1929) and Turkey (1934).

## 3. Monetary Policy: Instruments and Issues

1. However, the empirical evidence on the efficacy of selective credit controls is conflicting. Thus, in the case of India, which has had the longest experience of selective credit controls, one study found that 'they have been of limited effectiveness owing to the substitutability of different sources of finance' (Vaez-Zadeh and Pereira Leite, 1986, p. 558), whereas another study using an inventory behaviour model (1965–86), concluded that 'selective credit controls are effective . . . past credit levels have a strong bearing on their current levels . . . stocks held under selective credit controls are in general nonspeculative in character' (Bhujanga Rao, 1993, p. 175). In Korea, 'selective credit controls did indeed facilitate, albeit slightly, the investment activity of small and medium-sized enterprises . . . with only minor repercussions on other sectors and expenditure categories' (Pereira Leite and Vaez-Zadeh, 1986, p. 125).

## 4. Exchange Arrangements and Policies

1. 'For example, a country in the Far East whose own policies give it reasonable price stability might well want to have fixed rates on its two main trading partners with low inflation rates: the U.S. and Japan. That was the arrangement it had up to 1971 as a result of observing its own par value. But, at present, that choice is not open to it. As long as the yen/dollar rate floats, the country can peg on the yen and undergo a floating dollar, or peg on the dollar and suffer a floating yen; it can select any gradation of halfway houses; or it can float its own currency. But what might well have been its really preferred choice, a fixed rate on both currencies, would not be among the available options' (J. J. Polak, 1988, p. 134).

2. 'This is more than a theoretical nicety. Notice, for example, the unsatisfactory way in which the Fund classifies the Deutschmark. The Fund table describes the Deutschmark as linked to other (EMS) currencies, and thus does not include it in the last group, the floaters; yet, everyone knows that perhaps the most important floating rate in the system is the Deutschmark/U.S. dollar rate' (J.J. Polak, 1988, p. 134).
3. For instance, the Deputy Governor of the Reserve Bank of India in his address to the Third City of London Central Banking Conference, organized by the City Forum Limited, London, on 21 March 1994, remarked: 'Central bankers the world over are generally reticent about the management of their foreign exchange reserves – and this is how it should be,' S. S. Tarapore (*Reserve Bank of India Bulletin*, November 1994, p. 1485).
4. A former Governor of the Bank Negara Malaysia, Tun Ismail bin Mohamed Ali, once remarked to the author, 'For me as a central banker no level of reserves is really adequate.'
5. Reportedly, 100 central banks, or 70 per cent of the total surveyed, seek to establish benchmarks for monitoring performance, which are set up by the bank's investment committee, which usually meets monthly or more frequently, with participation of the governor, deputy governor or other senior officials and may employ external advisers. The Bank of Greece, for instance, allocates CG, First Boston some $200 million with instructions to yield 1 1/2 per cent above a US Treasury bond within strict risk parameters (*Central Banking*, vol. 5, no. 2, Autumn 1994, p. 73). The Reserve Bank of India's foreign reserves management procedures provide for: (1) a weekly investment committee meeting, chaired by the head of the reserves management department, and including the economic department; (2) a monthly strategy meeting chaired by the Governor/Deputy Governor; and (3) overall review of the policy and approach at still higher level at periodic intervals of, say, six months (P.B. Kulkarni, 1990, p. 307). The author was Chief Officer, Department of External Investment and Operations, Reserve Bank of India.

## 5. Regulation and Supervision

1. An apt instance in point is the decisive and masterly handling of the affairs of the Colombo branch of the BCCI (*c.* 1991) by the then Governor of the Central Bank of Sri Lanka, Dr Karunatilake, who was fully aware of all the facts of the situation, *qua* governor, and whose timely actions prevented any losses being suffered by the Sri Lankan depositors. The Colombo branch of the BCCI reopened on 1 August 1991 under the management of the privately-owned Seylan Bank, acting on the initiative of the Central Bank. These concerted actions were helped by the fact that the supervisory function was vested in the Central Bank.
2. A former Governor of the Bank of Israel remarked ruefully that 'around 50 per cent of his time was taken up with supervisory matters'

(Bruno, 1994, p. 15). While this order of magnitude may not be necessarily typical, it is strongly indicative of the dimensions of a basic central banking function. The Supervision and Examination Sector is, reportedly, the largest in the Central Bank of the Philippines, consisting of some 1600 people (*c.* 1980), most of whom are field examiners. The management of the supervision and examination 'is not a simple undertaking' and calls 'not only for the religious observance of professional and ethical standards, but of proper utilization of time and energy within an approved period' Jaime C. Laya (former Deputy Governor and Minister of the Budget of the Republic of the Philippines, 1980, pp. 200–1).

3. These citations from an International Monetary Fund publication are merely statements of both aspects of the case, on which the IMF itself does not take any position.
4. A former Governor of the Reserve Bank of India remarked in no uncertain terms:

> the record of the RBI's Banking Department leaves something to be desired and I would hope for a broader representation of outsiders, including those from commercial banks and other financial institutions on the staff of the new body. The supervisory body should also have a separate Board or Committee of Governance on which the Securities and Exchange Board of India as well as the Deposit Insurance Corporation and other interested organizations should be represented. (I.G. Patel, 1994, p. 50)

5. It is richly ironical that the Reserve Bank of New Zealand should suggest that each bank 'be required to display prominently a credit rating on its premises if it has a rating, if not, it must disclose this fact' (IMF, 1994, p. 14). Some years ago, when one of the prominent credit rating agencies, Moody's, had lowered New Zealand's rating from triple A it evoked a storm of protest from the government. The moral: credit ratings are a useful but by no means infallible guideline.
6. The crisis periods in the sample countries were as follows: Argentina (1980–2); Chile (1981–3); Uruguay (1982–5); Philippines (1983–6, bill market crisis in 1981); Thailand (1984–6); Malaysia (1985–6) (Sundararajan and Baliño, 1991, p. 9).

## 6. Developmental Role

1. The replies to the questionnaire were appropriately upbeat as none of them reported the pathology of the payments system as in India where a former Governor of the Reserve Bank of India observed in no uncertain terms:

> The payments, settlement and clearance system is in a shambles . . . a malady . . . afflicts not just individual banks but indeed the financial system as a whole. I am referring to the deplorable

situation that prevails in respect of payments and settlement and clearance and, indeed, in the balancing of books of all institutions. It is nothing short of scandalous and a mockery of the very notion of liberalization when the Unit Trust refuses to accept out-of-station cheques, when shares take God knows how long to register, and the books of the banks, including the Reserve Bank, do not balance expeditiously except perhaps miraculously at the end of the accounting year! The problem goes much deeper than lack of mechanization and needs to be tackled on a war footing, if financial liberalization is to be anything more than a glint in our eye and adequate supervision more than a mere incantation. (I.G. Patel, pp. 40, 44)

## 7. Informal Finance

1. Communication from Mrs Tanya Sirivedhin, Director of Economic Research, Bank of Thailand.
2. The Reserve Bank of India Act, 1935 (5.55) made it incumbent on the Bank to report within three years and to prepare the necessary legislation on the inclusion of indigenous bankers in the second schedule of the Act so as to bring this sector, financing 90 per cent of total credit requirements, within the ambit of Bank. The then Finance Member of the Government of India, Sir George Schuster, recognized that 'one of the greatest problems of the future for India' is not one of 'displacing the indigenous bankers . . . but of making the fullest use of them by adapting their methods so that they may fit in with the modern banking system and the central bank . . .' (*History of the Reserve Bank of India, 1935–51*, pp. 111–12).
3. As early as *c.* 1913, Keynes had observed 'that the main movements of the interest rate up and down, which result from the central facts of the Indian seasons and harvests, must be the same in both markets, and that the native money market must ultimately depend on the European for additional supplies of cash' (1971, p. 19–140).
4. There were hardly any fruitful developments in the matter of linking the indigenous bankers with the organized banking structure [in India] because 'the shedding of nonbanking business by indigenous bankers' was regarded 'as a prerequisite for the "link up" ' (*History of the Reserve Bank of India*, p. 488). Ironically, Reserve Bank governors seem to wax eloquent on the merits of informal finance only in their retirement. One of them recognized that:

   while informal sources of finance play an important role, the trend of policy has, however, been to treat it as an enemy of the people! . . . There is a case to look at informal finance afresh with a less jaundiced eye and use it rather than condemn it to benign neglect . . . Is it too much to hope that someone will listen? (S. Venkitaramanan, 'Informal Finance', *The Times of India*, 4 June 1995, p. 4)

## 8. Research and Advisory Role

1. The Monetary Law Act No. 58 (MLA) sets out the constitution and functions of the Central Bank of Ceylon (later the Central Bank of Sri Lanka) which was established in 1950 to replace the Currency Board system. Its responsibilities as an Advisor to Government are assigned in specific sections of the MLA. Section 64 requires the Monetary Board (MB) of the Bank to recommend corrective measures to the government in the event of domestic monetary or economic instability and also to report abnormal monthly movements in the money supply or the cost of living. Section 116 requires the MB to submit to the minister on or before 15 September in each year a confidential report to the minister of finance for use in the preparation of the Budget speech, which analyses the monetary situation and policy and the effects of the current fiscal policy upon the ability of the central bank to maintain monetary and exchange rate stability of the Sri Lankan Rupee. Besides these specific statutory obligations, the Central Bank also responds to numerous requests for advice from ministries, departments and public sector agencies on issues which 'are not even remotely connected with the principal business of the bank' and 'relate to the real sectors of the economy and matters which specialized financial institutions such as development banks and merchant banks are in a better position to handle,' p. 57 (*Ninth Interim Report of the Presidential Commission on Finance and Banking on the Central Bank of Sri Lanka*, sessional paper, no. XII–1993 (Colombo: Government Publications Bureau, 28 December 1992).
2. 'It would be manifestly absurd to say that . . . Government must necessarily ask for the advice of the Reserve Bank. Sometimes, advice is asked for . . . [but] there is an area which is very clearly the direct concern of Government.' H.V.R. Iengar, 1962, pp. 160–1.
3. A former Governor of the Bank of Thailand, Dr Puey Ungpakhorn, was under constant pressure from government and the public alike to head commissions of inquiry into virtually every public grievance.
4. The author enjoyed this privilege as Economic Advisor to the Bank of Libya (1959–60) by special dispensation of the then Governor, Dr Aly Aneizi, although there was no statutory provision for it.
5. The author vividly recalls a conversation with the late Sir Maurice Parsons (then Deputy Governor, Bank of England) during his visit to the Reserve Bank of India (RBI). When asked what he would look for in a good central banker, he said unhesitantly, 'How well does he know his markets?' The RBI initiated in the mid-1950s, at the instance of J. V. Joshi (Executive Director), a programme of assigning different commodity markets (for example, cotton, textiles, sugar, foodgrains), to individual research officers, a commendable experiment, which in the event fizzled out for a variety of reasons. It had a certain tentativeness about it which augured ill for its future; no use was made of the reports prepared by the enthusiastic officers, most of whom, including the author, were ignorant of Gujerati and its several dialects which are the accepted linguistic media of the market and the business

world in Bombay. Then as now the best informed commercial newspaper was the Gujerati daily, *Vyapar*. The RBI also lost even good listening posts later, as when Governor Iengar following the strictures passed on him by the Life Insurance Corporation of India (Chagla) Tribunal, withdrew, in a fit of pique, the RBI's representatives on the Bombay Stock and Bullion Exchanges. His successor, P. C. Bhattacharya, went one better by abolishing the London branch of the RBI as an economy measure on the ground that the State Bank of India branch in London could supply the same economic intelligence, which in the event was understandably not forthcoming as the Bank of England could hardly be expected to treat a commercial bank on a par with the RBI for supplying confidential data and information.

6. 'In Norway, the Ministry of Finance can and does exercise pressure on economists in the [Central] Bureau [of Statistics] to use models that are more likely to yield the projections the Government wants to see. In the United States, the Bureau of Labor Statistics has in periods been subjected to even stronger pressures' (Elster, 1994, p. 6). In the Philippines the Central Bank series on urban wages was discontinued by order of President Marcos in 1980 because of the 'embarrassment the data caused to the Government' by revealing a remarkable decline in real wages during the 1970s (Boyce, 1993, p. 27).

## 10. Transition Economies

1. For details see H. Poenisch, 'The New Central Banks of Eastern Europe,' *Central Banking*, 4 (1991) pp. 9–20. The author, a staffer of the Austrian National Bank, was Adviser to the People's Bank of China in 1989.
2. John Chown in his review of Marshall I. Goldman, *Lost Opportunity* (*Why Economic Reforms in Russia have not succeeded*) (New York: Norton, 1994), in *The Times Literary Supplement*, no. 4790, 20 January 1995, p. 10.

## 12. Organizational Reform

1. The following were Interim Governors of the Reserve Bank of India: (1) K.G. Ambegaonkar, 14 January–28 February 1957 (6 weeks); (2) B.N. Adarkar, 4 May–15 June 1970 (5 weeks); (3) N.C. Sengupta, 19 May–19 August 1975 (3 months); (4) M. Narasimham, 2 May–30 November 1977 (6 months); (5) A. Ghosh, 15 January–4 February 1985 (19 days). Even among the regular appointees, K.R. Puri, had a term of one year and 9 months and two others, L. K. Jha and Manmohan Singh, had terms of less than 3 years.
2. The late J. M. Garland, then Economic Advisor to the Commonwealth Bank of Australia, told the author in Sydney in 1958 that Governor Coombs, although himself an economist of distinction, always respected the expertise of the Economic Adviser and there was never even a hint of his trying to upstage his economists. He always

emphasized collegiality in decision and policy-making. A striking counter point is provided by the relationship between Per Jacobsson, one-time Managing Director of the International Monetary Fund, and his Director of Research, E. M. Bernstein, which is best described in the words of his biographer

> That PJ was an economist in his own right meant that there were adjustments to be made in relation to the economic research staff. Previously, that department had been largely autonomous. Now the Managing Director was influencing research, and writing his own speeches. The Head of the Department, Edward M. Bernstein, saw his influence, which had been very considerable throughout the IMF's existence, inevitably decrease. Though there was no open conflict, it was apparent to their colleagues that the minds of PJ and Bernstein worked in different ways: it was a question of how they tackled the problems. And PJ was not a person to alter his basic methods and approaches; he willed conformity in this respect on his collaborators. Bernstein apparently decided that he could not take the changes. When he intimated to PJ that he would be leaving the IMF, PJ's personal reaction was: 'I understand him: perhaps it was my enthusiasm that made him feel how tired of these subjects he was . . . He has done yeoman work in educating the officials of the Fund.' In January 1958 Bernstein announced his departure: (Erin Jacobsson, 1979, pp. 299–300).

3. John Mendzela joined the Reserve Bank of New Zealand from the private sector in early 1988 and worked there until mid-1992, serving as Senior Advisor and Chief Manager, Accounting Department. His brief was to develop systems for external accountability, Board monitoring of senior management and internal delegation of responsibility, as well to advise on effectiveness and efficiency. This section draws heavily on his working paper on 'Improving the Management of a Central Bank – A Case Study' WP/94/37, International Monetary Fund, April 1994.
4. There was a very shortlived exchange of personnel at the Research Officers level between the Reserve Banks of India and Australia in the early 1960s following the SEANZA Central Banking Courses.

## 13. Independence: Rhetoric and Reality

1. There is a very extensive literature on central bank independence the bulk of which deals with industrial countries, although some of them have sections or references to developing countries, for example, Cukierman *et al.*, 1992, and Cukierman, 1992. The latter is the most systematic single-volume discussion of the subject, which has also been covered in Alesina and Summers, 1993; Bruno, 1994; Cargill, 1995; Effros, 1994; Goodhart, 1994; Goodman, 1991; Havrilesky and Granato, 1993; Maxfield, 1994; Posen, 1993; Toniolo, 1990. Oddly, most

of the published statistical studies are based on an unpublished but frequently cited paper by Bade and Parkin, 1982. The only systematic analysis in the context of the developing countries is by Maxfield, 1994. The contemporary literature overlooks that the debate on independence of central banks dates back to the 1920s. Kisch and Elkin 1932, pp. 18–21) emphasized central banks' freedom from political pressures. The most succinct and perceptive discussion of the pros and cons of central bank independence is by Plumptre (1947, pp. 23–9).

2. This extract is from the official evidence submitted by then Governor Iengar to the Radcliffe Committee, Memoranda of Evidence, vol. I, p. 252, and para. 2, p. 255.
3. The peak of RBI credit to the Government of India was predictably followed by the trough in the Governor's status as recorded in the diaries of a distinguished visiting Australian economist (*c.*1959)

> Saturday morning was again spent at the Bank. First, a three-quarters of an hour interview with the Governor [Iengar] during which we talked about Indian economic problems. He was keenly interested to hear what was going on in Delhi, . . . clearly, the Left hand in Delhi does not always let the 'Right' hand in Bombay know about all it is doing . . . much to my surprise, he ended what had already been more than the courtesies demanded by asking me whether I would be free to lunch with him alone on Monday to continue the discussion . . . I had . . . at 1 pm a very pleasant *tête-à-tête* lunch with the Governor in his private dining room behind his office. We talked about all sorts of things, but he was, it became increasingly clear, anxious about two: one, to convey to me, and presumably through me to the Planning Commission in Delhi, his anxiety about a recent decision of the Congress Executive about credit cooperatives; two, to find out a bit more about Delhi thinking about the Third Plan. An odd procedure for the Governor of the Central Bank to have to use!. (Arndt, 1987)

But would foreknowledge of Delhi's thinking have really mattered for an institution which had ceased to be effective for all practical purposes?

4. Even the RBI Employees' Union has shown greater awareness of its lack of autonomy than ruling Governors when 'they started to lobby and agitate in front of the Ministry of Finance (MoF) in Delhi for improvement in their working conditions. Even the periodic RBI wage settlements were negotiated after those of the nationalized banks which had to be approved by the MoF. Clearly, the RBI lacked even the autonomy to negotiate its wage settlements with its own unions' (J. Sinha, a staff officer, in an unpublished memorandum, 1993, p. 48).
5. L.H. White's article, 'Privatize Central Banks to Stimulate Growth' (*Economic Affairs*, 1986, pp. 38–42), despite its title, is concerned mainly with the 'privatization of the financial sector . . . as part of the agenda for genuine liberalization, decentralization, and separation of economic affairs from political power,' p. 42.

# Bibliography


Abdeen, A. M. and D. N. Shook (1984) *The Saudi Financial System* (Chichester: John Wiley & Sons).

Abrams, R. K. and J. Cortés-Douglas (1993) 'Introduction of a New National Currency: Policy, Institutional, and Technical Issues', IMF Working Paper, WP/93/49.

Acharya, S. and M. Srinivasa (1983) 'Informal Credit Markets and Black Money: Do They Frustrate Monetary Policy', *Economic and Political Weekly*, XVIII: 1751–6.

——and —— (1984) 'Informal Credit Markets and Monetary Policy', *Economic and Political Weekly*, XIX, 1593–98

Agenor, P. and N. U. Haque (1994) 'Macroeconomic Management with Informal Financial Markets', PPAA/94/12 (Washington, DC: International Monetary Fund, 1994).

Alesina, A., and L. H. Summers (1993) 'Central Bank Independence and Macroeconomic Performance: Some Comparative Evidence', *Journal of Money, Credit, and Banking*, 25: 151–62.

Alexander, W. E. and F. Caramazza (1994) 'Money versus Credit: Role of Banks in Monetary Transmission', in T. J. T. Balino and C. Cottarelli (eds) *Frameworks for Monetary Stability* (*Policy issues and Country Experiences*) (Washington, DC: International Monetary Fund).

Alexander, W. E. *et al.*, *The Adoption of Indirect Instruments of Monetary Policy*, occasional paper 126 (Washington, DC: International Monetary Fund, 1995).

Alsop, J. W. (1992) *I've Seen the Best of It*, memoirs with Adam Platt (New York: W.W. Norton).

Amin, S. H. (1986) *Islamic Banking and Finance: The Experience of Iran* (Tehran: Vahid).

Anyadike-Danes, M. K. (1995) 'Comment on "Measuring the Independence of Central Banks and Its Effect on Policy Outcomes" by Cukierman, Webb, and Neyapti', *The World Bank Economic Review*, 9: 335–40.

Arndt, H. W. (1965) 'Central Banking in Developing Countries: Some Lessons of Australian Experience', *Indian Economic Journal*, XII: 232–43.

—— (1978) 'Leslie Galfried Melville' Citation for an Honorary Degree (Canberra: Australian National University).

—— (1987) *Asian Diaries* (Singapore: Chopmen).

Arrow, K. J. (1974) *The Limits of Organization* (New York: Norton).

Asian Development Bank (1990) *Asian Development Bank Outlook* (Manila).

Aslund, A. (1995) *How Russia Became a Market Economy* (Washington, DC: The Brookings Institution).

Asseily, A. E. (1967) *Central Banking in Lebanon: A Central Bank for the Economic Development of the Country* (Beirut: Khayat Book and Publishing Co.).

Bade, R. and M. Parkin (1995) 'Central Bank Laws and Monetary Policy', unpublished (cited in Cargill, 1995, pp. 159, 171).

Baka, W. (1990) 'Recent Developments in Poland', in *Central Banking Issues in Emerging Market Economies* (Kansas City: Federal Reserve Bank of Kansas), pp. 57–64.

Baka, W. (1994/95) 'Respect the National Bank', *Central Banking*, 5: 65–72.

Baliño, T. J. T., A. Dhawan and V. Sundararajan (1994) 'Payments System Reforms and Monetary Policy in Emerging Market Economies in Central and Eastern Europe', IMF *Staff Papers*, 41: 383–410.

—— and C. Cottarelli (eds) (1994) *Frameworks for Monetary Stability (Policy Issues and Country Experiences)* (Washington, DC: International Monetary Fund).

Balogh, T. (1974) *The Economics of Poverty* (London: Weidenfeld and Nicolson).

Bank of England (1994) *Reorganisation at the Bank of England* (Press Notice) London.

Bank of England (1995) Symposium on *Central Banking in Developing Countries* (London: Bank of England).

Basu, S. K. (1967) *Central Banking in the Emerging Countries (A Survey of African Experiments)* (New York: Asia Publishing House).

Bank Negara Malaysia, *Annual Report, 1994* (Kuala Lumpur).

Benard, W. J. (1993) 'Dutch Influence on Central Banking in the Netherlands Antilles', *Money Affairs*, VI: 101–10.

Bennett, A. G. G. (1993) 'The Operation of the Estonian Currency Board', IMF *Staff Papers*, 40: 451–70.

—— (1994) 'Issues and Experiences', in T. J. T. Baliño and C. Cottarelli (eds) *Frameworks for Monetary Stability* (Washington, DC: International Monetary Fund) 186–212.

Bhattacharyay, B. N. (1988) 'Development of Financial Infrastructure', *Savings and Development*, 4: 307–19.

Bhujanga Rao, G. (1993) 'Trade Credit and Selective Credit Controls: An Empirical Analysis', *Indian Economic Review*, 28: 175–90.

Binhadi, (1992) 'Bank Supervision in a Liberalized Financial System: The Indonesian Case', Paper, The 19th SEANZA Central Banking Course, Bank of Japan, Tokyo.

Blackman, C. N. (1979) 'The Role of the Central Bank in the Formulation and Implementation of Economic Policy in Small Developing Countries', in *The Role of Central Banks in Economic Decision Making* (Jerusalem: Bank of Israel) pp. 157–78.

—— (1981) 'Management of Foreign Exchange Reserves in Small and Developing Countries', *Social and Economic Studies*, 30: 156–71.

—— (1989) 'New Directions for Central Banking in the Caribbean', *Social and Economic Studies*, 38: 219–39.

—— (1993) 'Toward a Theory of Central Bank Management with Special Reference to the Caribbean', *Money Affairs*, 6: 89–100.

Blowers, G. A. and A. N. McLeod (1952) 'Currency Unification in Libya', IMF *Staff Papers*, II: 438–65.

Bod, P. (1994) 'Targets and Instruments of Monetary Policy in Hungary', in T. J. T. Baliño and C. Cottarelli (eds) *Frameworks for*

*Monetary Stability* (Washington, DC: International Monetary Fund) pp. 423–42.

Bordo, M. D. (1989) 'Lender of Last Resort: Some Historical Insights', NBER Working Paper Series, no. 3011 (Cambridge, Mass.: National Bureau of Economic Research) pp. 1–31.

Boughton, J. J. (1991) 'The CFA Franc Zone: Currency Union and Monetary Standard', IMF *Working Paper* 91/13.

—— (1993) 'The Economics of the CFA Franc Zone', in P. R. Masson and M. P. Taylor (eds) *Policy Issues in the Operation of Currency Unions* (Cambridge University Press) pp. 96–110.

Bowles, P., and G. White (1994) 'Central Bank Independence: A Political Economy Approach', *The Journal of Development Studies*, 31: 235–64.

Boyce, J. K. (1993) *The Philippines, The Political Economy of Growth and Impoverishment in the Marcos Era* (Basingstoke: Macmillan in association with the OECD Development Centre).

Boyes, W. J., W. S. Mounts, and C. Sowell (1988) 'The Federal Reserve as a Bureaucracy: An Examination of Expense Preference Behavior', *Journal of Money, Credit, and Banking*, 20: 181–90.

Breton, A. and R. Wintrobe (1978) 'A Theory of Moral Suasion', *Canadian Journal of Economics*, XI: 210–19.

Brimmer, A. F. (1971) 'Central Banking and Economic Development', *Journal of Money, Credit, and Banking*, III: 780–92.

Brown, G. A. (1994) 'Jamaica's Transition from Direct to Indirect Instruments of Monetary Policy', in P. Downes, and R. Vaez-Zadeh (eds) *The Evolving Role of Central Banks* (Washington, DC: International Monetary Fund) pp. 326–40.

Bruno, M. (1991) *Crises, Stabilization, and Economic Reform: Therapy by Consensus* (Oxford: Clarendon Press).

—— (1994) 'Political Autonomy of Central Banks: Theory and Practice', Keynote Lecture at Conference on the Constitutional Status of Central Banks in Eastern Europe, University of Chicago Law School, 22 April (revised draft, 1 July), mimeograph.

Cairncross, A. K. (1973) *Control of Long-Term Capital Markets*, (Washington, DC: The Brookings Institution).

Capie, F., C. A. E. Goodhart, N. Schnadt (1994) 'The Development of Central Banking' in *The Future of Central Banking* (The Tercentenary Symposium of the Bank of England) (Cambridge University Press) pp. 1–123.

Caprio, G., Jr., I. Atiyas, and J. A. Hanson (eds) (1994) *Financial Reform: Theory and Experience* (Cambridge University Press).

—— , D. F. I. Folkerts-Landau and T. D. Lane (eds) (1994) *Building Sound Finance in Emerging Market Economies* (Washington, DC: International Monetary Fund, World Bank).

Cargill, T. F. (1995) 'The Statistical Association Between Central Bank Independence and Inflation', *Banca Nazionale del Lavoro: Quarterly Review*, ILVIII: 159–72.

Carisano, R. (1992) *Deposit Insurance: Theory, Policy and Evidence* (Aldershot, Brookfield, USA: Dartmouth).

Carling, R. G. (1994) 'Reform of Monetary Instruments in Southeast Asia', in T. J. T. Baliño and G. Cottarelli (eds) *Frameworks for Monetary Policy* (Washington, DC: International Monetary Fund) pp. 443–57.

Castello-Branco, M. and M. Swinburne (1992) 'Central Bank Independence', *Finance and Development*, 29: 19–21.

*Central Banking* (1993) 'City of London Central Banking Conference', III: 43–51.

—— (1995) 'How Much Gold is Enough', V: 72–6.

Chandavarkar, A. G. (1960) 'Central Banking in Libya', *The Banker's Magazine*, 189: 495–8.

—— (1964) 'Some Special Aspects of the Open Market Operations of the Reserve Bank of India', *Reserve Bank of Indian Bulletin*, December: 1–9.

—— (1972) 'Government Balances as a Monetary Policy Instrument in the Less Developed Countries', *Economic and Political Weekly*, VII: 1785–90.

—— (1985a) 'Keynes and Central Banking', *The Indian Economic Review*, XX: 283–98.

—— (1985b) 'The Non-Institutional Financial Sector in Developing Economies and Macroeconomic Implications for Savings Policies', *Savings and Development*, 2: 129–41.

—— (1985c) 'Financial Pull of Urban Areas', *Finance and Development*, 22: 24–7.

—— (1987a) 'Developmental Role of Central Banks', *Finance and Development*, 24: 34–7.

—— (1987b) *The Informal Financial Sector in Developing Countries: Concepts, Evidence, and Policy Implications*, The South-East Asian Central Banks (SEACEN) Research and Training Centre, occasional paper no. 2.

—— (1988) 'Promotional Role of Central Banks', *International Journal of Development Banking*, 6: 3–14.

—— (1989) *Keynes and India* (Basingstoke: Macmillan).

—— (1992) 'Of Finance and Development: Some Neglected and Unsettled Questions', *World Development*, 20: 133–42.

Chandler, L. V. (1962) *Central Banking and Economic Development* (Bombay: University of Bombay).

Chant, J. F. and K. Acheson (1972) 'The Choice of Monetary Instruments and the Theory of Bureaucracy', *Public Choice*, XII: 13–33.

—— (1973) 'Mythology and Central Banking', *Kyklos*, 26 (26): 362–79.

Cho, Y. J. (1990) 'McKinnon-Shaw Versus the Neo-Structuralists on Financial Liberalization: A Conceptual Note', *World Development*, 18: 477–80.

Clauson, G. L. M. (1944) 'The British Colonial Currency System', *The Economic Journal*, LIV: 1–23.

Coats, W. L., Jr. and D. R. Khatkhate (eds) (1980) *Money and Monetary Policy in Less Developed Countries* (Oxford: Pergamon).

Cole, D. and Y. C. Park (1983) *Financial Development in Korea, 1945–1978* (Cambridge, Mass.: Harvard University Press).

Collins, M. (1993) *Central Banking in History*, vols I, II, III (Aldershot: Edward Elgar Publishing Co.).

Collyns, C. (1983) *Alternatives to the Central Bank in the Developing World*, occasional paper no. 20 (Washington, DC: International Monetary Fund).

Cooper, R. N. (1990) 'Currency Convertibility in Eastern Europe' in Symposium *Central Banking Issues in Emerging Market-Oriented Economies* (Kansas: Federal Reserve Bank of Kansas City) pp. 141–8.

Cortés-Douglas, H. and R. K. Abrams (1993) 'Introducing New National Currencies', *Finance and Development*, 30: 26–30.

Cottarelli, C. (1993) *Limiting Central Bank Credit to the Government: Theory and Practice*, occasional paper no. 110 (Washington, DC: International Monetary Fund).

—— (1994) 'Should an "Independent" Central Bank Control Foreign Exchange Policy?' in T. J. T. Baliño and C. Cottarelli (eds) *Frameworks for Monetary Stability* (Washington, DC: International Monetary Fund), pp. 330–56.

Crow, J. W. (1990) 'Monetary Policy and Inflation', in *Central Banking Issues in Emerging Market Economies* (Kansas City: Federal Reserve Bank of Kansas) 9–22.

Cukierman, A. (1992) *Central Bank Strategy, Credibility, and Independence: Theory and Evidence* (Cambridge, Mass.: MIT Press).

—— (1994) 'Central Bank Independence and Monetary Control', *The Economic Journal*, 104: 1437–48.

—— (1995) 'Political Influence on the Central Bank: International Evidence', *World Bank Economic Review*, 9: 397–424.

—— S. Edwards and G. Tabellini (1992) 'Seigniorage and Political Instability', *American Economic Review*, 82: (3): 537–55.

—— S. B. Webb and B. Neyapti (1992) 'Measuring the Independence of Central Banks and its Effects on Policy Outcomes', *World Bank Economic Review*, 6: 353–98.

Currie, L. (1981) *The Role of Economic Advisors in Developing Countries* (Westport, Conn.: Greenwood Press, 1981).

de Costa, E. P. W. (1985) *Reserve Bank of India (Fifty Years, 1935–85)* (Bombay: Reserve Bank of India).

Dalla, I., D. Khatkhate *et al.* (1995) *The Emerging Asian Bond Market* (Washington, DC: World Bank).

Deane, M. and R. Pringle (1995) *The Central Banks* (New York: Viking).

de Kock, M. H. (1974) *Central Banking* (New York: St. Martin's Press).

Desai, A. (1994) *My Economic Affair* (New York: Wiley Eastern Ltd., 2nd edn).

Deshmukh, C. D. (1948) *Central Banking in India – A Retrospect* (Poona: Gokhale Institute of Politics and Economics).

—— and R. V. Roosa (1965) *The Balance Between Monetary Policy and Other Instruments of Economic Policy in a Modern Society*, The Per Jacobsson Lectures (Washington, DC: International Monetary Fund).

Dott, S. and A. Shanmugham (1994) 'New Data on Payments Systems in Developing Countries', *Payments Systems Worldwide*, 5: 24–26.

Downes, P. (1989) 'Managing Foreign Exchange Reserves', *Finance and Development*, 26: 20–1.

—— and R. Vaez-Zadeh (eds) (1991) *The Evolving Role of Central Banks* (Washington, DC: International Monetary Fund).

Drake, P. W. (ed.) (1994) *Money Doctors, Foreign Debtors, and Economic Reforms in Latin American (From the 1890s to the Present).*

Drakopoulos, S. A. (1994) 'Hierarchical Choice in Economics', *Journal of Economic Surveys*, 8(2): 133–53.

Eddington, A. S. (1968) 'The Secluded Bursar', in *Specialists and Generalists (A Selection of Readings)* Committee on Government Operations, US Senate (Washington, DC: Government Printing Office) pp. 49–50.

Edwards, S. and G. Tabellini (1991) 'Explaining Fiscal Policies and Inflation in Developing Countries', *Journal of International Money and Finance*, 10: 16–48.

Effros, R. C. (1994) 'The Maastricht Treaty, Independence of the Central Banks and Influencing Legislation', in T. J. T. Baliño and C. Cottarelli (eds) *Frameworks for Monetary Stability* (Washington, DC: International Monetary Fund) pp. 279–308.

Elster, J. (1994) *The Impact of Constitutions on Economic Performance* (Washington, DC: World Bank).

Elster, J. (1988) *Ulysses and the Sirens*: Studies in Rationality and Irrationality (Cambridge: Cambridge University Press).

Espinosa-Vega, M. A. (1995) 'Multiple Reserve Requirements', *Journal of Money, Credit, and Banking*, 27: 762–73.

European Bank for Reconstruction and Development (1994) *Transition Report*, October (London: European Bank).

Fan, L-S. and C-M. Fan (1990) 'Modern Mercantilism, Central Bank Bankruptcy and Policy Dilemma: The Case of Taiwan', *Banca Nazionale Del Lavoro Quarterly Review*, 172: 91–100.

Fay, S. (1988) *Portrait of an Old Lady: Turmoil at the Bank of England* (Harmondsworth: Viking).

Federal Reserve Bank of Kansas City (1990) *Central Banking Issues in Emerging Market-Oriented Economies* (Kansas City: Federal Reserve Bank).

Feldman, R. A. and R. Mehra (1993) 'Auctions, Theory and Applications', International Monetary Fund, *Staff Papers*, 40: 485–511.

Fisher, J. L. (1953) *Report on the Desirability and Practicality of Establishing a Central Bank in Nigeria for Promoting the Economic Development of the Country* (Lagos: Government Printer).

Flanders, M. J. (1993) 'A Model of Discretion: The Gold Standard in Fact and Fiction', *The World Economy*, 16: 213–300.

Fleming, J. M. (1968) 'Targets and Instruments,' IMF *Staff Papers*, XV: 387–401.

Fleming, V. and S. Cole (1995) 'The Evolution of Central Banking in Post-Communist Countries', *Bank of England Quarterly Bulletin*, 35: 54–9.

Freedman, C. (1994) 'The Use of Indicators and the Monetary Conditions Index in Canada', in T. J. T. Baliño and C. Cottarelli (eds) *Frameworks for Monetary Stability* (Washington, DC: International Monetary Fund) pp. 458–78.

Frenkel, J. A. (1990) 'Currency Convertibility in Eastern Europe', in *Central Banking Issues in Emerging Market-Oriented Economies* (Federal Reserve Bank of Kansas City) pp. 149–56.

—— (1993) 'Top Economist Ponders a Changing World' (Interview), *Finance and Development*, 30: 2–5.

Friedman, M. and A. J. Schwartz (1963) *A Monetary History of the United States 1867–1960* (Princeton: Princeton University Press).

Fry, M. J. (1990) *Fiscal Approach to Central Banking*, University of Birmingham, International Finance Group, working paper 12: 1–23.

—— (1992) 'Can a Central Bank Go Bust?', *The Manchester School*, LX Supplement: 85–98.

—— (1993) 'The Fiscal Abuse of Central Banks', IMF Working Paper WP/93/58.

——, C. A. E. Goodhart and A. Almeida (1995) 'Central Banking in Developing Countries, in *Bank of England Symposium on Central Banking in Developing Countries* (London: Bank of England) pp. 1–74.

Galbis, V. (1993) 'High Real Interest Rates Under Financial Liberalization: Is There a Problem', IMF Working Paper WP/93/7.

Galbraith, J. K. (1975) 'How Keynes Came to America', in *Economics, Peace and Laughter* (Harmondsworth: Penguin).

Germidis, D., D. Kessler and R. Meghir (1991) *Financial Systems and Development (What Role for the Formal and Informal Financial Sector?)* (Paris: Development Centre, OECD).

Ghate, P. G. (1992) 'Interaction Between the Formal and Informal Financial Sector: The Asian Experience', *World Development*, 20: 859–82.

Goehuys, D. (1992) 'Islamic Banking Spreads Its Wings', *Central Banking*, 3: 41–4.

Goldman, M. I. (1994) *Lost Opportunity? (Why Economic Reforms in Russia Have Not Worked)* (New York: Norton).

Goodfriend, M. (1988) 'Bureau Analysis and Central Banking', a review essay, *Journal of Monetary Economics*, 22: 517–22.

Goodhart, C. A. E. (1984) *Monetary Theory and Practice* (London: Macmillan).

—— (1988) *The Evolution of Central Banks* (Cambridge, Mass.: MIT Press).

—— (1994) 'What Should Central Banks Do? What Should Be Their Macroeconomic Objectives and Operations?' *The Economic Journal*, 104: 1424–36.

Goodhart, C. A. E. (1995a) 'Why do Banks Need a Central Bank' in C. A. E. Goodhart, *The Central Bank and the Financial System* (Cambridge, Mass: MIT Press) pp. 3–18.

Goodhart, C. A. E. (1995b) 'Can We Improve the Structure of Financial Systems' in C. A. E. Goodhart, *The Central Bank and The Financial System* (Cambridge, Mass: MIT Press) pp. 19–39.

—— (1995c) 'Central Bank Independence', in C. A. E. Goodhart, *The Central Bank and the Financial System* (Cambridge, Mass.: MIT Press) pp. 60–71.

——, with Dirk Schoenmaker (1995) 'Institutional Separation Between Supervisory and Monetary Agencies', in C. A. E. Goodhart, *The Central*

*Bank and the Financial System* (Cambridge, Mass.: MIT Press) pp. 333–413.

——, F. Capie and N. Schnadt (1994) 'The Development of Central Banking', in F. Capie, C. Goodhart, S. Fischer and N. Schnadt (eds) *The Future of Central Banking* (Tercentenary Symposium of the Bank of England) (Cambridge, Mass.: University Press) pp. 1–123.

Goodman, J. B. (1991) 'The Politics of Central Bank Independence,' *Comparative Politics*, April: 329–49.

Greenspan, A. (1990) 'Overview', *Central Banking in Emergent Market Economies* (Kansas City: Federal Reserve Bank of Kansas) pp. 177–82.

Guasch, J. H. and T. Glaessner (1993) 'Using Auctions to Allocate and Price Long-Term Credit', *World Bank Research Observer*, 8: 169–94.

Guidotti, P. E. and C. A. Rodriguez (1992) 'Dollarization in Latin America: Gresham's Law in Reverse?' IMF *Staff Papers* 39: 518–44.

Guitian, M. (1994) 'Rules or Discretion in Monetary Policy: National and International Perspectives', in T. J. T. Baliño and C. Cottarelli (eds), *Frameworks for Monetary Stability*, (Washington, DC: International Monetary Fund), pp. 19–41.

Gupta, O. P. (1934) *Central Banking in India, 1773–1934, with Special Examination of the Reserve Bank of India Act 1934* (Delhi: Gupta).

Gurley, J. G., H. T. Patrick and E. S. Shaw (1965) *The Financial Structure of Korea* (United States Operations Mission to Korea, July 1965) (Washington, DC: US Agency for International Development).

Haan, J., D. Zelhorst and O. Roukens (1993) 'Seigniorage in Developing Countries', *Applied Financial Economics* (UK) 3: 307–14.

Haggblade, S. (1978) 'Africanization from Below: The Evolution of Cameroonian Societies into Western Style Banks', *Rural Africana New Series*, Fall: 35–6.

Hanke, S. H., L. Jonung and K. Schuler (1993) *Russian Currency and Finance: A Currency Board Approach* (London and New York: Routledge).

—— and K. Schuler (1990) 'Keynes and the Currency Reform: Some Lessons from Eastern Europe', *Journal of Economic Growth*, 4: 10–16.

—— and—— (1991) *Currency Boards for Eastern Europe* (Washington, DC: Heritage Foundation).

—— and—— (1993) 'Currency Boards and Currency Convertibility', *Cato Journal* (US), 12: 687–705.

—— and—— (1994) *Currency Boards for Developing Countries* (San Francisco: International Center for Economic Growth).

Hardy, D. C. (1993) 'Reserve Requirements and Monetary Management: An Introduction', IMF Working Paper, WP/93/35.

—— and A. K. Lahiri (1994) 'Cash Shortage in the Former Soviet Union?' IMF Working Paper, WP/94/67.

Havrilesky, T. (1990) 'A Public Choice Perspective on the Cycle in Monetary Policy', *Cato Journal*, 9: 709–18.

—— and J. Granato (1993) 'Determinants of Inflation Performance: Corporatist Structures vs. Central Bank Autonomy', *Public Finance*, 76: 249–61.

Heller, H. R. (1977) 'Choosing an Exchange Rate System', *Finance and Development*, 14 23–7.

—— (1991) 'Prudential Supervision and Monetary Policy', in P. Downes and R. Vaez-Zadeh (eds) *The Evolving Role of Central Banks* (Washington, DC: International Monetary Fund) pp. 57–68.

Hennessy, E. (1991) 'How Central Bankers are Trained,' *Central Banking*, 4: 32–6.

Hetzel, R. L. (1990) 'Central Banks' Independence in Historical Perspective: A Review Essay', *Journal of Monetary Economics*, 25: 165–76.

Hicks, J. R. (1977) *Economic Perspectives* (New York: Oxford University Press).

—— (1982) 'A French View of Money (1943)', in *Money, Interest and Wages: Collected Essays of Economic Theory*, vol. 2 (Cambridge, Mass.: Harvard University Press) pp. 132–9.

Hilbers, P. (1993) 'Monetary Instruments and Their Use During the Transition from a Centrally Planned to a Market Economy', IMF Working Paper, WP/93/87.

Hirsch, F. (1977) 'The Bagehot Problem', *The Manchester School of Economic and Social Studies* XLV: 241–57.

Hobsbawm, E. J. (1969) *Industry and Empire* (Harmondsworth: Penguin).

Hook, A. T. (1992) 'Managing Payment System Risk During the Transition from a Centrally Planned to a Market Economy', IMF Working Paper, WP/92/95.

Hooyman, C. J. (1994) 'The Use of Foreign Exchange Swaps by Central Banks', IMF *Staff Papers*, 41: 149–61.

Huang, C. J., J. C. Cheng, C. S. Chou and S. C. Lin (1992) 'The Substitutability of Monetary Assets in Taiwan', *Southern Economic Journal*, 58: 975–87.

Hughes, A. V. (1992) 'Central Banking at the Small End', *Central Banking*, 3: 23–8.

Humphrey, D. B. (1994) *Payment Systems (Principles, Practice and Implementation)*, Technical Paper no. 260 (Washington, DC: World Bank).

Humphrey, T. M. (1975) 'The Classical Concept of the Lender of Last Resort', Federal Reserve Bank of Richmond *Economic Review*, 61: 2–9.

—— (1989) 'Lender of Last Resort: The Concept in History', Federal Reserve Bank of Richmonds *Economic Review*, 75, 8–16.

Iengar, H. V. R. *Monetary Policy and Economic Growth* (Bombay: Vora & Co.).

International Monetary Fund (1994) *International Capital Markets* (M. Goldstein and D. Folkerts-Landau).

—— (1995) *Annual Report* (Washington, DC: IMF).

—— (1995) *Annual Report on Exchange Arrangements and Exchange Restrictions.*

—— (1995b) *International Capital Markets: Developments, Prospects, and Policy Issues* (D. Folkerts-Landau and T. Ito).

Iqbal, Z. and A. Mirakhor (1987) *Islamic Banking*, occasional paper 49 (Washington, DC: International Monetary Fund).

Iyengar, S. K. (1943) 'Central Banking in Hyderabad', *The Economic Journal*, LIII: 274–80.

—— and M. Mir Khan (Nawab Mir Nawaz Jung) (1944) *A.B.C. of Central Banking: The Problem, Position and Prospects in Hyderabad* (Hyderabad: Indian Co-operative Series, no. XI).

Jacobsson, E. E. (1979) *A Life for Sound Money – Per Jacobsson, His Biography* (Oxford: Clarendon Press).

Jayasankaran, S. (1994) 'On Being Accountable for the Accounting', *Malaysian Business Review*, April 16: 29–31.

Johnson, H. G. (1971) 'A Word to the Third World: A Western Economist's Frank Advice', *Encounter*, 37: 3–10.

—— (1973) 'The Problems of Central Banking', *UMBC Review* (Malaysia), IX: 67–73.

Jordan, J. L. (1994) 'A Market-Approach to Banking Regulation', *Cato Journal*, 13: 315–32.

Kaldor, N. (1970) 'The Case for Regional Policies', *Scottish Journal of Political Economy*, 17: 337–48.

—— (1971) 'Conflicts in National Economic Objectives', *The Economic Journal*, LXXXI: 1–15.

—— (1984) *The Failure of Monetarism* (Bombay: Reserve Bank of India).

Kemmerer, E. W. (1927) 'Economic Advisory Work for Governments', *The American Economic Review*, XVII: 1–12.

Kennedy, C. (1965) 'The Case for Equities as a Part of Official External Assets', *Social and Economic Studies*, 14: 245–51.

Keynes, J. M. *The Collected Writings of John Maynard Keynes* (London: Macmillan)

vol. I: *Indian Currency and Finance* (1913) [1972].

vol. IV: *A Tract on Monetary Reform* (1923) [1971].

vol. VI: *A Treatise on Money: The Applied Theory of Money* (1930) [1971].

vol. XV: *Activities 1906–14: Indian and Cambridge* (1971).

vol. XV: *Activities 1929–31: Rethinking Employment and Unemployment Policies*

vol. XIX: *Activities 1922–29: The Return to Gold and Industrial Policy* (1981a).

vol. XX: *Activities 1929–31: Rethinking Employment and Unemployment Policies* (1981b).

Khan, M. S. (1986) 'Islamic Interest-Free Banking', IMF *Staff Papers*, 33: 1–27.

—— (1995) 'Central Banking in an Islamic Economy', paper prepared for the Ninth Expert Level Conference on Islamic Banking, Jakarta, Indonesia, 7–8 April.

—— and A. Mirakhor (1987) 'The Financial System and Monetary Policy in an Islamic Economy', in M. S. Khan and A. Mirakhor (eds) *Theoretical Studies in Islamic Banking and Finance* (Houston: The Institute for Research and Islamic Studies) pp. 163–84.

—— and—— (1990) 'Islamic Banking: Experiences in the Islamic Republic of Iran and in Pakistan', *Economic Development and Cultural Change*, 38: 353–76.

—— and—— (1992) 'Islamic Banking', in P. Newman, M. Milgate and J. Eatwell (eds) *The New Palgrave Dictionary of Money and Finance* (London: Macmillan).

—— and—— (1993) 'Monetary Management in an Islamic Economy', *Journal of Islamic Banking and Finance*, 10: 42–64.

—— and V. Sundararajan (1992) 'Financial Sector Reforms and Monetary Policy', in V. A. Jaffarey (moderator), *Structural Adjustment and Macroeconomic Policy Issues* (Washington, DC: International Monetary Fund and Pakistan Administrative Staff College) pp. 58–79.

Khatkhate, D. R. (1972) 'Analytic Basis of the Working of Monetary Policy in Less Developed Countries', IMF *Staff Papers*, XIX: 533–58.

—— (1988) 'Assessing the Impact of Interest Rates in Less Developed Countries', *World Development*, 16: 577–88.

—— (1988) 'Assessing the Level of Interest Rates in Less Developed Countries', *Economic and Political Weekly*, XXIII (July): 1427–32.

Khazzoom, J. D. (1966) *The Currency Ratio in Developing Countries* (New York: Frederick A. Praeger, Inc.).

Kisch, C. H. and W. A. Elkin (1932) *Central Banks* (London: Macmillan).

Klamer, A. (1989) 'An Accountant Among Economists, Conversations with Sir John R. Hicks', *The Journal of Economic Perspectives*, 3: 167–180.

Klaus, V. (1990) 'Policy Dilemmas of Eastern European Reforms: Notes of an Insider', in *Central Banking Issues in Emerging Market-Oriented Economies* (Kansas City: The Federal Reserve Bank of Kansas City) pp. 51–56.

Kovanen, A. (1994) 'Foreign Exchange Auctions and Fixings: A Review of Performance', IMF Working Paper, WP/94/119.

Krishnaswamy, K. S. (1985) 'The Reserve Bank and Government: A Broad-Brush Picture', *Commerce* (Bombay), 7 September: 33–8.

Kroc, R. (1972) 'Management Strategy of a Central Bank in a Developing Country', *Finance and Development*, 9: 42–7.

Kulkarni, P. B. (1990) 'Foreign Exchange Reserve Management', *The 18th SEANZA Central Banking Course*, Reserve Bank of India, Bombay, pp. 297–307.

—— (1992) 'Management of Gold Reserves by Central Banks', *Discount and Finance* (Bombay), IV March 28: 1–8.

Lamfalussy, A. (1994) *Central Banking in Transition*, Per Jacobsson Lecture (London: Bank of England).

Laski, H. J. (1968) 'The Limitations of the Expert', in *Specialists and Generalists (A Selection of Readings)*, Committee on Government Operations, US Senate (Washington, DC: US Government Printing Office) pp. 50–9.

Lastra, R. M. (1992) 'The Independence of the European System of Central Banks', *Harvard International Law Journal*, 33: 475–519.

Laya, J. C. (1980) 'Bank Supervision and Examination in the Philippines', *SEANZA Lectures* (Jakarta: Bank Indonesia).

Leone, A. M. (1991) 'Effectiveness and Implications of Limits on Central Bank Credit to the Government', in P. Downes and R. Vaez- Zadeh (eds) *The Evolving Role of Central Banks* (Washington, DC: International Monetary Fund) pp. 363–413.

Leone, A. M. (1994) 'Institutional and Operational Aspects of Central Bank Losses', in T. J. T. Baliño and C. Cottarelli (eds), *Frameworks for*

*Monetary Stability (Policy Issues and Country Experiences)* (Washington, DC: International Monetary Fund) pp. 738–55.

Levitsky, J. and R. N. Prasad (1987) *Credit Guarantee Schemes for Small and Medium Enterprises*, Technical Paper no. 58 (Washington, DC: World Bank).

Lindbeck, A. (1976) 'Stabilization Policy in Open Economies with Endogenous Politicians', *American Economic Review*, 66: 1–19.

Lindgren, C. (1991) 'The Transition from Direct to Indirect Instruments of Monetary Policy', in P. Downes and R. Vaez-Zadeh (eds) *The Evolving Role of Central Banks* (Washington, DC: International Monetary Fund) pp. 307–25.

—— and D. E. Dueñas (1994) 'Strengthening Central Bank Independence in Latin America', in T. J. T. Baliño and C. Cottarelli (eds), *Frameworks for Monetary Stability* (Washington, DC: International Monetary Fund) pp. 309–29.

Loungani, P. and M. Rush (1995) 'The Effect of Changes in Reserve Requirements on Investment and GNP', *Journal of Money, Credit, and Banking*, 27: 511–26.

McKinnon, R. I. (1973) *Money and Capital in Economic Development* (Washington, DC: The Brookings Institution).

—— (1984) *Financial Repression and Economic Development* (Taipei, Taiwan: The Institute of Economics, Academica Sinica).

McLeod, A. N. (1994) 'Central Banking in Trinidad and Tobago, 1966–1969', *Banca Nazionale Del Lavoro Quarterly Review*, 190: 309–32.

Majumdar, B. (1979) *Central Banks and Treasuries: A Study of the Relations Between the Bank and the Fisc with Special Reference to India* (Bombay: Vora).

Mancera, M. (1990) 'Interview', *Central Banking*, 2: 39–40.

—— (1991) 'Role of Monetary Policy', in P. A. Volcker, M. Mancera and J. Godeaux, *Perspectives on the Role of a Central Bank* (Washington, D.C.: People's Bank of China, International Monetary Fund, United Nations Development Programme pp. 18–22.

Mas, I. and S. H. Talley (1990) 'Deposit Insurance in Developing Countries', *Finance and Development*, 27: 43–5.

Masson, P. R. and M. P. Taylor (1993) 'Currency Unions: A Survey of the Issues', in P. Mason and M. P. Taylor (eds), *Policy Issues in the Operation of Curency Unions* Cambridge University Press pp. 3–54.

Mathieson, D. J. and R. D. Haas (1995) 'Establishing Monetary Control in Financial System with Insolvent Institutions', IMF *Staff Papers*, 42: 184–201.

Mathur, R. (1988) 'The Delay in the Formation of the Reserve Bank of India: The India Office Perspective', *The Indian Economic and Social History Review*, XXV: 133–70.

Mauri, A. (1982) 'Some Comments on the Role of Central Banks in Less Developed Countries', *Annali della Facolta di Scienze Politiche dell Universita di Milano*, II: 297–314.

Maxfield, S. (1994) 'Financial Incentives and Central Bank Authority in Industrializing Nations', *World Politics*, 46: 556–87.

Meesook, K. M. (1978) *Regional Distribution of Commercial Bank Services in Thailand* (Bangkok: Bank of Thailand).

Meltzer, A. (1990) 'Comment from the Floor', in *Central Banking Issues in Emerging Market Economies* (Kansas City: Federal Reserve Bank of Kansas).

Mendzela, J. (1994) 'Improving the Management of a Central Bank – A Case Study', IMF Working Paper, WP/94/37.

Mills, H. R. (1961) *Report on Training Facilities at the Technician Level in South and South East Asia* (Colombo: Colombo Plan Bureau).

Mirakhor, A. (1988) 'The Progress of Islamic Banking in Iran', in C. Mallat (ed.) *Islamic Law and Finance* (London: Graham & Trotman).

Mittra, S. (1978) *Central Banking Versus Treasury: An International Study* (Washington, DC: University Press of America).

Montiel, P., P. Agenor and N. U. Haque (1993) *Informal Financial Markets in Developing Countries: A Macroeconomic Analysis* (Oxford: Blackwell).

*Morgan Stanley Central Banking Directory* (1994) (London: Morgan Stanley Co.).

G. Myrdal, (1957) *Economic Theory and Underdeveloped Regions* (London: Duckworth).

—— (1965) 'Development and Underdevelopment', 50th Anniversary Lecture (Cairo: National Bank of Egypt).

Nascimento, J. C. (1994) 'Monetary Policy in Unified Currency Areas', IMF Working Paper, WP/94/11.

Neufeld, E. P. (1958) 'The Bank of Canada's Approach to Central Banking', *Canadian Journal of Economics and Political Science*, XXIV: 332–44.

Nicholson, M. (1972) *Oligopoly and Conflict* (University of Toronto Press).

Nordhaus, W. D. (1975) 'The Political Business Cycle', *Review of Economic Studies*, 42: 169–90.

Norman, M. (1932) 'Foreword', in Kisch and Elkin (eds) *Central Banks* (London: Macmillan).

North, D. C. (1994) 'Economic Performance Through Time', *American Economic Review*, 84: 359–68.

Oakeshott, M. (1985) 'The Rule of Law', in *History and Other Essays* (Oxford: Basil Blackwell).

O'Grady Walshe, T. (1991) 'Managing a Central Bank: Goals, Strategies and Techniques', in P. Downes and Reza Vaez-Zadeh (eds) *The Evolving Role of Central Banks* (Washington, DC: International Monetary Fund pp. 93–120.

Olakanpo, J. O. W. (1965) *Central Banking in the Commonwealth: A Comprehensive Study of Monetary Problems and Techniques* (Calcutta: Bookland Private Ltd).

Osband, K. and D. Villanueva (1993) 'Independent Currency Authorities: An Analytic Primer', IMF *Staff Papers*, 40: 202–16.

Owen, D. P. and O. Solis-Fallas (1989) 'Unorganized Money Markets and "Unproductive" Assets in the New Structuralist Critique of Financial Liberalization', *Journal of Development Economics*, 31: 341–55.

Patel, I. G. (1994) 'Some Reflections on Financial Liberalization', *International Journal of Development Banking*, 12: 39–52.

Patinkin, D. (1965) 'The Paths to Economic Progress', in D. Krivine (ed.) *Fiscal and Monetary Problems in Developing States* (New York: Frederick A. Praeger) pp. 392–407.

Pereira Leite, S. and R. Vaez-Zadeh (1986) 'Credit Allocation and Investment Decisions: The Case of the Manufacturing Sector', *World Development*, 14: 115–25.

Plumptre, A. F. W. (1947) *Central Banking in the British Dominions* (University of Toronto Press).

Poenisch, H. (1991) 'The New Central Banks of Eastern Europe', *Central Banking*, 4: 9–20.

Polak, J. J. (1988) 'The Choice of an Exchange Rate Regime', in D. Sutalaksana (ed.) *Development Issues in the Current International Monetary System* (Singapore: Addison-Wesley Publishing Co. pp. 132–48.

Popper, K. (1977) *The Unended Quest* (Glasgow: Fontana/Collins).

Posen, A. S. (1994) 'Why Central Bank Independence Does not Cause Low Inflation: There is no Institutional Fix', in R. O'Brien (ed.) *Finance and the International Economy* (New York: Oxford University Press).

Premchand, A. (1993) *Public Expenditure Management* (Washington, DC: International Monetary Fund).

—— (1995) *Effective Government Accounting* (Washington, DC: International Monetary Fund).

Presidential Commission on Finance and Banking, The Sri Lanka (1992) *Final Report: Part II: The Central Bank* (Colombo: Government Publications Bureau).

Pringle, R. (1993/94) 'The views from the peoples Bank of China', *Central Banking*, IV: 67–76.

Quah, D. and S. P. Vahey (1995) 'Measuring Core Inflation' *The Economic Journal*, 105: 1130–44.

Quintyn, M. (1994) 'Government Versus Central Bank Securities in Developing Open Market Operations', in T. J. T. Baliño and C. Cottarelli (eds) *Frameworks for Monetary Stability* (Washington, DC: International Monetary Fund) pp. 691–737.

Quirk, P. J. (1994) 'Capital Account Convertibility: A New Model for Developing Countries', in T. J. T. Baliño and C. Cottarelli (eds) *Frameworks for Monetary Stability* (Washington, DC: International Monetary Fund) pp. 373–96.

—— *et al.* (1987) *Floating Exchange Rates in Developing Countries: Experience with Auction and Interbank Markets*, occasional paper no. 53 (Washington, DC: International Monetary Fund).

—— *et al.* (1995) *Capital Account Convertibility (Review of Experience and Implications for IMF Policies)*, occasional paper 131 (Washington, DC: International Monetary Fund).

Raj, K. N. (1948) *The Monetary Policy of the Reserve Bank of India: A Study of Central Banking in an Underdeveloped Economy* (Bombay: Asia Publishing House).

Rana, P. B. (1995) 'Reform Strategies in Transitional Economies: Lessons from Asia', *World Development*, 23: 1157–69.

Rangarajan, C. (1988) 'Central Banking and Economic Development: Indian Experience', *Reserve Bank of India Bulletin*, XLII: 645–8.

Repse, E. (1993) 'Be Ready to be Blamed for Everything: How Latvia Introduced its Currency', *Finance and Development*, 30: 28–9.
Reserve Bank of India (1957) *Functions and Working* (Bombay: Reserve Bank of India).
—— (1970) *History of the Reserve Bank of India, 1935–1951* (Bombay: Reserve Bank of India).
Robertson, D. H. 'The Role of Persuasion in Economic Affairs', in S. R. Dennison and J. R. Presley (eds) *Robertson on Economic Policy* (Basingstoke: Macmillan) pp. 156–69.
Robinson, D. J. and Peter Stella (1988) 'Amalgamating Central Bank and Fiscal Deficits', in M. I. Blejer and Ke-Young Chu (eds) *Measurement of Fiscal Impact: Methodological Issues*, occasional paper 59 (Washington, DC: International Monetary Fund) pp. 20–31.
Robinson, M. A. (1959) *The National Debt Ceiling (An Experiment in Fiscal Policy)* (Washington, DC: The Brookings Institution).
Rodriguez, C. A. (1993) *Quasi-Fiscal Deficits: Latin American Lessons for South Asia*, Report no. IDP–129, August (Washington, DC: World Bank).
Rostowski, J. (1994) 'Interenterprise Arrears in Post-Communist Economies', International Monetary Fund Working Paper, WP/94/43.
Rowley, C. and R. Elgin (1985) 'Towards a Theory of Bureaucratic Behavior', in D. Greenaway and G. K. Shaw (eds) *Public Choice, Public Finance and Public Policy* (Essays in Honor of Alan Peacock) (Oxford: Basil Blackwell) pp. 31–50.
Rutherford, M. (1994) *Institutions in Economics (The Old and the New Institutionalism)* (Cambridge University Press).
Saal, M. I. and L. M. Zamalloa (1995) 'Use of Central Bank Credit Auctions in Economies in Transition', IMF *Staff Papers*, 42: 202–24.
Sahay, R. and C. Vegh (1995) 'Inflation and Stabilization in Transition Economies: A Comparison with Market Economies,' *Finance and Development*, 32: 36–9.
Samuelson, P. A. (1966) 'Reflections on Central Banking', in J. E. Stiglitz (ed.) *The Collected Scientific Papers of Paul A. Samuelson*, vol. II (Mass.: MIT Press).
Sandilands, R. (1990) *The Life and Political Economy of Lauchlin Currie: New Dealer, Presidential Advisor and Development Economist* (Durham, NC: Duke University Press).
Sargent, T. J. and N. Wallace (1981) 'Some Unpleasant Monetarist Arithmetic', Federal Reserve Bank of Minneapolis, *Quarterly Review*, 5 : 1–17.
Sayers, R. S. (1947) *Modern Banking*, 7th edn (Oxford: Clarendon Press).
—— (1959) 'Central Banking in Underdeveloped Countries', in *Central Banking After Bagehot* (London: Oxford University Press) pp. 108–33.
—— (1961) 'The Role of the Central Bank in a Developing Economy', in *Problems of Development* (Paris: Organization for European Economic Co-operation, European Productivity Agency, January) pp. 33–45.
—— (1976) *The Bank of England, 1891–1944*, vol. 2 (Cambridge University Press).
Schadler, S. (1994) 'Capital Movements and Surveillance', in T. J. T. Baliño and C. Cottarelli (eds) *Frameworks for Monetary Stability* (Washington, DC: International Monetary Fund) pp. 357–94.

—— *et al.* (1995) *IMF Conditionality: Experience Under Stand-By and Extended Arrangements, Part I: Key Issues and Findings*, occasional paper 128 (Washington, DC: International Monetary Fund).

Schwartz, A. J. (1992) *Do Currency Boards Have a Future?* (London: Institute of Economic Affairs).

SEACEN Centre (1986) *Reports and Papers of Seminar on Unorganized Money Markets*, 20 March 1985, Yogjakarta, Indonesia (Petaling Jaya, Malaysia).

Selgin, G. A. and L. H. White (1994) 'How Would the Invisible Hand Handle Money?' *Journal of Economic Literature*, XXXII: 1718–49.

Sen, S. N. (1967) *Central Banking in Underdeveloped Money Markets*, 4th edn (Calcutta: Bookland Private Ltd.).

Sen, S. R. (1957) *The Economics of Sir James Steuart* (Cambridge, Mass.: Harvard University Press).

Shaw, E. S. (1973) *Financial Deepening in Economic Development* (New York: Oxford University Press).

Siddiqi, M. N. (1982) 'Islamic Approaches to Money, Banking, and Monetary Policy: A Review', in M. Ariff (ed.), *Monetary and Fiscal Economics of Islam* (Jeddah: International Centre for Research in Islamic Economics) pp. 25–42.

Sinha, J. (1994) 'Financial Incentives, Central Bank Autonomy, and Inflation – A Study of the Reserve Bank of India' (unpublished).

Sirisena, P. T. (1990) 'Supervision in Developing Countries: A Case Study of Sri Lanka', paper, the 18th SEANZA Central Banking Course, Reserve Bank of India, Bombay.

Skorov, G. (1992) 'From Economic Reform to Hyperinflation', *Central Banking*, 3(3): 28–38.

Snoek, H. (1989) 'Problems of Bank Supervision in LDCs', *Finance and Development*, 26: 14–16.

Snyder, E. P. (1986) Testimony before Committee on Banking, Finance and Urban Affairs, Ninety-Ninth Congress (Washington, DC: Government Printing Office).

Solow, R. M. (1994) 'Advise and Dissent', *The New Republic*, 211: 41–3.

Southard, F. A., Jr. (1968) 'The Central Bank in the Policy Making Process', *Finance and Development*, 5: 17–19.

Staff Report of the Committee on Banking and Currency (1972) *Foreign Experience with Monetary Policies to Promote Economic and Social Priority Programs*, 92nd Congress (Washington, DC: US Government Printing Office).

Streeten, P., and T. Balogh (1957) 'A Reconsideration of Monetary Policy', *Bulletin of the Oxford University Institute of Statistics*, 19: 331–9.

Summers, B. J. (1991) 'Clearing and Payment Systems: The Central Bank's Role', in P. Downes and R. Vaez-Zadeh, *The Evolving Role of Central Banks* (Washington, DC: International Monetary Fund).

Sundararajan, V. and T. J. T. Baliño (1991) 'Issues in Recent Banking Crises', in V. Sundararajan and T. J. T. Baliño, *Banking Crises: Cases and Issues* (Washington, DC: International Monetary Fund) pp. 1–57.

—— and G. Sensenbrenner (1994) 'Linkages Between Payments Systems Reforms and Monetary Policy: The Recent Experience in Russia and

Other Former Soviet Union Countries', in T. J. T. Baliño and C. Cottarelli (eds), *Frameworks for Monetary Stability* (Washington, DC: International Monetary Fund) pp. 611–54.

—— A. Vasudevan and L. Molho (1988) 'Financial Reform and Monetary Control in Indonesia', IMF Working Paper, no. 88/4.

Supinit, V. (1991) 'Interview' by Dick Wilson, *Central Banking*, 3: 15–23.

Talley, S. H. and I. Mas (1990) *Deposit Insurance in Developing Countries*, WPS 548 (Washington, DC: World Bank).

Tamagna, F. M. (1965) *Central Banking in Latin America* (1st English edn) (Mexico: Center for Latin American Monetary Studies).

Tarapore, S. S. (1994) 'Foreign Exchange Reserves Management: An Indian Perspective', *Reserve Bank of India Bulletin*, November: 1483–9.

Teijero, M. O. (1989) *Central Bank Losses: Origins, Conceptual Issues, and Measurement Problems, Policy*, Planning and Research Working Paper no. 293 (Washington, DC: World Bank).

Thatcher, M. (1993) *The Downing Street Years* (New York: HarperCollins).

Thurow, L. (1972) *Foreign Experience with Monetary Policies to Promote Economic and Social Priority Programs*, Staff Report prepared for the Committee on Banking and Currency, US House of Representatives, 92nd Congress, May.

Tobin, J. (1982) *Central Banks and Government Budget* (Bombay: Reserve Bank of India).

—— (1984) 'On the Efficiency of the Financial System', *Lloyds Bank Review*, 153: 1–16.

Toma, E. F. and M. Toma (eds) (1986) *Central Bankers, Bureaucratic Incentives, and Monetary Policy* (Boston: Kluwer Academic Publishers).

Toniolo, G. (1990) 'Central Banks' Independence in Historical Perspective' (A Review Essay), *Journal of Monetary Economics*, 25: 165–75.

Tuya, J. and L. Zamalloa (1994) 'Issues on Placing Banking Supervision in the Central Bank', in T. J. T. Baliño and C. Cottarelli (eds), *Frameworks for Monetary Stability* (Washington, DC: International Monetary Fund) pp. 663–90.

Tybout, J. (1984) 'Interest Controls and Credit Allocations in Developing Countries', *Journal of Money, Credit, and Banking*, 16: 474–87.

US Congress (1985) *The Federal Financing Bank and the Debt Ceiling*, Hearing before Committee on Banking, Finance and Urban Affairs, House of Representatives, Ninety-Ninth Congress, 31 October (Washington, DC: Government Printing Office, 1986).

Uzair, M. (1982) 'Central Banking Operations in an Interest-Free Banking System', in Mohammad Ariff (ed.) *Monetary and Fiscal Economics of Islam* (Jeddah: International Centre for Research in Islamic Economics, King Abdulaziz University) pp. 211–29.

Vaez-Zadeh, R. (1991) 'Implications and Remedies of Central Bank Losses', in P. Downes and R. Vaez-Zadeh (eds) *The Evolving Role of Central Banks* (Washington, DC: International Monetary Fund) pp. 69–92.

—— and S. Pereira Leite (1986) 'Effectiveness of Selective Credit Controls: An Empirical Test Applied to India', *The Journal of Development Studies*, 22: 558–72.

Venkitaramanan, S. (1992) 'Central Bank Independence,' *Central Banking*, 3: 19–21.

—— (1995) 'Informal Finance', *The Times of India*, 4 June: 4.

Vicente, M. G. (1993) 'Devolution of Central Bank Functions for Countryside Development', *Central Bank Review*, Philippines, XLV: 27–9.

Villaneuva, D. (1988) 'Issues in Financial Sector Reform', *Finance and Development*, 25: 14–17.

—— and A. Mirakhor (1990) 'Strategies for Financial Reforms: Interest Rate Policies, Stabilization, and Bank Supervision in Developing Countries', IMF *Staff Papers* 37: 509–36.

Volcker, P. A. (1990) *The Triumph of Central Banking*, The 1990 Per Jacobsson Lecture (Washington, DC: Per Jacobsson Foundation).

—— M. Mancera and J. Godeaux (1991) *Perspectives on the Role of a Central Bank* (Proceedings of a Conference held in Beijing, China, 5–7 January 1990) (Washington, DC: People's Bank of China, International Monetary Fund, United Nations Development Programme).

Wagle, N. M. (1937) *Recent Progress of Central Banking in the British Dominions* (unpublished M.Sc. Econ. Thesis, University of London).

Walsh, C. E. (1993) 'Central Bank Strategies, Credibility and Independence: A Review Essay', *Journal of Monetary Economics*, 32: 287–302.

Walters, A. and S. Hanke (1992) 'Currency Boards', in P. Newman, M. Milgate and J. Eatwell *The New Palgrave Dictionary of Money and Finance* (London and Basingstoke: Macmillan).

Wattleworth, M. (1983) 'Credit Subsidies in Budgetary Lending', DM/83/40, International Monetary Fund, 26 May.

White, L. H. (1986) 'Privatize Central Banks to Stimulate Growth', *Economic Affairs*, 6: 38–42.

Williamson, J. (1982) 'A Survey of the Literature on the Optimal Peg', *Journal of Development Economics*, 11–12: 39–61.

—— (1995) *What Role for Currency Boards* (Washington, DC: Institute for International Economics).

Wilson, P. W. (1991) *A Question of Interest* (The Paralysis of Saudi Banking) (Boulder: Westview Press).

World Bank (1983) *World Development Report 1983* (New York: Oxford University Press).

—— (1989) *World Development Report 1989* (New York: Oxford University Press).

—— (1990) *The Long-Run Perspective Study of Sub- Saharan Africa, vol. 4, Proceedings of a Workshop on Regional Integration and Corporation* (Washington, DC: World Bank).

—— (1992) *Philippines Capital Market Study, vol. 1: Main Report* (Washington, DC: World Bank).

—— (1993) *Handbook on Financial Sector Operations* (1st edn) (Washington, DC: World Bank).

—— (1993) *The East Asian Miracle* (Washington, DC: World Bank).

Worrell, D. (1991) 'Making Caribbean Central Banks More Independent', *Social and Economic Studies*, 40: 147–54.

Yazdani, S. and G. P. Hill (1993) 'Islamic Credit: The Iranian Experience', *Journal of Agricultural Economics*, 44: 301–10.

Zaidi, I. and A. Mirakhor (1991) 'Stabilization and Growth in an Open Islamic Economy', *Review of Islamic Economics*, 1: 1–20.

Zengyin, T. (1991) 'Role of Regulational and Supervision of the Central Bank', in P. A. Volcker, M. Mancera and J. Godeaux, *Perspectives on the Role of a Central Bank* (Washington, DC: People's Bank of China, International Monetary Fund, United Nations Development Programme) pp. 45–6.

Zhengying, Z. (1991) 'Implementation of Monetary Policy', in P. A. Volcker, M. Mancera and J. Godeaux, *Perspectives on the Role of the Central Bank* (Washington, DC: People's Bank of China, International Monetary Fund, United Nations Development Programme).

Zuberi, H. A. (1992) 'Interest-Free Banking and Economic Stability', *Pakistan Development Review*, 31: 1077–87.

# Index